The Parliaments
of
Elizabethan England

The Parliaments of Elizabethan England

EDITED BY
D. M. Dean
AND
N. L. Jones

BASIL BLACKWELL

JN
525
P37
1990

Copyright © Basil Blackwell Ltd 1990

First published 1990

Basil Blackwell Ltd
108 Cowley Road, Oxford, OX4 1JF, UK

Basil Blackwell, Inc.
3 Cambridge Center
Cambridge, Massachusetts 02142, USA

British Library Cataloguing in Publication Data

A CIP catalogue record for this book is available from the British Library.

Library of Congress Cataloging in Publication Data

The Parliaments of Elizabethan England/edited by D. M. Dean and N. L. Jones
  ISBN 0–631–15267–9
  1. England and Wales. Parliament—History—16th century.
  2. Great Britain—Politics and government—1558–1603. I. Dean, D. M. (David M.) II. Jones, Norman L. (Norman Leslie), 1951–'
JN525.P37   1990
328.42'09—dc20   89–38415
                                                    CIP

Typeset in 11 on 12½pt Baskerville
by Footnote Graphics, Warminster, Wiltshire
Printed in Great Britain by TJ Press Ltd., Padstow

Contents

Abbreviations

APC	J. R. Dasent (ed.), *Acts of the Privy Council of England* (32 vols, London, 1890–1907)
BIHR	*Bulletin of the Institute of Historical Research*
BL	British Library
CJ	*Journal of the House of Commons*
Dean, 'Bills and Acts'	D. M. Dean, 'Bills and Acts, 1584–1601' (unpublished PhD dissertation, University of Cambridge, 1984)
D'Ewes	Sir Simonds D'Ewes, *The Journals of all the Parliaments during the Reign of Queen Elizabeth* (London, 1682)
EHR	*English Historical Review*
Elton, *Parliament*	G. R. Elton, *The Parliament of England, 1559–1581* (Cambridge, 1986)
Elton, *Studies*	G. R. Elton, *Studies in Tudor and Stuart Politics and Government* (3 vols, Cambridge, 1974, 1983)
Hartley, *Proceedings*	T. E. Hartley (ed.), *Proceedings in the Parliaments of Elizabeth I*, vol. 1, *1559–1581* (Leicester, 1981)
HJ	*Historical Journal*
HLRO	House of Lords Record Office
HMC	Historical Manuscripts Commission
HPT	The History of Parliament Trust, *The House of Commons, 1558–1603*, ed. P. W. Hasler (3 vols, London, 1981)
LJ	*Journal of the House of Lords*
MP	Main Papers, House of Lords Record Office
Neale, *Commons*	J. E. Neale, *The Elizabethan House of Commons* (London, 1949)
Neale, *Parliaments*	J. E. Neale, *Elizabeth and Her Parliaments* (2 vols, London, 1953, 1957)
OA	Original Acts, House of Lords Record Office

PRO	Public Record Office
RO	Record Office
Salis. MSS	Historical Manuscripts Commission, *Calendar of the Manuscripts of the Most Hon. The Marquis of Salisbury, K. G., Preserved at Hatfield House, Hertfordshire* (London, 1883–)
SP	State Papers, Public Record Office
SR	A. Luders (et al., eds), *Statutes of the Realm* (11 vols, London, 1810–28)
STAC	Star Chamber, Public Record Office

Contributors

Dr David Dean, Lecturer in History, Goldsmiths' College, University of London

Norman Jones, Professor of History, Utah State University

Sir Geoffrey Elton, Regius Professor Emeritus of Modern History, University of Cambridge

Michael A. R. Graves, Associate Professor of History, University of Auckland, New Zealand

Wallace T. MacCaffrey, Higginson Professor of History, Harvard University

J. D. Alsop, Associate Professor of History, McMaster University, Canada

T. E. Hartley, Senior Lecturer in History, University of Leicester

Conrad Russell, Professor of History, King's College, London

Introduction: Representation, Ideology and Action in the Elizabethan Parliaments

D. M. DEAN AND N. L. JONES

This book arose out of our conviction that the Elizabethan parliament needed to be located in its context, identifying what it did and how it did it. For too long parliamentary historians have regarded parliamentary politics in isolation and only in relation to the centre of government. Such studies have been obsessed by the whiggish search for the origins of modern parliamentary democracy. As a result, many important questions that would have explained parliament's importance to contemporaries have been unasked or, if asked, were asked in such a way as to provide only limited perspectives. Each of the essays in this volume seeks to redress this imbalance by asking questions that locate Elizabethan parliamentary activity firmly within the English polity.

Geoffrey Elton sets the scene by tracing the triumph of common law over canon law in the pre-Elizabethan parliaments. Michael Graves examines the work of parliament from the perspective of the privy council. Wallace MacCaffrey examines parliament's role in the crown's making of foreign policy and Jim Alsop its role in meeting the crown's financial needs. David Dean investigates the use of parliament by the localities and Norman Jones places religious legislation in the context of wider religious change and convocation. With Terry Hartley's study of the sheriff and elections we move altogether out of the actual sessions of parliament into the politics and procedures of choosing representatives to serve in the lower house. Conrad Russell, whose well-known chapter on 'Westminster and the Wider World' set out the wider context of parliamentary sessions for the 1620s, offers some reflections on the early Stuart implications of developments in Elizabeth's reign.[1]

[1] Conrad Russell, *Parliaments and English Politics, 1621–1629* (Oxford, 1979), ch. 1.

Elizabethan parliaments were gatherings of members of the ruling elites; how they were elected and contemporary assumptions about representation are therefore essential to our understanding of their parliamentary activities. We are incapable, moreover, of understanding their actions in parliament if we examine only the parliamentary record. Their work in the houses must be seen in the fullest setting of their ideological and material perceptions and interests.

The elected members of Elizabethan parliaments, in conjunction with the Lords and their monarch, had the power to bind all subjects, but in no meaningful way did they do this by consent. As the rightful governors of the realm, they saw it as their duty to provide for the welfare of the common weal, drawing upon their experience as secular and ecclesiastical authorities. Participation in parliament was one of the many duties such men expected to undertake in fulfilment of the responsibilities of their ordained place in society, serving their nation, their monarch, their interests and their God.

It is these concerns which are articulated time and time again in the parliamentary debates which survive. More modern notions of representation are notably absent from their discourse. None of the three Elizabethan parliamentary theorists, Sir Thomas Smith, William Lambarde and John Hooker, identified MPs as the representatives of a body of electors. As John Hooker said: 'But in the Knights, Citizens and Burgesses: are represented the Commons of the whole Realme, and every of these giveth not consent onely for him self: but for all those also for whom he is sent.'[2] Hooker knew his subject well: he kept a diary of the 1571 parliament in which the matter of borough representation was raised. His pronouncement does not, as Vernon Snow thought, argue that 'the whole realm is represented in the House of Commons' but rather that the whole parliament represents the entire realm.[3] Thus it does not contradict Sir Thomas Smith's opinion that whatever

the people of Rome might do either in *Centuriatis comitijs* or *tributis*, the same may be doone by the parliament of Englande, which representeth and hath the power of the whole realme both the head and the bodie. For everie Englishman is entended to bee there present, either in person or by

[2] Vernon F. Snow (ed.), *Parliament in Elizabethan England, John Hooker's Order and Usage* (New Haven and Yale, 1977), p. 182.
[3] For the debate see Hartley, *Proceedings*, pp. 225–31.

procuration and attornies, of what preheminence, state, dignitie, or qualitie soever he be, from the Prince (be he King or Queene) to the lowest person of Englande. And the consent of the Parliament is taken to be everie mans consent.[4]

To both Smith and Hooker, MPs were attorneys delegated with the authority to give counsel and consent on behalf of the community but this did not require that they consult those in whose names they spoke.[5] As Hooker makes clear, such an attorney gave consent on behalf of those '*for* whom he is sent' not '*by* whom he is sent'. Of course some members for boroughs did consult with those boroughs for advice and assistance but this was part of a contractual understanding and, in most cases, concerned matters of direct import for the borough. Such members need not exercise any such consultation when offering their consents or dissents on matters of more general social, economic or political concern. The situation of the bishops was strikingly similar, for they too were in contact with the representatives of the clergy meeting in convocation but were in no way accountable to them. Members were thus, in a very real sense, private men representing private interests: peers spoke for themselves, borough members for the borough elites, bishops for the clergy and knights of the shire for the county elites. Real accountability was impossible until there was general acceptance of the notion of public payment for public service, regular parliamentary sessions to enable the role of MP to emerge as an occupation and the fuller sense of constituency and party which arguably emerged only with the extension of the franchise.

These perceptions are made clear in the one rare moment when Elizabethan members debated the nature of representation. In 1571 they were faced with the question of whether or not a member must reside in the place for which he spoke. Thomas Norton was of the opinion that they need not be residents, stressing the election 'of such which were able and fitt for soe great a place' and thus would provide 'good service' for the entire realm, rather than 'the private regard of place or priviledge of any person'. This argument almost won the day until another member, probably Thomas Atkins of

---

[4] Mary Dewar (ed.), *De Republica Anglorum by Sir Thomas Smith* (Cambridge, 1982), pp. 78–9. Cf. Snow, p. 182, n. 103.

[5] Sir John Neale pointed out that in the election writ itself MPs 'were to be given "full and sufficient power" to consent to the business of parliament for themselves and the communities they represented,' *Commons*, p. 158.

Gloucester, delivered a learned speech in favour of residency, arguing that none were 'soe fitt for every countrey as those who knowe the same'.[6] The debate thus revolved not around the question of local representation but rather the quality of advice; not around the issue of whether borough members spoke *for* the inhabitants of the borough but whether they should be local men able to bring their local knowledge to the assembly of the 'body of the whole realm'.

As the reign progressed, there are signs that borough elites, anxious to respond to the intrusions of central government in the localities during the war with Spain, placed greater emphasis on selecting members who possessed some understanding of local needs. The 1586–7 Warwick election dispute partly revolved around this very issue, with some borough members expressing a fear that one contender, Job Throckmorton, would be unable to serve the borough's particular interests. It can be argued that such concerns mark the beginnings of a sense of 'constituency' and that this can be detected in debates over the subsidy in 1593 and monopolies in 1601.[7]

The 1571 debate on the residency of burgesses was rounded off by Francis Alford who, after objecting to the youthfulness of some MPs (and suggesting a minimum age requirement of thirty years), proposed that as most towns had two burgesses one could be a local man and the other 'a man learned and able to utter the mynd of his opinion'. Thus 'hee seemed to conclude the lawe should bee in force for the one burgess and at liberty for th'other.'[8]

Alford's belief that a man 'learned and able to utter his opinion' need not be resident in the place that gave him his seat was a plea of self-justification. In his long parliamentary career he, a resident of London, sat for Mitchell in Cornwall, Reading in Berkshire and for Lewes and East Grinstead in Sussex.[9] When he spoke, and he spoke often, it was not as the representative of those places but as the learned civil lawyer, clerk of the Oxford market, rector of a Cambridgeshire church and a well-travelled man of the world.[10]

---

[6] Hartley, *Proceedings*, pp. 225–6, 229.

[7] See the article by David Dean, pp. 139–62 below.

[8] Hartley, *Proceedings*, p. 230.

[9] Most of Alford's seats were secured with the patronage of his cousin Thomas Sackville, Lord Buckhurst, HPT, I, pp. 116, 258–60.

[10] HPT, I, p. 335. Although he himself pleaded that he was 'not learned in the lawe' another member noted him as 'learned in the civill lawes', Hartley, *Proceedings*, pp. 210, 222.

Alford was an active member of the Commons, sitting in six Elizabethan parliaments before his death in 1592. In the same session in which he contributed to the residency of burgesses debate, he spoke on bills for the preservation of the Queen, against dispensations made by the archbishop of Canterbury and providing for the dissolution of Bristol's merchant adventurers; in later sessions Alford spoke on an impressive variety of matters from Mary, Queen of Scots to fraud, the ministry, vagabonds, grain and cloth.[11] In making his contributions his constituencies were irrelevant.

Of course, the visible Francis Alford represents only a very small part of his work as an MP. The Commons only sat in the morning, and in the world before the printing of bills most of the morning was spent hearing them read out by the clerk. Afternoons were usually devoted to committee work about which we know very little. In 1571 Alford sat on the subsidy committee and those dealing with bills concerning promoters, tellers and receivers, attainders, papal bulls, assurances of lands, fugitives and Bristol's merchant adventurers.[12] In the case of the latter interested parties were invited to put their case.[13] Alford, with the other members, heard their deliberations, discussed the problem, redrafted the bill and returned it to the house.

Besides these formal activities, members such as Alford would have continued debate outside parliament, in their lodgings or in the eating and drinking houses. Besides parliamentary business, other duties and interests, both personal and public, occupied members' time in London and Westminster. This was no less true of the bishops who moved between Convocation and the Lords, the judges who sat both in the Westminster courts and as advisors to the peers in parliament, and the privy councillors and courtiers who attended the royal court as well as parliamentary sessions.

Drawn from every county and enfranchised borough, parliament gave its members a sense of collective identity, a unity of purpose and a sense of shared experience, of 'nation', providing a vital means of communication between the central government and the governors of the localities. Parliament, in Professor Elton's celebrated phrase, was a 'point of contact'.[14] It enabled privy councillors,

---

[11] Hartley, *Proceedings*, pp. 205, 210, 222. On Alford see HPT, I, pp. 335–8.

[12] HPT, I, pp. 335–6.

[13] Hartley, *Proceedings*, p. 247.

[14] G. R. Elton, 'Tudor Government: The Points of Contact I. Parliament' in *Studies*, pp. 3–21.

bishops and judges to consult with those who were charged with ruling the country and provided the opportunity to demonstrate to them the value of certain laws, the reasons behind executive actions and the need to pay taxes. It was a means to cajole, coerce and convince. For the county and borough elites it provided the opportunity to express opinion and offer advice, to discuss problems and solutions with other rulers and to experience the wider world of Elizabethan government. As Neale wrote:

A matchless attraction it was to be in London at this time; to be 'of the parliament'; to move on the fringe of the Court, marvelling at its fashions and splendours; to see and hear the Queen; perchance to kiss her hand; to be at the heart of politics, and listen to famous men speaking in the House; to gather news from all quarters of the kingdom and the world. Such a one stood a tip-toe among his neighbours on his return home.[15]

Towns, corporations and individuals who lobbied to promote their interests in parliament had to deal with members unrestrained by party or constituency, but not all members were created equal. The support of the men who led the houses of parliament through their eloquence, learning, greatness, connections or office had to be obtained. Acquiring it was neither simple nor cheap. In 1571 Bristol spent £50 on its bill in which Francis Alford was involved.[16] In the same session the Curriers of London spent over £6 to defeat a bill promoted by the shoemakers. Their expenses included the cost of buying dinner for the Speaker's servants; a capon and a dozen quails for the London MP John Marshe; suppers for the burgesses for Liverpool and Derby 'and dyvers other their freindes and acquayntaunces'; a gift of wine to a member for Southwark, Thomas Cure, who spoke 'againste the showmakers bill' in the Commons; and sums of money to one of the members for York and a servant of the Commons's clerk, Francis Spelman, 'for that he shoulde give us warninge if eny matter were moved against the companie'.[17] In

[15] Neale, *Commons*, p. 150.
[16] This was paid in 1572, Bristol RO MS 04026/9, f. 172. The struggle which lay behind this measure is discussed by D. H. Sacks, 'Trade, Society and Politics in Bristol circa 1500–circa 1640' (unpublished doctoral dissertation, Harvard University, 1977) pp. 596–611.
[17] D. M. Dean, 'Public or Private? London, Leather and Legislation in Elizabethan England', *HJ*, 31 (1988), 543, 545. Such payments are recorded in the financial accounts of the companies, mostly held at the Guildhall Library, London. For the Curriers' activity in 1571, see MS 14, 346/1, ff. 69v–71.

order to secure an act in 1571 to make the River Lea navigable, the City of London spent some £40; the costs of a private measure greatly exceeded those of a public bill.[18]

Such interests were not merely lobbying on particular matters of local concern but also on matters of national application and importance. The lobbying of interest groups reveals the fact that all parliamentary activities were managed. Without the help of those like the Speaker or the clerk who managed the Commons or of leading lawyers and influential courtiers and councillors, a bill had little chance of passage. As the satirist of 1566 exclaimed after lampooning the leaders of the House of Commons, 'for the rest they be at devotion, and when pressed they cry a good motion.'[19] The sheep-like nature of many members meant that the houses were effectively run by small minorities, making their operation much smoother than might have been the case and accounting for the low attendance that marked Elizabethan parliaments. Despite the Commons's attempts to make its members attend, all evidence suggests that most sittings saw no more than half the membership in the house.

The leadership of the houses formed an elite within an elite, and it is nearly impossible to separate their actions into public and private categories. Many men, like Thomas Norton, who held no royal office, functioned on behalf of the privy council in parliamentary matters. This makes determining the origins of a bill a very difficult matter and much ink has been spilt in trying to identify the difference between official and unofficial bills, public and private measures.[20] Even more vexing is the problem of identifying the work of servants of the crown with crown policy. As implied by their acceptance of fees, the problem for the historian is to discover whether officials spoke for themselves alone, for the Queen, for the privy council or for some private interest. It is not necessarily the case that a privy councillor, for example, spoke or acted in concert with other councillors, the council as a whole or his Queen. In 1559 the Marquis of Winchester the lord treasurer, actually voted against the royal supremacy and seems to have suffered no

---

[18] Elton, *Parliament*, pp. 56–7.
[19] Elton, *Parliament*, pp. 351–4. Alford was described as 'the bold' in the lampoon.
[20] See, for example, Elton, *Parliament*, pp. 43–87; Elton, 'Enacting Clauses and Legislative Initiative, 1559–81' in *Studies*, pp. 142–55; D. M. Dean, 'Enacting Clauses and Legislative Initiative, 1584–1601', *BIHR*, 57 (1984), 140–8.

disfavour. Despite the Queen's dislike of parliamentary discussions of religion, privy councillors supported many of the religious measures of 1566 and 1571. In 1593 a royal official, James Morice, attorney of the court of wards, saw fit to initiate a measure attacking the clerical oath, clearly without the support of any other official besides Robert Beale, secretary to the privy council, who also spoke on the subsidy in a way which angered both Queen and council.[21] They understood that the duty to give counsel in parliament was a private duty. Yet, at the same time, the officials of the crown frequently worked together to promote the interests of the government. Such cooperation was achieved without the recognition that to promote such a policy implied the solidarity of a party platform. No Elizabethan councillor lost office if he dissented from the position adopted by the majority of the council.

Indeed, the liberty of speech in both houses was central to the proper functioning of the high court of parliament. As the few but famous cases in which the Commons's liberty of speech was infringed reveal, it was considered necessary that all could speak freely and without restraint. To speak without fear of retribution was essential to members' ability to give wise and honest counsel to the monarch and to make good law. As one member put it while speaking of the succession in 1566:

Therefore, to prevent the evills of trayterous flattery and divellish dissimulacion and many other inconveniences, the providence of God, I say, hath ordeined by lawe that in this House every one hath free speech and consent, and that he doth iniury to the whole realme that makes any thing knowne to the prince that is here in hand without consent of the House, or that bringeth any message from her Majestie into this House to draw us from free speech and consent.

In the case where a law was made 'to endanger the present state of the prince', the author noted, it could be no law for God 'hath ordeined by lawe that all things agreed upon by the Parliament are dead and noe lawes, untill she [the Queen] hath quickened them and given them life by her royall assent.'[22]

At the beginning of the reign most Elizabethans shared a model of government which equated political order with divine order. As

---

[21] See Neale, *Parliaments*, II, pp. 267–9, 304–5 and the recent article by Patrick Collinson, 'Puritans, Men of Business and Elizabethan Parliaments', *Parliamentary History*, 7 (1988), 187–211.

[22] Hartley, *Proceedings*, p. 130.

Hooker later expressed it in his *Laws of Ecclesiastical Polity*, the laws that parliament made 'do take originally their essence for the power of the whole realm and the church of England, than which nothing can be more consonant unto the law of nature and the will of our Lord Jesus Christ.'[23] As the lord keeper informed the assembled parliament in 1563, it had two responsibilities, the maintainance and enhancement of God's glory and honour and the maintainance and upholding of the Queen's honour and estate, the common weal. 'And because Gode's lawe and doctrine beinge the first braunche, is of it selfe every way perfitt and absolute, therefore the whole faulte and lacke toucheinge that braunche must lighte altogether upon our selves that oughte to take the benefitte of it.'[24]

Assuming that human law must conform with divine and natural law, they believed that there was a natural order in the political hierarchy and that the lower orders naturally had no say. Legitimacy came from God, not the governed, and the magistracy was responsible to God for the governed. If their laws and actions conformed to God's will then all would prosper. As Hooker reminded them:

We are to note, that because whatsoever hath necessary being, the Son of God doth cause it to be, and those things without which the world cannot well continue, have necessary being in the world: a thing of so great use as government amongst men, and human dominion in government, cannot choose but be originally from him, and have reference also of subordination to him.[25]

This was the belief enunciated time and time again during parliamentary debates. The Commons's proposed petition on the succession in 1566 drew attention to their suit which 'shuld tend to the glory of God, to your Majesties' honor and suerty, and to the tranquillitye and perpetuall quietnes of all your realme'.[26] In 1571 Thomas Norton, speaking on usury, used a familiar dictum from Gratian. He argued that 'since it is doubtfull what is good, that wee shoulde be mindfull of the true old saying *quod dubitas ne feceris* [don't do what is doubtful] and for that *quod non ex fide est, peccatum est* [what is not from faith is sin]'.[27]

---

[23] David Little, *Religion, Order and Law* (Chicago, 1984), p. 162.
[24] Hartley, *Proceedings*, p. 81.
[25] Little, *Religion*, p. 156.
[26] Hartley, *Proceedings*, p. 155.
[27] Hartley, *Proceedings*, pp. 236–7.

This way of reasoning about the making of law explains why religion was so important in Elizabethan parliaments. It was the standard against which human law was judged. Built into the legal system was the belief that the process in all courts, including the high court of parliament, existed to discover truth. Since all truth was unitary, it all, ultimately, referred back to God, the fount of justice and right, the punisher of injustice and wrong. God and truth were the central issues and they underlie many of the lawmaker's assumptions. In 1601 Francis Darcy warned the Commons that if they did not take steps to curb drunkenness the Almighty would 'laye his heavye hand of wrathe and indignacion uppon this Land'.[28] Upon them, Edward Glascock told them in the same session, would fall God's wrath if they did not remedy the sin of swearing by parliamentary statute, for the Almighty had promised to punish those who did not drive blasphemy from their houses. Glascock's very words were written into the preamble of the bill.[29] Here there is no sense of accountability *to* the represented but rather *for* the represented: the Almighty was able to punish, electors were not.

Perhaps the clearest statement of the duty of human law to conform to divine law comes from that great parliament man William Fleetwood. In the 1571 usury debate he reminded the Commons that the central issue under discussion was God's will. Usury was damnable according to Scripture 'and therefore whether it were good or not good, it was noe good question.' Even the Queen could not allow it by royal dispensation because it was *malum in se*, a thing forbidden by God. Based on a distinction rooted in English law and theology, his comment laid out one of the basic ground rules for lawmakers.[30]

God's law was also seen to animate the Elizabethan poor law. The preamble of the 1572 act referred to the growing numbers of rogues, vagabonds and sturdy beggars who were responsible for 'horryble Murders, Theftes and other greate Outrages, to the highe

---

[28] BL Stowe MS 362, ff. 84v–5.

[29] D'Ewes, pp. 660–1; PRO, SP 12/282/56.

[30] Hartley, *Proceedings*, p. 236. It is worth noting the similar perspective offered by Thomas Egerton, solicitor general between 1581–92, attorney general 1592–4 and lord keeper 1596–1603 (and then lord chancellor until his death in 1617), S. E. Thorne (ed.) *A Discourse upon the Exposicion and Understandinge of Statutes, with Sir Thomas Egerton's Additions* (San Marino, California, Huntington Library, 1942), pp. 168–9 and n. 205.

displeasure of Almightye God and to the greate annoye of the Common Weale'; the legislators of the 1597–8 and 1601 statutes omitted such elaborate statements of the lawmakers' desire to serve both God and their fellow Englishmen. Yet, for the famous Cambridge puritan divine William Perkins, God's work was still being done: the 1597–8 act against vagabonds was, he thought, 'an excellent Statute, and beeing in Substance the very law of God, is never to be repealed.'[31]

The trouble was that as the century drew to a close there was less and less agreement on how God's will was to be discovered and who had the duty to enforce it. The belief that the divinely ordained hierarchy had the duty to conform with God's will and to enforce it had led to attempts in parliament to reform the church, culminating in the disturbed sessions of 1584–5 and 1586–7. The failure of the 'bill and book' attempt in the parliament of 1586–7 had forced those who believed that the state should conform to a godly model to begin the development of a theology of dissent that raised conscience over law as the dictator of action. They began separating church from state in self-defence. William Perkins summed up the new attitude when he wrote:

Men in making lawes are subject to ignorance and errour: and therfore when they have made a law (as neere as possibly they can) agreeable to the equitie of Gods law, yet can they not assure themselves and others, that they have failed in no point or circumstance. Therefore it is against reason, that humane lawes being subject to defects, faults, errours, and manifold imperfections, should truly bind conscience, as God lawes doe, which are the rule of righteousness.[32]

Perkins's stand on the majority of man-made laws, as concerning 'things indifferent', was that they contained errors and therefore could not bind the conscience as did God's law. Such a position could be taken much further by those arguing for separation from the established church and it was such men whom Richard Hooker had in mind when writing the *Laws of Ecclesiastical Polity*, printed

---

[31] *SR*, IV, p. 590, cf. pp. 896, 899, 962. Perkins's comments stem from his assessment of vagabondage as no lawful calling according to Scripture, William Perkins, *Workes* (Cambridge, 1616), I, p. 755. His comment, and Robert Allen's that God's 'good hand' was evident in the enforcement of the statute, are cited by Margo Todd, *Christian Humanism and the Puritan Social Order* (Cambridge, 1987), pp. 165–6.

[32] William Perkins, *Workes* (Cambridge, 1612), I, pp. 529–30.

at the same time as an intense parliamentary debate over separatists in the 1593 session.[33]

This apparent shift in attitudes towards the making of law thus
combined with the general theological and ideological confusion
which followed the Reformation, and encouraged a debate about
the roots of law. By the 1590s there were signs that irreconcilable
theological differences over the purpose and role of government
were increasingly making secular considerations the only acceptable way of justifying legislation. By the early seventeenth century
questions which had once been answered theologically in parliament were being left to the divines as irrelevant in determining the
nature of law. As the relationship between people and their God
became increasingly individualistic, there was less and less need for
forcing the community to conform to God's law. Consideration of
secular order became paramount, eclipsing fear of divine retribution.

Such shifts are clearly discernible in the debates over usury
between 1571 and 1640, but they may well have wider application.[34]
In the 1593 debate over the bill prohibiting merchants alien from
retailing wares, one participant argued that the matter was to be
determined by two methods: through the laws of nature and God
and through the profit and commodity of the commonwealth. The
former taught that they should treat others as they themselves
would like to be treated, and biblical texts were cited in favour of
charity and generosity towards strangers. On the other hand, some
members of the house had argued against the bill on the grounds
that 'charity without policy was but folly' and so the speaker felt
that the final test was whether or not the bill was bad 'policy'. Thus
he proceeded to demonstrate, through an analysis of the retailing

---

[33] See W. Speed Hill (ed.) *The Folger Library Edition of the Works of Richard
Hooker* (Cambridge, Mass., 1977), I, pp. xiii–xx. Most pertinent are Hooker's
remarks, echoing those of John Whitgift during the 1572 Admonition Controversy,
that the separatists were too rigid in their insistence that ecclesiastical law be
agreeable to Scripture, *Laws*, book 3, ch. 9 (Hill, pp. 235–9). Such matters were
prominent in the 1590s debate in Cambridge, Peter Lake, *Moderate Puritans and
the Elizabethan Church* (Cambridge, 1982), ch. 9.

[34] Norman Jones's *God and the Moneylenders. Usury and Law in Early Modern
England* (Oxford, 1989) discusses these matters in relation to the debate over
usury. For a recent account of the shifts in the conformist and presbyterian debate,
with clear implications for parliamentary activity, see P. G. Lake, *Anglicans and
Puritans? Presbyterianism and English Conformist Thought from Whitgift to Hooker*
(London, 1988).

trade, that the problems blamed on the merchant strangers (falling prices and rising unemployment) were not caused by them. The crucial part of the debate revolved around such economic arguments, albeit supported by, and in the context of, the scriptural obligation to be charitable.[35]

Recent work in Elizabethan parliamentary history has shown that the traditional interpretation which located the rise of modern freedom in the Elizabethan age, whether in terms of the rise of the House of Commons, the birth of a loyal opposition or the existence of party, was wrong. Nevertheless, the parliaments of Elizabeth were the nurseries for legal and constitutional developments which shaped the future of the English-speaking peoples and those whom they conquered. Elizabethan statutes determined the legal definitions of, for example, murder, bankruptcy, perjury, charity, usury, poor relief and rape until modern times. More importantly, the decisive shift from medieval concepts of the relationship between God, the law and the state to more modern, secular rationales began in the Elizabethan period. For the next sixty years Stuart men and women were engaged in a search for a political consensus to replace the one which was being eclipsed by the end of Elizabeth's reign.

[35] BL Lansdowne MS 55/63, ff. 188–90. Although endorsed as pertaining to the 1589 subsidy debate, the speech clearly relates to the 1593 debate over the bill against strangers retailing foreign wares. The dating of the speech and the debate are discussed fully in David Dean's forthcoming study of the legislation of the later Elizabethan parliaments.

1

Lex Terrae Victrix: The Triumph of Parliamentary Law in the Sixteenth Century*

G. R. ELTON

Even before the sixteenth century, the king's high court of parliament had become England's legislative instrument: that part of the king's government which defined the law of the land by making and repealing statutes that constituted the ultimate definition of the common law. The fact that law developed and changed much more commonly in the course of litigation or discussion among judges and counsel is here irrrelevant. The pronouncements of parliament may have been rare by comparison and may often have summed up innovations carried forward in the courts, but when it set its seal upon some item of the law it established a certainty far more definite than the precedents created by judgements. In the course of the sixteenth century, that certainty and control over the law grew noticeably more positive, as printing fixed the text of statutes and compelled all concerned to respect their precise wording. All this has been set out before,[1] but one important issue deserves further attention. Parliament might hold ultimate authority over the common law, but its universal authority over the realm for that very reason depended on the exclusive authority of the common law within that realm. At the beginning of the century that authority was still limited by the independent force of rival legal systems, ranging from local customs to the canon law of the

---

* This is an adapted and slightly expanded translation of my article, 'Lex terrae victrix: Der Rechtsstreit in der englischen Frühreformation,' *Zt. der Savigny-Stiftung*, Kanonistische Abteilung LXX (1984), 217–36. I am grateful to Professor Martin Heckel for permission to reuse this material, hitherto not very accessible to English-speaking historians.
[1] See e.g. G. R. Elton, *The Tudor Constitution* (2nd edn, Cambridge, 1982), pp. 235–40.

Universal Church, with all of which systems the common law had before this engaged in battles without ever winning an outright victory. A hundred years later, local custom and canon law still operated in certain areas of litigation but by then they had all come to accept the superiority of the common law and in particular had all come to accept the power of that law's legislative instrument to dictate to them too. A proper understanding of what happened requires a study of the Reformation but one which asks questions different from the religious, political or social ones usually investigated.

It is true that the English Reformation in the reign of Henry VIII can be analysed in various ways and that most of them have been tried. Among historians who regret that it ever happened it has commonly been seen as an unhappy consequence of the King's wayward lechery. Others have treated it as an act of state by means of which the monarchy overcame the last independent rival in power within the realm. Even for those scholars who will admit genuinely religious origins and judge the event within the general setting of the European Reformation, uncertainties and differences persist. Medievalists seem content to treat it as merely a continuation, at best consummation, of long-standing and highly predictable developments: an episode in the history of the nation so clearly derived from its past that its importance must not be overstressed. Did it witness the triumph of laity over clergy, of the king over the last limitation upon his absolute powers, of a new faith over an old? Lately there has been a tendency to believe that nothing much happened at all because the whole country cannot be shown to have swiftly turned Protestant, as though only instant conversion could justify speaking of the Reformation at all.[2] The very diversity of reactions and interpretations demonstrates the magnitude of that break with Rome, that emergence of an independent national church, even as the size of the event fully justifies the wide range of views about it. But among those views, which turn upon politics, faith and personalities, one line of approach has not been prominent, even though it lies nearest to the language and concepts current at the time. The Reformation has not been investigated as an event in the history of the law. Yet whatever else may have happened, in the first instance there occurred a collision and conflict of laws.

[2] Christopher Haigh (ed.), *The English Reformation Revised* (Cambridge, 1987); J. J. Scarisbrick, *The Reformation and the English People* (Oxford, 1984).

It is necessary to distinguish the various stages of the Henrician Reformation with some care. The central issue in debate altered twice quite drastically, with the result that both the battleground and the aims of the combatants moved into different planes. In the beginning the real question arose from the King's request that the Pope should terminate his marriage with Catherine of Aragon. Then, when the curia, under pressure from Catherine's nephew Charles V, refused a service in itself by no means unusual, there resulted that 'break with Rome' which had not in the first place been intended: the King took over the headship of his territorial church and became pope in his own country, in order that his personal problems might be resolved by agencies staffed by his own subjects. The necessity of finding a justification in law for the unquestionably revolutionary transfer of dignities then called forth a search for the legal foundations of the supremacy. At each stage of this progressive crisis different questions of law arose, different even though they were interdependent and developed one from another. If we are to discover which kind of law – and therefore what kind of polity – in the end emerged victorious, we must study the three stages and their juristic problems separately. The final outcome was by no means inevitable or even visible from the first.

In that first crisis of the divorce only one of the existing European legal systems played any part: no rival concepts of law collided here but only mutually opposed interpretations of the canon law. All agreed that the Scripture (Leviticus 20:21) prohibited marriage with a brother's widow, provided the earlier union had been consummated. Hence the debate over the delicate question of whether Prince Arthur had in fact consummated his marriage with Catherine, and hence Henry's highly dubious attempts to prove an alleged fact which the Queen resolutely denied. Dubious or not, there is no reason to think that the Pope would not have accepted those proofs if he had been free of imperial pressure. It was his unwillingness to pronounce judgement that provoked the first conflict – still a conflict not between legal systems but between personalities. As the King explained to the Pope, the parties were in dispute over the same law: '*Nostris et vestris sunt iidem libri, adsunt iidem interpretes*'[3] (we share the same books and are served by the same interpreters).

A second problem arose in the course of this first stage: had

---

[3] Henry VIII to Clement VII, 28 December 1531: *Records of the Reformation*, ed. N. Pocock (1870), II, pp. 148–9.

Julius II's bull of dispensation removed the obstacles to the king's marriage? If it had, the King had lost his right. In order to obtain his ends, Henry therefore found himself compelled to deny the papal power to dispense from the law of God, an issue also contained within the purview of the canon law of the church. Both parties investigated the canonistic precedents, and English propaganda placed special emphasis upon the favourable verdicts collected from various European universities in the years 1530 and 1531. As late as December 1533 the authoritatively concise *Articles devised by the whole consent of the King's most honourable council* based their case on this point. Neither the pope nor any other human being, it was stated, could do away with the laws of God and nature (meaning *lex divina* and *lex naturae* in their technical sense), with the result that Leviticus 20 allowed the King, who professed to have innocently fallen into sin, no escape from the dilemma of his invalid marriage.[4]

This interpretation of the *lex divina* naturally contradicted the papal claim, embedded in the canon law of Rome, to be able to dispense also from the law of Scripture. Henry's interpretation deprived the curia of part of its instruments for the government of the church. In addition, at a time when the sack of Rome (1527) had seriously impaired the main sources of papal income, the Pope could not afford to surrender a financially very profitable claim. With the canonists unable to agree and the Pope unwilling to dissolve his marriage, Henry put forward another concept of the canon law which would enable him legitimately to rid himself of his wife. He maintained that the divorce could be pronounced by the authorities of the church in England; such a judgement, he alleged, could not be appealed to Rome nor was Rome entitled to advoke the case from England. To support this proposition, Henry again cited only rules of the canon law, especially the canons of the early councils; at this point, no sort of schismatic notions were put forward. It was simply stated and proved from the documents of the law of the church that the provinces of the church did not in any way move towards separation from the Universal Church when they claimed that measure of independence which the law granted them. The king emphasized both the sound sense of this and the precedents allegedly in support of what he regarded as a perfectly normal entitlement: '*Mari et montibus a Roma disiungimur, et tamen*

[4] Ibid., p. 525.

Romam citamur, quod nunquam auditum apud nos est, regem fuisse citatum' (sea and mountains separate us from Rome, and yet we are cited to appear at Rome; that a king should be so cited was never heard amongst us). Such papal proceedings were oppressive when applied to a private person, but *'in principe vero non ferendum'* (for a prince unbearable).[5] In this respect, too, the English propaganda always repeated reliance on the same canonistic principles, as for instance in the *Articles of the Council*: the decision to entrust the trial of the matrimonial dispute to the archbishops in England rested, it was claimed, upon the principle enunciated by the councils of the church 'that cases of strife or controversy being once begun in any region shall there and in the said region be finally determined, and none other where.'[6]

Thus the issues involved in the grand case of the divorce itself – the case which triggered off the Reformation in England – remained from first to last problems in the interpretation of the canon law, with Henry maintaining that the claims of what he called the papal canon law could not be reconciled to the law of God upon which that of the church was meant to depend. As late as 1534, at a time when the second stage had long been reached, it was asserted that the King would never, of course, have proceeded against the pope 'except he had seen the law of God clearly on his side.'[7]

At this point, however, such a position no longer constituted the truth of the conflict. In 1527–9, and possibly into the spring of 1531, it was genuinely intended to reconcile the differences between King and Pope upon an agreed solution within the canon law; the King was really convinced that the support offered to him by carefully selected universities in England, France and Italy would persuade Rome of the truth (as he saw it). The years of negotiations, during which Henry VIII displayed a barely believable patience, lived by this illusion. Meanwhile, however, it had become clear to others – especially to Thomas Cromwell, rising star within the administration – that this line of operations could not lead to success. What may be called the fraternal strife with the Pope over the true meaning of canonistic detail developed irresistibly into a dispute concerning the general papal claims to authority in the church. And thus the schism appeared at the gates.

[5] Ibid., p. 150.
[6] Ibid., p. 525.
[7] Ibid., p. 545 (*The little treatise against the muttering of some papists in corners*).

As we have already seen, the King's choice of proofs insensibly slid from the positive provisions of the canon law into the abstract laws of God and nature. Everyone agreed that the positive law of the church had to derive from those superhuman laws, with the implication that disagreements concerning the canon law should be resolved by reference to the laws of God and nature. The consequences of this somewhat naive conviction cause little surprise. While the canon law could be read in books, only opinions existed about the actual contents of those laws created by God; the law of nature more especially would readily adapt itself to any reading that might prove useful. Thus Christopher St German declared as early as 1523 that the common law of England derived directly from the law of nature – or, as he glossed it, the law of reason.[8] The pope's power to dispense could be disputed within the framework of the canon law; but if one wished to question the pope's claim to act as the ultimate court in the affairs of the English church one needed to resort to other-worldly laws and confront the 'papal-canon law' with the law of God.

In this manner Henry made himself supreme head of the Church of England. The foundation of proof that he offered for his claim was entirely a priori and ran thus. The Universal Catholic Church consists of parts organized in polities ruled by kings. As souls the inhabitants (subjects) form a church which in extent agrees entirely with the commonwealth composed of their bodies. Over them, acting as God's deputy, there rules a monarch simultaneously king of the commonwealth and supreme head of the church. This theory of the constitution (reminiscent of early medieval views of *Landeskirchen*) appears fully worked out in the preamble of Cromwell's act of appeals (January 1533) whose enactment was concerned only with the prohibition of all appeals from English to foreign courts. The importance of this act has repeatedly been called in question, simply because the principle stated in the preamble did not lead to equally resounding practical consequences in the body of the act, but this is to misunderstand what was going on. When a statute which did little more than extend the provisions of the old praemunire laws opened with a comprehensive constitutional definition, it did so because that definition was new and needed to be resoundingly proclaimed. The clergy had accepted the supremacy

---

[8] Christopher St German, *Doctor and Student*, ed. T. F. T. Plucknett and John Barton (Selden Society, 1974), pp. 13–19.

title in 1531 and had thus removed all theoretical difficulties standing in the way of Henry's claim. Thus, when Cromwell insisted that 'this realm of England is an empire ... governed by one supreme head and king ... unto whom a body politic compact of all sorts and degrees of people ... be bounden and owe to bear next to God a natural and humble obedience'[9] he was not trying to make new law but stating a newly established foundation for the character of the unitary realm of England – an empire so recognized in the world and therefore totally independent of all external authority. However long the prehistory may have been of efforts to subject the Church of England to the royal authority and rule, the schismatical achievement of 1533 was nevertheless totally novel and called for the provision of proof.[10] By choosing statute for making that proclamation Cromwell placed the authority of the common law behind a particular political philosophy. But what grounds in law, beyond mere assertion, could be alleged to substantiate Henry's claim?

In the act of appeals Cromwell did not allege any named law; instead, and at first sight surprisingly, he produced the evidence of 'diverse ... histories and chronicles' which allegedly testified to the existence and constitution of that unitary state. The reference was, in fact, to the collection of historians' statements which had been in process of being compiled for some three years and was intended to provide support for the new situation; in the propaganda of the 1530s it came to be reused several times.[11] However, Cromwell apart (and he too on this occasion only), no one seems to have regarded these voices from the past as sufficient justification for the replacement of the pope by the king: to this day, that act of 1533 remains the only one to call for the testimony of historians as the foundations of a political theory. Both the acceptance in 1531 of the royal supremacy by the Convocations and the 1534 act of supremacy[12] in effect ignored the search for theoretical foundations: both simply accept the supremacy as universally known and

[9] 24 Henry VIII c. 12, *SR*, III, p. 427.

[10] It seems to me that John Guy, 'Thomas Cromwell and the intellectual origins of the Henrician Reformation', *Reassessing the Henrician Age*, ed. A. Fox and J. A. Guy (Oxford, 1986), pp. 151–78, does not sufficiently distinguish between a prehistory of ideas and a decision to make a proclaimed reality of them.

[11] G. D. Nicholson, 'The nature and function of historical argument in the Henrician Reformation' (unpublished PhD dissertation Cambridge, 1977).

[12] 26 Henry VIII c. 1, *SR* III, p. 492.

long since existing. Henry VIII's own position was very uncompli-
cated and straightforward: he was supreme head of the church as
vicar of God and hence by the grace of God. The most impressive
treatise in support of this revolution, Stephen Gardiner's *Oratio de
vera obedientia* (1535),[13] very elegantly developed this confident
claim without trying to justify it in law: mainly directed at the
spiritualty and foreign readers, and strictly clericalist, it had no
difficulty in swallowing the King's papal position. And Gardiner
should be read as mirroring exactly what Henry thought. Apart
from having been the King's secretary from 1529 to 1534, he had
been deeply involved ever since 1527 in the preparation of the
documents for the divorce process; in addition, out of favour since
the middle of 1532, he intended his book to help restore him in the
King's good grace. Remembering all this, we have here the fullest
statement of Henry's fundamental convictions. England, he held,
was an independent body politic in both its spiritual and secular
aspects, so that its ruler combined within himself the offices of king
and spiritual head. Such was the will of God, for of course only God
could appoint his deputy on earth; no earthly source of power
either could or did contribute in any way.

According to this 'high-church' theory, therefore, the royal
supremacy rested on the law of God, in precisely the way that the
Pope had proved the existence of his supremacy, though the King
could offer only less persuasive quotation from Scripture (mostly
from the Old Testament) than the Pope's '*hic est Petrus*' and such
like. The King simply took over the papal position inasmuch as it
concerned his own empire or independent and unitary state. As the
act of appeals – rather unnecessarily introducing the evidential
labours of historians – pointed out, he thus possessed powers of
judicature over both laity and clergy: authorities on both sides
derived their powers solely from him. These theoretical expositions
raised hardly any problems of either philosophy or theology so long
as the right divine extended only to matters spiritual, but behind
that monolithic thesis there lurked major practical difficulties
which were bound to lead to an ever more manifest conflict
between rival legal systems.

These difficulties sprang from the fact that in England *rex solus*
(the king in his own person) did not have legislative powers; he

---

[13] Cf. *Obedience in Church and State: Three Political Tracts by Stephen Gardiner,*
ed. P. Janelle (Cambridge, 1930).

could make new law and abolish old only in conjunction with the Lords and Commons in parliament. It was in this period that it became generally accepted that the king himself formed one of the constituent parts of the parliament. That principle plainly underlay Christopher St German's detailed explanation of the powers which parliament could exercise over the church,[14] and it was expressly enunciated by Henry himself in 1542.[15] As a member of the parliament the king could do things he could not do as a personal ruler. As supreme head (local pope) he was absolute and could issue decrees for matters spiritual; as king he could exercise this fundamental function in the state only as one member of one (sovereign) mixed body. Now it was recognized at once that without the cooperation of parliament it would be impossible to equip the royal supremacy with practical reality. True, in 1506 the judges had laid it down that a secular law (such as an act of parliament) could not bestow a spiritual jurisdiction upon a layman even if he was king, and Thomas More lost his life because he rejected the act of supremacy precisely on those grounds.[16] This impediment was ignored, or (as in St German's 'New additions') comprehensively eroded: the Reformation constituted a constitutional revolution just because it terminated this limitation upon royal power. For the king needed such secular laws in order to write the divinely granted supremacy into the law of his land. The doctrine behind that supremacy made it a sin against God to deny the king's claims, and that sin could be punished by an ecclesiastical court using the canon law, with excommunication as the ultimate sanction. But the secular head of the church could rest easy only if he was able to prevent subversion or deal with it by means of the punishments available in the common law: the sin had to be defined as a crime over which the courts of the common law exercised jurisdiction. And only parliamentary statute could add to the crimes (treasons and felonies) solely triable there.

The statutes of the Reformation Parliament, as is well known, tried hard to observe the necessary distinctions. None of them ever remotely attempted to ground the supremacy on anything but the ordinance of God which they accepted as starting point for enacting

---

[14] 'New additions' (1531): see *Doctor and Student*, pp. 317–40. The parliament is there (p. 317) recognized as consisting of king, Lords and Commons.

[15] *Tudor Constitution*, p. 277: '... the Parliament, wherein we as head and you as members are conjoined and knit together into one body politic'.

[16] Ibid., p. 237.

stated consequences and imposing penalties upon various forms of
resistance or disobedience. Since the King was supreme head, it
followed that he had powers of taxing the clergy of his church,
appointing its bishops, controlling dispensations, and so forth, all
of which powers could be defined and protected in the law without
ever calling in question the purely divine creation of the King as
God's vicar on earth for his dominion. The act of supremacy rode
over the problem of the grounds on which Henry rested his
supremacy by simply accepting this detail as given: 'Albeit the
king's majesty justly and rightfully is and oweth to be supreme
head of the Church of England.' Thereafter it proceeded to register
that fact for two reasons stated, namely for public awareness of that
fact and for 'the increase of virtue in Christ's religion within this
realm of England'. Thus the enactment declared that the King and
his successors were to be accepted as supreme heads of the church
and were to have full power to deal with all 'errors, heresies,
abuses, offences, contempts and enormities' correctable by a
'spiritual authority or jurisdiction'. The act did not claim to have
created either title or ensuing powers but only to register both.[17] It
wished merely to publish the facts, so that all subjects should know
their duty. In the same spirit the act of six articles of 1539 rested the
King's desire to establish doctrinal uniformity in the realm on his
duty as 'by God's law supreme head immediately under Him of this
whole Church and Congregation of England'.[18]

Yet that very act also contained hints that the strict separation
between the authority given to the King by God and the declaring
of certain practical consequences by the authority of parliament
(King, Lords and Commons) would prove increasingly difficult to
maintain. The act of supremacy had registered the King's power to
control doctrine by the right of his position in the church and by
means of his spiritual jurisdiction. The act of six articles took care
once again to confine what was done by the authority of parliament
to the creation of penalties enforceable at common law. But the
preamble (rightly) noted that the articles of belief there protected
had been defined not by the King alone but by his consent as well
as the assent of Lords and Commons. The long line of major and

[17] 26 Henry VIII c. 1, *SR* III, p. 492.
[18] 31 Henry VIII c. 14, *SR* III, p. 739. The addition of 'Congregation' to
'Church' deserves more attention than it has received. It meant that this
supposedly altogether reactionary act employed both the traditional and the
Erasmian translation of *ecclesia*.

unprecedented enactments which had established the theory of the supremacy in the reality of daily lives, and which had helped to extend royal power into a domain hitherto closed to it, had from the first set up a manifest tension within the King's position which the most careful of phrasing could not disguise. His dignity as supreme head he owed to God and God's law; the reality of his powers as supreme head he owed to the common law, enlarged for this purpose by the relevant legislative authority. Thus the supremacy contained within itself a potential strain between two legal systems, a strain which could become dangerous if head and subject were to find themselves differing over the interpretation of the basic principles, or if the exercise of that supremacy were ever to be called in question at law.

All this, of course, was to happen later in the century. But from the first there existed in effect two intepretations of the theory of the supremacy, one high and one low, one theological and the other legal; even though both often enough agreed harmoniously, the possibilities of a conflict could not be ignored. The point was put plainly quite early on by Lord Chancellor Audley, Cromwell's chief assistant in the drafting of those revolutionary statutes, in conversation with Stephen Gardiner. Familiar though the quotation may be, it is worth citing again at length:

'Thou art a good fellow, bishop,' quoth he (which was the manner of his familiar speech), 'look at the act of supremacy and there the king's doings be restrained to spiritual jurisdiction; and in another act it is provided that no spiritual law shall have place contrary to a common law or act of Parliament. And this were not,' quoth he, 'you bishops would enter in with the king and by means of his supremacy order the laity as ye listed. But we will provide,' quoth he, 'that the praemunire shall ever hang over your heads ...'[19]

Thus Audley regarded the authority of the (king-in-)parliament as ultimately superior to that of the king as spiritual head. It is worth noting that it was in effect Audley who created the ambiguities of the act of six articles when he advised Henry to settle the truth of the sacrament of the altar by act of parliament because no authority in the general opinion exceeded that of that instrument.[20] Thus he held that the law of parliament (which is the common law)

[19] *The Letters of Stephen Gardiner*, ed. J. A. Muller (Cambridge, 1933), p. 392.
[20] Ibid., p. 369.

in the last resort defined what free powers the supreme head might exercise. From the first, therefore, parliament intervened in matters which theoretically lay entirely between God and king. The hidden conflict was accidentally summed up in one of the marginal notes which the translator added to the English version of Gardiner's *De vera obedientia*. That translation, of course, was published when Gardiner, now lord chancellor to Queen Mary, had altogether changed his opinions concerning the supremacy; since the editor meant to cause Gardiner the maximum of political embarrassment his annotations formed a distinctly hostile commentary on the text. Thus, where Gardiner had declared the supremacy to be *'inexistens'* (inherent) in the king, the margin carries the explanation 'the king's supremacy by parliament'.[21]

It might be thought that this dispute among the laws manifested itself only in the course of time and especially became serious in the reign of Mary who meant to divest herself of a title now seen as grounded upon parliamentary statute. However, even under Henry VIII and despite his majestic behaviour, the common law began to attack along the edges of a purely personal supremacy decreed by the law of God. Cromwell revealed his own position in the act concerning Peter's pence and dispensations (1534), for the drafting of which he was responsible.[22] After declaring that England, which recognized the king as supreme head under God, owed obedience only to such laws as had been accepted as there valid by the people 'at their free liberty' and with the king's permission, the act went on:

It standeth therefore with natural equity and good reason that in all and every such laws human ... your royal majesty, and your Lords spiritual and temporal, and Commons, representing the whole state of your realm in this your most high court of Parliament, have full power and authority ... to abrogate, annul, amplify and diminish ...

Cromwell could hardly have expressed more plainly the principle of an absolute legislative power vested in the tripartite parliament and extended to all spiritual as well as secular concerns of the 'empire' of England. The theory of the general legislator, here incorporated into a statute, included the assertion that the foundations

---

[21] Janelle, *Obedience*, p. 115.
[22] 25 Henry VIII c. 21, *SR* III, pp. 464–71; *Letters and Papers ... of Henry VIII*, VII, no. 49.

and the exercise of the ecclesiastical government even belonged, so far as the positive law was concerned to the parliament. In this definition Cromwell represented the views of the common lawyers, a sector to which he himself belonged. Though so far as legal practice was concerned the supremacy seems to have mattered only because parliament had declared resistance to it to amount to treason, the common law had found in Christopher St German a champion who even before the break with Rome aspired to winning for it full control over any other law used in the realm.[23]

Even before the supremacy was fully worked out, signs appeared that the role of the parliament might offer competition to the role of God. Thus in 1531 an act attended to the pardon which the King in his person and without the parliament had granted to the clergy because their jurisdiction had allegedly offended against the old statutes of praemunire.[24] The act recited the royal pardon and confirmed it 'by the authority of Parliament', which does not interfere with the original and purely personal action of the King. However, before the enactment there occurs a strange sentence in which parliament (without any truth or justification) is made to claim more participation than the official doctrine or the facts of the case allowed to it. There we learn that the King had exercised his mercy 'of his mere motion, benignity and liberality, by authority of this his Parliament'. The first act of succession (1534) contained a similar ambiguity or duplicity. It reported that the king's first marriage had been found invalid in the trial before the archbishop of Canterbury (that is, by an action under the canon law); but it then went on to declare 'by authority of parliament' that the marriage was definitely null and against the law of God.[25] Again and again, the acts contain hints that the endeavour to keep the legal foundation of the supremacy (the law of God) separate from its exercise as defined in the positive law of the realm could not be sustained. The supremacy owed its practical force and therefore its real existence to acts of parliament, and the drafters of the acts not infrequently, though with an obscurity caused by embarrassment, admitted as much.

The most interesting example of the dilemma arose out of the

---

[23] *The Reports of Sir John Spelman*, ed. J.H. Baker (2 vols, Selden Society, 1977–8), I, pp. 57–8; *Christopher St German on Chancery and Statute*, ed. J.A. Guy (Selden Society, 1985), p. 21.

[24] 22 Henry VIII c. 15, *SR* III, pp. 334–8.

[25] 25 Henry VIII c. 22, *SR* III, pp. 471–4.

need to determine what sort of spiritual law was to be used in the schismatic church. On the one hand, the church courts continued as before, except that now they derived their jurisdiction from the royal supreme head; on the other, the canon law of the Universal Church, hitherto also the law of those courts, was held to be papistical and therefore to be rejected.[26] Nevertheless, while there existed ecclesiastical courts they needed an approved ecclesiastical law. In the 1530s some common lawyers, with hesitant support from Cromwell, tried to abolish those rivals and transfer all actions to their own courts, but the bishops, as Audley later put it, entered with the King. Thus the old spiritual jurisdiction remained in existence and, at least down to the outbreak of the civil war, also active.[27] Where, however, could one find a canon law which did not come from Rome and incorporate the papal supremacy? In the spring of 1532 Cromwell provoked in the Commons a general attack which Henry then used to force an equally general submission upon the clergy in their convocations.[28] This submission was obtained outside the parliament and without its participation. When the representatives of the clergy signed the submission they accepted two resolutions touching the law of the church: new canons could only be proposed by Convocation and depended for their validity on ratification by the king, while the existing law was to undergo a revision by a royal commission (sixteen laymen and sixteen clerics) so as to cleanse it of all papal traces.

Even in 1532 Cromwell would have preferred a parliamentary victory to one gained by the monarch as *rex solus*, and two years later he managed to get the submission confirmed by statute.[29] Although that confirmation altered nothing in the relations between king and canon law, the normal formula touching the authority of parliament was to have consequences: once again, however guardedly one brought in parliament, once in it was bound to assert itself. Setting up that commission underwent years

---

[26] The theory that the medieval church in England possessed its own law and could choose whether to abide by papal decrees – the theory, that is, invented in the Reformation Parliament – was discredited as unhistorical in F. W. Maitland's *Roman Canon Law in the Church of England* (London, 1898).

[27] G. R. Elton, *Reform and Renewal: Thomas Cromwell and the Commonweal* (Cambridge, 1973); R. A. Houlbrooke, *Church Courts and the People during the English Reformation 1520–1570* (Oxford, 1979).

[28] G. R. Elton, *Reform and Reformation: England 1509–1558* (London, 1977), pp. 151–5.

[29] 25 Henry VIII c. 19, *SR* III, pp. 460–4.

of delay, although a small committee of canonists associated with Cromwell produced as early as 1535 a proposal which turned out to be too general and imprecise for use in the courts.[30] The church itself wished to put an end to uncertainty and petitioned for the promised enquiry. This led in 1536 to a further statute in which the foundations for this reform were drastically changed.[31] While in 1532 the whole matter had been consigned to the personal action of the King, he was now instructed, by the authority of the parliament, to set up the commission, with the additional provision that his power to do so should endure only for three years from the end of this parliament. The task thus remained in his hands but he executed it by order of a time-limited statute and not as a free function of his supremacy. The statute also laid down principles for the reform of the canon law which, even though they did not go counter to his own views, yet made him the agent of the parliament: nothing in the law to be approved was to offend against both the royal prerogative and 'the customs, laws and statutes of the realm'. Beyond any doubt, therefore, the canon law in future was to stand under the control of the common law and not that of the quasi-papal supreme head. The victory of the common law, which had become ever more manifest since 1531, here received official confirmation, but neither the submission of 1532 nor the confirming act of 1534 had made mention of any such thing.

Thus the canon law, to be newly worked over by clerical experts, now became dependent on the approval not only of the supreme head (as the submission had laid down) but more specifically of the king-in-parliament. In practice nothing was to happen for quite some time. The situation grew worse in 1535 when the study of the 'papal' canon law was abolished at both the universities.[32] Soon the dearth of trained canonists produced in 1545 a parliamentary licence for civilians to practise in the church courts.[33] Several times also the intended commission was mentioned again in statutes, but no action was taken until 1551. In that year, under the guidance of Cranmer – theologian not lawyer – the commission produced a general code called *Reformatio Legum Ecclesiasticarum*; however, this failed to obtain the necessary ratification in parliament. In

[30] F. D. Logan, 'The Henrician canons', *BIHR* 47 (1974), 99–103.

[31] 27 Henry VIII c. 5, *SR* III, pp. 548–9.

[32] *Documents Illustrative of English Church History*, ed. H. Gee and W. J. Hardy (Oxford, 1896), pp. 269–74.

[33] 37 Henry VIII c. 17, *SR* III, p. 1009.

1571, in the course of a campaign to secure confirmation of the law to be applied in the church courts, this collection was put into print, with John Foxe as editor.[34] Though the campaign had some support in the Commons, it achieved nothing.[35] Now and again, piecemeal reforms of the canon law were attempted by means of royal orders or episcopal decrees, as well as, more drastically, by such acts of parliament as that of 1540 which liberalized the church's prohibited degrees affecting intended marriages.[36] Only in 1604, after Elizabeth's death, did the church manage to agree to a general code of canon law, though this too never received the approval of parliament. Nevertheless it became operable in the ecclesiastical courts, though this had little meaning by this time; before long, those courts in effect ceased their activity with the exception of testamentary causes, long since subjected to common-law principles of inheritance, which were taken from them only in 1857. Though neither the papal nor the Protestant canon law was ever formally abolished and the courts continued to sit, the common law with the assistance of parliament had not only subdued the rival system but had effectively demolished it.[37]

Thus the old battle between the canon and common laws came to an end. The politically more ominous dispute concerning the legal foundations of the royal supremacy remained unresolved – hanging in mid-air – during Henry VIII's reign. As we have seen, the original motion of a purely personal power, equal to the papal *potestas*, was soon forced to admit the practical necessity of cooperating with parliament: the essential character of the supremacy silently transmuted from an attribute of the *rex solus* to one particular to *rex in parliamento*. Official statements soon came to place the *lex parliamentaria* at least by the side of the *lex divina* in explaining the origin of the royal supremacy. While Henry VIII reigned, this concession hardly mattered in practice. That particular supreme head ruled by force of his personality, though his growing trust in the principles maintained by Cromwell (a trust which survived Cromwell's fall) caused him to concede an increasing parliamentary participation in the development of the Church of

[34] Houlbrooke, *Church Courts*, p. 17.

[35] Elton, *Parliament*, pp. 99, 208.

[36] Houlbrooke, *Church Courts*, p. 18; 32 Henry VIII c. 38, *SR* III, p. 792.

[37] Cases in the courts continued, and the high commission in particular exercised a serious jurisdiction down to 1641, but the law employed was a form of canonistic custom controlled by common and statute law.

England. In the most important task that fell to the ruler of the church – the definition of the officially authorized faith and liturgy – Henry used both statutes and personal announcements, a double action possible only because down to 1547 there could be no question of a reform in fundamentals. Even so, it is worthy of note that after 1540 every exercise of the royal power related to uniformity in belief actually rested upon statute, for it was then enacted by the authority of parliament that the King could, by letters patent, proclaim all changes recommended by the bishops, such patents to be obeyed and observed as though ordained in the act.[38]

After the old King's death the situation altered quickly, and with it the relationship between the personal and parliamentary rule over the church also changed. Though, naturally, no one thought of abolishing or denying the law of God, it became in a manner superfluous. From 1549, only the law of the land, through acts of parliament, determined what kind of church should obey its supreme head. The chief reason for this lay in the decision at last to bring in a proper Reformation, and the reverse decision of Queen Mary to be rid of the Reformation completed a development which Cromwell and his jurists had foreseen and prepared as early as the 1530s.

So far as legislation was concerned, parliament under Edward VI in the two acts of uniformity (1549, 1552) prescribed by means of successive Books of Common Prayer the only legitimate form of divine service.[39] Both laws derived the universal force of the regulations solely from the authority of the king-in-parliament. The foundations of the English church were built by parliament in statutes which carried the official liturgies as appendices. The preface of the Prayer Book also based its claim to obedience and exclusive use on parliamentary authority. That the church now existed totally under the parliament's rule and not only the king's appeared plainly in the fact that the first book, never even submitted to the ecclesiastical authorities, passed after vigorous debates in both houses of parliament; the second underwent a similar experience, though its details had emerged from long arguments among the theologians.[40]

---

[38] 32 Henry VIII c. 26, *SR* III, pp. 783–4.
[39] 2 & 3 Edward VI c. 1; 5 & 6 Edward VI c. 1.
[40] A. G. Dickens, *The English Reformation* (London, 1964), pp. 218–20, 247–9.

In 1553 this church built on parliamentary foundations confronted a Catholic Queen. Mary, of course, wished to forget and abolish everything that had happened since the opening of the Reformation Parliament, and at first she hoped simply to declare invalid any laws which did not agree with what she regarded as the laws of God. She meant to proclaim from above that any such measures contrary to *the* law had never had any force and therefore also no existence. If she had succeeded, she would have helped the law of God, and with it the canon law of the Universal Church, to an undisputed victory over the law of the land. She found her privy council unwilling. For practical reasons, they thought it necessary to observe that principle which, years before, Audley had explained to Gardiner: an act of parliament could be abrogated only by another such act.[41] In consequence, and very much against her inclination, the Queen had after all to turn to the parliament if she was to rid herself of the incubus of the Reformation and the title she hated. She had to take this step in spite of her own unwavering conviction that God had himself ordained the outcome. The restoration of the papal church in England thus depended quite as completely on the authority of parliament (and therefore on the authority of the common law) as had the introduction of the Protestant church in her brother's reign.[42] Nor was this a mere formality, as parliament proved when it delayed the restoration until it had obtained guarantees concerning the secularized church lands. The Queen had to come to terms with the fact that what she held to be the truths of the faith had to defer to the legislative authority of the parliament as well as to the political interests represented in it. Though the exercise of the Protestant religion had become more or less impossible before the passing of the repeal, it could not be punished, nor could the rule of what to her was the only true religion be brought back without an act of parliament. At the beginning of her reign a good Catholic might have been sentenced to death under the law as it stood, while a manifest heretic would have had to be apologetically set at liberty by any court. The same problem, of course, reappeared on Elizabeth's accession when it was decided to reintroduce the reformed church: the acts of 1559 for supremacy and uniformity in their turn established the Church of England by the authority of parliament.[43]

[41] *Gardiner's Letters*, ed. Muller, pp. 369–70.
[42] 1 Mary st. 2 c. 3, *SR* IV, p. 202.
[43] 1 Elizabeth I cc. 1, 2.

I have several times emphasized that the *lex parliamentaria* should not be treated as an independent law; rather it formed the most comprehensive method available for changing the common law by addition, subtraction or piecemeal improvement. The standpoint of the observer determines the view one takes of the outcome of these conflicts of laws. In politics the parliament won the day: that is to say, the omnipotence of the king-in-parliament became fundamental to law and affairs in England. In matters of the law the common law won a total victory when it subjected the church with its law to itself and incorporated God's decree concerning the vicariate on earth into its own system. This elevated and now virtually unrivalled position received confirmation also in other aspects of the age. In 1533, for instance, parliament tackled the problem of heresy trials.[44] It did not claim to be able to define heretical beliefs, a duty it continued to leave to the church, except that it expressly exempted attacks on the papacy from this crime against God. We may safely presume that the bill came from the government, and it is probable that Cromwell was behind it. Its terms conferred upon parliament the task of controlling the conduct of such trials. The act complained of the complexities with which the church had allegedly burdened the pursuit of heretics – complexities which could catch even the wisest and best learned of men unawares. It was declared outrageous that the methods of the church courts left their victims with less chance to prove their innocence than did the law of treason – 'treasons committed to the peril of your most royal majesty upon whose surety dependeth the whole wealth of the realm'.[45] In future, therefore, persons suspected of heresy were to be indicted according to the rules of the common law. Even though this precaution was to be revoked in 1539, the heresy act should nevertheless be regarded as another victory for the common law over its ecclesiastical rival. Even in cases of treason, that law of the land had then not obtained total control; in treason, an accusation, which by the rules of the common law ought to have been effective only if made by presentment

---

[44] 25 Henry VIII c. 14, *SR* III, pp. 454–5.

[45] This phrasing, which appears to treat an attack on the king as something much worse than one on the truth of God's religion, recalls the answer sent by the vice-chancellor of Cambridge in the middle of the nineteenth century to the railway company which proposed to run trains to Cambridge on Sundays. Such a proposal, the promoters learned, was 'unpleasing to Almighty God and offensive to the Vice-Chancellor'.

or indictment by a grand jury, could still be raised by assertions about general fame or the king's special knowledge. In line with his thinking about heresy trials, Cromwell put an end to such exceptions also in his treason law of 1534 which specified the methods of the common law in charges even of high treason.[46] Of course, since parliament constituted the ultimate authority over that law, that provision did not eliminate the punishment of treason by acts of attainder without trial – the weapon which Cromwell's enemies employed against him in 1540.

From the 1530s onwards there are thus plenty of signs that the builders of the unitary state meant to erect it, so far as possible, on a monopoly vested in the common law. The possibility that the equity of chancery might become a rival rather than a subordinate assistant to the common law vanished when the latter by statute took over jurisdiction in uses (1536), while the 1540 statute of wills for the first time introduced a common-law jurisdiction over testaments, hitherto exclusively the domain of the church courts. These are just examples of well-known facts – the facts which account for the English law's successful resistance also to propaganda in favour of the civil law of Rome.[47] The elevation of parliament to legal sovereignty testifies to the determination of the lawyers predominant in Henry VIII's government to equip the common law with a general competence over all legal affairs as well as with an instrument of permanent self-renewal. These ambitions underlay the interesting developments in the native law which for decades had been reforming itself from within, in order to overcome threats of competition by offering litigants a better and safer answer to their problems than was available elsewhere and by different methods.[48] The Reformation Parliament set the seal upon these transformations, and statute took over as the primary means of reform. After 1540, the year in which Cromwell, political architect of that victory, suffered execution, the legislative supremacy and omnipotence of the king-in-parliament remained beyond contesting. Some will call this the end of the Middle Ages and others the beginning of the early modern state, while some, rightly pointing to the medieval prehistory of parliament and common law upon which Cromwell erected his successful 'revolution', will maintain

[46] 26 Henry VIII c. 13, *SR* III, pp. 508–9.

[47] Cf. G. R. Elton, *F. W. Maitland* (London, 1985), pp. 79–88.

[48] Cf. the account of these developments in J. H. Baker's Introduction to his edition of *Spelman's Reports* (see n. 23 above).

that the Middle Ages lasted at least until the middle of the nineteenth century. It is true that the law reformers of the Victorian age found themselves still coping with some survivals from the days of Edward I or Edward III, but the bulk of the statutes whose continued effect troubled them belonged to the reigns of Henry VIII and his successors.

In these developments, the battle against the Roman curia and its own *lex communis* played the leading role, if only because here territory was won which previously had been expressly outside the competence of England's *lex communis*, and also because the incorporation of the papal functions in the crown of England might easily have led to a more specifically royal canon law founded on the will of God. Enough people, and they included the King, would have preferred this. The war opened, as we have seen, with a debate concerning only interior problems of the canon law. That stage of the dispute could therefore be settled by the methods and principles of that law, with the King, supported by the theologians and canonists of his realm, simply transferring the papal powers to himself. The support of lay jurists was his also, but on conditions. The traditions of England were not so easily bypassed. Both political calculations, which preferred to involve the realm in the revolution, and the legal necessity to entrust its enforcement to the courts of the common law, unexpectedly rendered impossible the first intention to erect the supremacy solely on the abstract laws of God and nature. As Cromwell recognized, only the positive law, valid in court, mattered in the last resort. Thus there resulted the decisive contest of laws, between the *lex ecclesiae* and the *lex terrae*. *Lex terrae* won, and the royal supreme head saw himself compelled to rule his church by the same constitutional methods that already applied to his rule of the commonwealth. Instead of employing the inheritance of Rome in the construction of an absolute monarchy, it became necessary to whittle the papal precedents down until they fitted a monarchy that ruled under the common law. In theory as well as practice, the early Reformation in England produced the sovereignty of the tripartite parliament and of the law over the making of which it presided.

This transformation thus set the stage for the function and role of parliament in the reign of Elizabeth I. A unitary realm where one law ruled both monarch and subjects had replaced a community of partly independent orders within one country, looking to various laws for guidance and in which the powers of the crown varied in diverse spheres of action. The maker of this one law, however, was now a mixed body whose decisions stood out by being unappealable and final. This achievement eliminated the possibility, always lurking around during the process of unification, that ultimate power might fall to a single person; however hard some writers, especially from within the clergy and the court, were later to try to elevate the lawful prerogative of the crown into that principle of absolutism which in the subsequent century gained ground all over the European continent, the triumph of the common law and its maker could not be evaded. On the other hand, a sovereign lawmaking power so organized undoubtedly posed serious difficulties as well as opportunities. The opportunities existed for any interest, indeed any individual, within the realm seeking irrefutable solutions to their problems and desires by operating the legislative machinery of parliament; the difficulties arose from the fact that such operating called for complex managerial skills and political compromises. The developed institution called the king-in-parliament stood ready to make laws and in consequence received proposals for such laws in numbers which far exceeded anything that the machinery was capable of processing. Thus the history of parliament became primarily a history of bills and acts, a history which recorded the interchange of internal and external pressures. Much of this remains to be worked out, and much harm has been done by historians who lacked a proper understanding of what lawmaking in that parliament actually meant.[49] Secondly, the potential embodied in the machinery created a visible and public platform for debating the political, ecclesiastical, economic and social concerns that went to the making of law by means of parliament. Here, too, superficial views, derived largely from entrenched convictions and an unbalanced assessment of pronouncements issuing from such competing interests, have traditionally distorted the reading of parliamentary, and indeed of national, history. The principle of one law for all, victorious over all rivals and applicable to all aspects of life, may have looked like a striking simplification of what had gone before, but its effect was to complicate the employment and handling of that law and its maker well beyond the experience of the past. It was in the parliaments of Elizabeth I that the problems now raised as well as the opportunities now offered first came to be a major concern in political life.

[49] I have tried to expound this kind of analysis for the first half of Elizabeth's reign: *The Parliament of England 1559–1581* (Cambridge, 1986).

2

Managing Elizabethan Parliaments

M. A. R. GRAVES

The management of parliaments was not the concern solely of the privy council. After all, management was no more than a means to specific ends. Those ends were various, not only the transaction of government business, but also the advancement of governing class and sectional interests, the airing and redress of their grievances and the exploitation of parliament as a propaganda platform, most notably by the presbyterians during the 1580s. The ultimate yardstick of managerial success was the enactment of parliamentary objectives in statute, whether these were grants of taxation, alterations in religion, commonweal matters or measures to benefit particular economic lobbies, localities, families or individuals. In other words, not only the government but all kinds and manner of interests sought to manage parliaments to their own ends.

However, for private parliamentary lobbies the managerial road to legislative success was difficult. It was littered with obstacles, fraught with dangers, and the incidence of failure was high. This can be illustrated quantitatively by the success and failure rates of Elizabethan parliaments. First, only a relatively small proportion of bills introduced into either house eventually became laws: for example, 40 out of 98 (or 41 per cent) in 1559, and 83 out of 354 (23 per cent) in 1572–81. A longer perspective reveals a similar picture. So, in the first seven Elizabethan parliamentary sessions (1559–81), only 252 bills (or 28 per cent) of the 885 which were read in either house, were successful. The success rate (28 per cent or 158 out of 573) in the latter half of the reign did not improve. Secondly, whilst new laws required the assent of both houses, as well as of the Queen, promoters of bills were free to decide in which one to place them first. As the House of Commons represented local communities and economic interests, it was natural that the sponsors of their measures should entrust their advancement to their elected knights or burgesses. In addition, individual members introduced bills of general application on a variety of commonweal matters. The result was what sometimes became a near-unmanageable volume of unofficial legislation, in short sessions which averaged only ten to eleven weeks, and many of them failed due to sheer lack of time rather than outright rejection.[1]

The catalogue of problems which faced their sponsors did not end there. Bills had to run the gauntlet of both houses, in each of which they might be criticized or opposed. This was particularly true if a measure threatened the interests of other localities or rival economic lobbies.[2] The City of London's economic power and ambitions, for example, were a common object of suspicion, hostility and even opposition. At the same time, the city itself was constantly vigilant for threats to its own economic position and its members were sometimes entrusted with the defeat or repeal of harmful measures.[3] London, however, was not alone in practising the mixed managerial arts of surveillance, canvassing, persuasion, propaganda and opposition. Yarmouth, Exeter and other cities and towns were no less active in seeking the aid of noble connections, canvassing support in the Commons and laying out money for the purpose. In 1571 the practice of employing feed members to further particular measures caused 'much ado' and a Commons enquiry, but the practice continued – just another weapon in the managerial armoury of parliamentary lobbies.[4] Jobbery and tactics, both crude

[1] M. A. R. Graves, *The Tudor Parliaments. Crown, Lords and Commons, 1485–1603* (London, 1985), pp. 122–3, 139, 141; Elton, *Parliament*, p. 52; Dean, 'Bills and Acts', pp. 80, 84, 252–3.

[2] Many examples are to be found in Dean, 'Bills and Acts', ch. 6, *passim*, and Elton, *Parliament*, pp. 316–18.

[3] Hartley, *Proceedings*, pp. 225, 253, 370, 390; M. A. R. Graves and R. H. Silcock, *Studies in Early Modern English History, 1558–1660* (Auckland, 1986), pp. 218–22, 225–32; M. A. R. Graves, 'Thomas Norton, The Parliament Man: An Elizabethan M.P., 1559–1581', *HJ*, 23, 1 (1980), 26; M. A. R. Graves, 'The Management of the Elizabethan House of Commons: The Council's Men-of-Business', *Parliamentary History*, 2 (1983), 22–3; Dean, 'Bills and Acts', p. 201; D. M. Dean, 'Public or Private? London, Leather and Legislation in Elizabethan England', *HJ*, 31 (1988), 525–48; I. Archer, 'The London Lobbies in the Later Sixteenth Century', *HJ*, 31 (1988), 17–44.

[4] Dean, 'Bills and Acts', pp. 201–2; HMC, 73rd Report, pp. 51–2; Hartley, *Proceedings*, pp. 255–6. For other examples of parliamentary activity by local interests see e.g. Hartley, *Proceedings*, pp. 209–11, 247; Neale, *Commons*, pp. 388–92; Elton, *Parliament*, pp. 69–70, 76–86.

and sophisticated, jostled each other in the legislative marketplace, as a diversity of interests competed with each other and for available time.

Of course the fate of bills did not depend just on the strength or lack of opposition to them in the two houses. The activating force of parliament was the Queen, who maintained a watching brief and was prepared to intervene personally in its proceedings. But she entrusted the detailed management and daily supervision to her privy council.[5] Therefore the success of members' legislative activities was, to a large extent, dependent on its approval, or at least its acquiescence. So bill promoters and lobbies frequently petitioned the council or canvassed the active support of individual councillors or other prominent royal servants. Lord Burghley in particular was the recipient of petitions and draft bills from parliamentary hopefuls, though he was not alone. However, an individual councillor's approval was not conciliar support and certainly it did not transform a private bill into an official measure. Likewise it could be imperilled by the opposition of councillors, by the Queen's preference for short sessions and by the priority which the council naturally accorded to official business. Occasionally, when royal necessity was impeded by private interest, direct official intervention could halt a bill in its tracks.[6] Even if unofficial bills passed both houses, they still required the royal assent. That was no formality, because Elizabeth vetoed seventy-two bills during the thirteen sessions of her reign, and the great majority of victims were of unofficial origin. However, with a few exceptions (notably the great bill against Mary Stuart in 1572), she did not exercise her veto in an arbitrary manner. Instead, more often than not, she acted on conciliar advice, especially that of Burghley. How else could Elizabeth, locked in the gilded cage of her court, have weighed up the pros and cons of bills for rebuilding Cringleford village and against the deceitful packing of hops with a 'mixture of dross, sand or leaves'? Moreover, it was well known that a councillor's advice could be self-interested. So in 1581 the joint Dorset borough of Weymouth and Melcombe Regis was advised not to proceed

[5] Elton illustrates Elizabeth's willingness to intervene in order to stop discussion on prohibited subjects such as religion, or to stay the progress of bills offensive to her. But, he adds, the incidence of intervention 'does not exactly demonstrate frequent or highly improper interference', Elton, *Parliament*, p. 123.

[6] Ibid., p. 123; HMC, 18th Report, pp. 93–5; *CJ*, I, 102; Dean, 'Public or Private?', pp. 525–7.

with a bill because it would be harmful to Sir Christopher Hatton, one of the Queen's favourites, who 'surely would overthrow it when it should come to her Majesty's hands ...'.[7]

The lobbying and manoeuvring of competing private interests occupied much of parliament's time. However, their managerial activities were usually confined to the particular issues and bills which concerned them. Once those matters had been frustrated or succeeded, they played no further part in managerial politics. In contrast, the Elizabethan council had an encompassing, ongoing responsibility to guide the activities of parliaments in the royal and national interest. After all they were summoned only when the crown needed money, laws and, less frequently (as in 1572 and 1586–7), advice. Yet it has to be asked why parliamentary management by the privy council was necessary. The first thought which must spring to mind is that royal proposals and policies were, like private bills, liable to provoke opposition and conflict. Indeed an earlier generation of historians argued that this was what happened: within a House of Commons, growing more powerful and critical, there emerged an organized puritan opposition with its own radical legislative programme. In these circumstances the prime purpose of conciliar management would have been to anticipate and neutralize such opposition.[8] However, the present generation of scholars has convincingly rejected the picture of a dynamic puritan opposition operating in a House of Commons which was, in turn, becoming increasingly difficult to manage. Even the presbyterian campaigns, which undoubtedly occurred in the 1580s, were small-scale affairs and easily stifled at birth. Therefore the reason for the privy council's ongoing managerial activity must be sought elsewhere.[9]

The answer is to be found, partly at least, in the nature of the membership of parliaments. The loyalties of the Elizabethan bishops and peers, knights and burgesses who rode into Westminster were very different from those of modern MPs. Many of them had specific obligations to perform on behalf of their families, social or

[7] Elton, *Parliament*, pp. 123–6; Dean, 'Bills and Acts', pp. 80, 208; HMC, 5th Report, p. 579b; Neale, *Commons*, pp. 388–9.

[8] Neale, *Parliaments*; W. Notestein, *The Winning of the Initiative by the House of Commons*, Proceedings of the British Academy, vol. XI (London, 1924).

[9] G. R. Elton, 'Parliament in the Sixteenth Century: Functions and Fortunes', *HJ*, 22 (1979), 255–278; G. R. Elton, 'Parliament', in *The Reign of Elizabeth I*, ed. Christopher Haigh (London, 1984), pp. 79–100; M. A. R. Graves and R. H. Silcock, *Revolution, Reaction and the Triumph of Conservatism* (Auckland, 1984), pp. 335–69; Graves, *Tudor Parliaments*, ch. 1, 6, 7, 8.

occupational groups or the local communities which they represented. But their prime allegiance was to the crown, not to political
parties – for there were none. It is necessary to discard modern
notions of 'government' and 'opposition' and of a 'whipped' or
disciplined majority, which will guarantee the enactment of an
official legislative programme. Therefore, whilst the privy council
did not have to contend with an organized parliamentary opposition, it could not look to a disciplined majority to do its bidding.
Instead, parliaments were a microcosm of an Elizabethan governing class of independent-tempered men who wore authority easily
and naturally and who were themselves accustomed to giving
orders. Occasionally the privy council resorted to selective disciplinary measures (sometimes on the Queen's personal initiative),
such as the sequestration or imprisonment of those puritan maver-
icks William Strickland (1571) and Peter Wentworth (1576, 1586–
7 and 1593), and of Anthony Cope and other presbyterian cam-
paigners in 1586–7. But the official heavy hand could be used only
with members who did not enjoy widespread parliamentary support. For most of the time the council had to depend on the
organization of business and the presentation of popular (or at least
acceptable) policies, on the arts of persuasion, and on the natural
loyalty to the Queen. Two houses of independent-tempered men
could not be handled in any other way.

Nevertheless the Commons posed a serious problem to Elizabeth's
parliamentary managers, not because it was growing more powerful
and intransigent, but because it was becoming larger, busier and, in
the process, more inefficient. Not only did it increase from 400 to 462
members, but also 50 per cent or more of them were parliamentary
novices needing guidance and instruction from old hands. The
situation was worsened by the input of bills by private interests. The
result was, as we have seen, a frequent logjam, and indeed some bills
did not even reach the floor of the house. In 1601 Robert Wingfield
moved that 'seeing the subsidy was granted, and they yet had done
nothing, it would please her Majesty not to dissolve the parliament
until some acts were passed.' His plea highlighted the importance
which members attached to unofficial bills, especially those entrusted
to them by those who had elected them and to whom they might have
to answer afterwards.[10]

---

[10] BL Lansdowne MS 41/16, f. 45; Heywood Townshend, *Historical Collections*,
or *An exact Account of the Proceedings of the four last Parliaments of Q. Elizabeth of
Famous Memory* (London, 1680), p. 204.

The time-conscious conciliar managers had other problems too. For example, the Queen, Lord Keeper and Commons Speaker repeatedly admonished the Commons for its time-wasting prolixity, the frivolous or provocative speeches of members and lengthy debate on unofficial bills. Elizabeth summed up her interpretation of the official position when, in 1571, she advised the Commons through Lord Keeper Bacon: '[H]er Highness thinketh ... that they should leave to talk [rhetoric] and speak [logic], to leave long tales which is rather an ostentation of wit then to any effect, and to deal with these things as there were to be proponed ... that they might the sooner return home.' Such strictures had little effect. Thirty years later the Commons was still being cautioned not to spend its time 'in idle and vain matter, painting the same out with froth and volubility of words ... and by troubling the house of purpose with long and vain orations to hinder the proceeding in matters of greater and more weighty importance.'[11]

Even when allowance is made for the remarkable capacity of sixteenth-century audiences to sit attentively through sermons and speeches of formidable duration, there was a limit to the endurance of many Commons members. As they were not provided with the printed text of bills,[12] the conduct of business was almost entirely dependent on the spoken word, from the literal first reading of bills, through debates, committees[13] and their reports to the house. The ennui which this engendered, together with the tedious, technical and often complex nature of lawmaking, may have contributed to the continuing problem of absenteeism, which frequently impaired the efficiency and threatened the productivity of the house. Committees in particular were often so poorly attended that their conveners had to adjourn them and ask the Commons to afforce them. On the other hand, there were always enough knights and burgesses to carry on business in the house. Indeed it might be argued that it was well rid of the drones and pleasure-seekers. In 1572 an experienced parliament man made the caustic observation

[11] Hartley, *Proceedings*, p. 244; Townshend, p. 183; D'Ewes, p. 601b.

[12] Interested members could purchase copies from the clerks, but the standard fee of one penny for ten lines could make serious inroads into a knight's daily wage of four shillings and, even more, into a burgess's two shillings.

[13] Committees were time-consuming and often unproductive. In 1584 William Fleetwood attended one along with at least sixty other members, 'all young gents, and at our meeting in the afternoon twenty at once did speak and there we sat talking and did nothing until night ...' BL Lansdowne MS 41/16, f. 45.

that 'new men ... are commonly most adventurous, and can be gladdest of large parliaments to learn and see fashions, where the old continuers have among other things learned more advisedness.' He touched upon an important precondition of parliamentary efficiency: that what mattered was not quantity but quality, and in particular experience, dedicated service and the legislative skills of the lawyers. Unfortunately some lawyer members were notorious absentees, enticed away by the profit motive to plead their clients' causes in the central law courts next door. Therefore the same anonymous advisor offered the cynical suggestion that, if a contentious matter was assigned to a committee, the longer it will be 'ere the matter come in again, specially if you will appoint lawyers in term time.'[14] However, as we shall see, this did less than justice to the more conscientious parliamentary service of other members of the legal profession.

Nevertheless privy councillors, charged with the duty to transact essential royal business, faced continuous organizational problems in the lower house. And their difficulties were compounded by the way in which their royal mistress harried parliaments on to an early end. So, as they struggled to combat the Commons' inefficiency and accommodate both official and private legislative objectives, they dutifully advised it to make haste. A common argument employed to justify the necessity for speed was the 'lateness of the year' and the approach of the plague season. When parliament met in April 1571 and May 1572 this must have struck a responsive chord in members. Yet the same sinister argument was used as early as February in 1593. On other occasions a loving Queen was careful not only of members' health, but also of the great costs which they incurred in London, whilst in December 1601 she informed the Lords that she was ending parliament in time for them to return home for Christmas.[15]

The fact that the Queen's hustling tactics added to the privy council's managerial problems should alert us to the danger of assuming that Tudor government was a monolithic structure, characterized by unity of purpose. Undoubtedly it was the councillors' duty to advise the Queen on policies, to execute them in

[14] HPT, I, pp. 67–101; Graves, *Tudor Parliaments*, pp. 118–19; 'A Discourse importing the assembly of a Parliament', BL Harleian MS 253, ff. 32, 35. For the probable identification of the author of these advices in 1572, see below p. 54 and n. 32.

[15] Graves, 'Management', p. 15; Townshend, pp. 58, 140.

accordance with her wishes and to oversee the daily administration of her realm. One of their multifarious responsibilities was to recommend the calling of a parliament and then, when it assembled, to manage it in her interest. However, this neat picture of a body of dutiful servants, working together in obedience to her commands, is far removed from reality.

First, both the privy council and parliament were interwoven in the social fabric. They were not two unrelated bodies of men apart from that fabric and with corporate lives of their own untouched by it. The upper tiers of Elizabethan society, from which bishops and peers, parliamentary knights and burgesses, and privy councillors were drawn, were imbued with a competitive dynamic. Great personages attracted to themselves clienteles of lesser men in mutually beneficial associations. These patron-client connections were essentially social mechanisms. However, when they competed for supremacy in a county or when they intruded into the power centres of government, in particular court and council, they acquired a political, factional aspect. Factions became instruments in the perpetual competition for office, power and royal patronage. Therefore, it was inevitable that the privy council, the linchpin of government, became the ultimate arena and prize of such factions, divided one from another by rivalry for royal favour, sometimes by personal antipathies and (less often) by genuine differences of policy.

During the first thirty years of the reign, the privy council tended to polarize into two loose factional alignments headed by the Queen's chief minister, William Cecil (Lord Burghley), and her favourite, the Earl of Leicester. They were rivals for the Queen's confidence and sometimes disagreed on policy. On the other hand, they were essentially moderate men whose differences did not prevent frequent cooperation in the royal interest. However, Leicester's death in 1588 was the beginning of a gradual transformation of Elizabethan politics. Burghley, the Elizabethan Nestor whose benevolent, paternal role within the Elizabethan aristocracy had earned him the friendship or at least respect of many, was ageing and often ill. Indeed in the new climate of the 1590s he was viewed by an increasing number as a conservative dinosaur – Nestor had become Polonius. A whole generation of experienced privy councillors – Sir Walter Mildmay (1589), Sir Francis Walsingham (1590), and Sir Francis Knollys (1596) – died off. A new generation replaced them, under the leadership of the political heirs of Leicester and Burghley: the former's stepson (the Earl of Essex) and the latter's younger son (Robert Cecil). Their rivalry was worked out in an often bitter competition in court and council. Yet there is no evidence that the destabilized politics of the 1590s had a significant impact on parliament. This is not to say that, whilst conciliar disunity in Elizabeth's reign did not result in open and unseemly parliamentary conflict, it did not manifest itself in more subtle ways: diplomatic absences, thunderous silences when active support was crucial or manipulation offstage. The Commons's punishment of one of its members, Arthur Hall, in 1581, for privately printing a tract offensive to the house turns out, on closer inspection, to be an oblique attack mounted by several councillors and their allies on Hall's ex-guardian and friend, Lord Burghley. Likewise, in 1597, the lord treasurer's successful motion in the upper house, that such lords as were absent should be admonished to explain themselves, immediately obliged Essex to justify his truancy. Conciliar disunity often ran just below the surface.[16]

Even when the council was in harmony on a particular policy, the Queen was not bound to take its advice – and often she did not. Frustrated councillors repeatedly wrung their hands as she refused to marry, name a successor, eliminate Mary Stuart, make war on Spain or consent to ecclesiastical reform and harsher anti-Catholic laws. Sometimes Elizabeth did give way, but only belatedly and after periods of sustained pressure: for example, more biting laws against recusants and Jesuits, and the executions of Norfolk and Mary Stuart. It is significant, however, that such conciliar successes were achieved during, or as a consequence of, parliamentary sessions. Privy councillors, unable to overcome Elizabeth's obstinacy on their own, recruited the help of the governing class to which they belonged, which monopolized the Lords and Commons and which shared their prejudices, fears and concerns. Together they would make common cause in order to convert a foolish, obstinate woman to their chauvinistic world-view. This introduces yet another dimension to the privy council's managerial activities and problems. Its responsiblity, in parliament as elsewhere, was to serve the Queen, in this case by obtaining the taxes and laws necessary for effective royal government. Similarly, despite the personal misgivings of some councillors, it dutifully smothered the presbyterian

---

[16] *LJ*, II, 196, 198; G. R. Elton, 'Arthur Hall, Lord Burghley and the Antiquity of Parliament', in *History and Imagination. Essays in honour of H. R. Trevor-Roper*, ed. H. Lloyd-Jones, V. Pearl, and B. Worden (London, 1981), pp. 88–97.

agitations of the 1580s, publicly dissociated itself from the rasher actions of radical Protestants, such as William Strickland in 1571, and urged parliament to give priority to royal business. Yet, at the same time, councillors were ready to harness the energies of the two houses in order to compel Elizabeth to act on matters of great moment and urgency. So, whenever a parliament met, they had to juggle a number of objectives in the hope that they did not drop any of them.[17]

How did the Elizabethan privy council manage parliaments in the pursuit of this ideal? We might assume that its first priority was to ensure an adequate conciliar presence in each house. However, Tudor politics did not focus upon parliaments. The council's prime functions were to advise and administer and its parliamentary service was just one amongst its infinite variety of activities. Whenever Elizabethan parliaments met they were of the highest importance and yet, if they were laid end to end, they would occupy no more than three years in a reign of forty-five years. The acid test of royal government was not its performance in these brief, occasional meetings but its record in the continuous daily relationship with local governing elites. In this sense Professor G. R. Elton is right in stressing that the traditional concentration on parliaments is misplaced.[18]

Doubtless Elizabeth would have welcomed Professor Elton's advice, because she understood the realities of Tudor government rather better than Wallace Notestein, Sir John Neale and the rest of their generation did. Men were appointed to the council board for all kinds of reasons: for their advice or administrative skills; as a reward for loyal service; due to kinship (e.g. Henry Lord Hunsdon and Sir Francis Knollys), or personal favour (e.g. Leicester, Hatton and Essex), or because they were powerful regional magnates (e.g. the Earls of Bedford and Shrewsbury). Some, such as Sir William Knollys, George 2nd Lord Hunsdon and, above all, Sir Robert Cecil, were the political heirs of Elizabeth's first generation of ministers. Their choice may have been the result of Elizabeth's deep attachment to the familiar, as well as deliberate political grooming by their fathers. One thing is certain, that councillors were not chosen with parliaments in mind.

Furthermore, as Elizabeth's reign wore on, a sizeable conciliar

[17] Elton, *Parliament*, pp. 354–77, esp. pp. 376–7; Graves, 'Management', pp. 12–13, 24–9.

[18] Elton, *Parliament*, p. ix.

presence in the two houses became less and less necessary. Some historians have treated the declining number elected to the Commons as an act of political irresponsibility. So Notestein was critical of James I, who 'neglected to retain in the Lower House enough Councillors, and Councillors of ability'.[19] As this was the continuation of a process occurring between 1589 and 1601, when the number there shrank from eight to five, the same criticism should be levelled against Elizabeth. Moreover the parliamentary talents of her later councillors – Sir John Fortescue, Sir William Knollys, Sir John Stanhope, even Cecil – were markedly inferior to those of Burghley, Hatton, Mildmay, Walsingham and others of the previous generation. Yet once again this is to misunderstand why men became councillors, to misrepresent their parliamentary role as the reign progressed and to exaggerate the Commons's importance, as if it was the only house which mattered. The crucial facts about the council's membership are that it shrank from eighteen to thirteen during the reign, and that it became predominantly aristocratic – so, in 1601, all but five of the councillors sat in the Lords. This might have mattered more if an increasingly fractious, even unmanageable Commons had required even more careful stewardship by the council. In fact it did not, despite the monopolies furor of 1601, which was provoked by the lack of official remedial action after the ominous rumblings in the 1597 parliament. Indeed, as the reign progressed some of the major political issues, such as the Queen's marriage and Mary Stuart's threat, became irrelevant or disappeared. Similarly, presbyterian activity lapsed into passivity. The council's parliamentary horizons shrank and increasingly focused on the funding of the war with Spain.

At the same time, perhaps as a consequence of this financial priority, the government displayed a declining interest in lawmaking – or at least it conveyed the public impression that this was the case. From 1586–7 war revenue was the chief reason for parliaments, each of which was called shortly after the collection of the last instalment of the previous subsidy. In itself this is no proof that the official attitude to legislation had changed. The council had never confined itself to the specific purposes for which parliament had been summoned. Nevertheless official pronouncements on lawmaking did change significantly. In the earlier Elizabethan parliaments, the lord keeper had declared that there was a 'want of

[19] Notestein, p. 33.

laws which needeth to be provided for'. This gave way to a growing
concern with the excessive number of burdensome laws and, by the
1590s, there were calls from the Queen, Lord Keeper, Commons
Speaker and prominent lawyers to reduce their number. Committees were appointed and in 1601 an act was passed to this end.
However, all is not quite as it seems. An ongoing official worry was
that private legislation could threaten the passage of official
business. Furthermore the volume of new laws did not appreciably
fall. In December 1588, for example, the privy council appointed a
statutory review committee which scrutinized 'unnecessary or
deiective' laws and which was probably responsible for five new
acts of parliament in 1589. And in 1597–8 the government was
active in the initiation of measures to alleviate the current economic
crisis. In other words conciliar responses in practice were sometimes at variance with official pronouncements, although the
increasing frequency with which such concern was expressed does
in itself suggest a change of attitude.[20]

Whether or not this was the case, the privy council certainly
displayed a growing willingness to devolve responsibility on
knights and burgesses for making the Commons in particular more
efficient and productive. The development of committees for privileges and the resolution of disputed elections in the later Eliza-
bethan-Jacobean parliaments posed no threat to conciliar control.
The emergence of the general committee, in which formal rules of
debate were discarded and the Commons Speaker was replaced by
a chairman, should be regarded in the same light. It was a
procedural device, designed to improve efficiency and not to wrest
parliamentary initiative from the council, which indeed must have
welcomed it. This was not a register of a decline in the council's
parliamentary control, but rather of its self-confidence. Detailed
parliamentary management, as distinct from general surveillance,
could be left to its active agents, though whether those agents
continued to be drawn from the clients of prominent councillors
and their loyalist 'men-of-business',[21] as they had been in the
earlier Elizabethan parliaments, remains to be seen.

Nevertheless there were continuing managerial problems in the
Commons. In contrast, it might be assumed that the Lords can be

---

[20] P. Williams, *The Tudor Regime* (Oxford, 1979), pp. 453–6; M. A. R. Graves,
Elizabethan Parliaments, 1559–1601 (London, 1987), pp. 62–5; *APC*, XVI, pp.
416–18; Dean, 'Bills and Acts', p. 166.

[21] See below, pp. 57–9.

dismissed in a couple of lines, simply because it was a 'safe' chamber. Its members were hereditary peers, many of whom were Tudor creations and who had a natural loyalty to an hereditary monarchy, and bishops who were servants of Elizabeth, supreme governor of the church. Its membership – about eighty – included a strong conciliar element (ranging from eight to thirteen), other prominent servants and the associates of Lord Burghley, the chief minister for forty years. Burghley himself sat there for nine parliamentary sessions (1571–97). However, to pass over the Lords because it was politically reliable is to miss the crucial point about its importance: that it was the more efficient chamber. Its size and the number of bills introduced there were much smaller. It was also the older house, its procedures were well established and its conduct of business was more decorous, whilst its life members had more parliamentary experience. Furthermore, its deliberations were aided by the Queen's legal counsel (the attorney and solicitor general), her master of the rolls, judges and serjeants-at-law, who were summoned on writs of assistance and gave learned advice when required. The house was more reliable because of its greater efficiency, not its political subservience.[22]

Nevertheless the Commons, as an elected assembly, might seem to have been more independent and less susceptible to outside influence. In practice this was not so. Many 'great men', especially peers, were electoral patrons. They secured the return of clients who were usually loyal supporters of the privy council (though less so during Essex's meteoric career in the 1590s). The most notable example was Francis, 2nd Earl of Bedford, who had a hand in the election of between twenty and thirty-five borough members to the parliaments of 1559–84. The proportion of burgesses who, to some degree, owed their seats to the favour of a 'great man' ranged from more than a quarter to a third. Some noble patrons were themselves councillors. Others acted in response to requests from friends and allies on the council. Bedford in particular often used his electoral influence on William Cecil's behalf. If we include those members who had parental links with the court or noble families, together with the thirty-two who were created peers or succeeded to peerages, then it becomes clear that the two houses were simply a parliamentary microcosm of the Elizabethan governing class. Many knights and burgesses were caught up in an intricate web of

[22] Graves, *Tudor Parliaments*, pp. 22–3, 26, 28–9, 31–2, 45–8.

social connections and a deferential hierarchy which intimately linked Lords and Commons. Whilst, as we have seen, the beneficiaries of electoral patronage were not whipped members of a political party or obedient followers of a faction leader, they were likely to demonstrate in parliament the same deference and sense of duty towards their superiors and benefactors as they did at other times. This gave the upper house considerable influence in the Commons and, in turn, assisted the council in its managerial activities there.[23]

The electoral influence of great men did not give rise to charges of sinister manipulation by an authoritarian government, even when it was exercised on behalf of prominent privy councillors. If fears were aroused or resentment stirred, it was because some burgesses felt that the autonomy of their particular boroughs was being threatened by excessive noble influence. As one of them warned in 1571, during a debate on the bill to legalize the election of carpetbaggers, 'lords' letters shall from henceforth bear all the sway ...'. Certainly there was no suggestion that such activities were an attempt to pack the Commons with royal creatures. It was a practice never contemplated, because it was unnecessary, it bore no relation to political realities and, in any case, it would have been impossible to achieve. Furthermore, in a less than ideal world, elected clients, conciliar agents and royal servants sometimes slipped from grace. In 1571, for example, the ambitious lawyer, Robert Bell, led a hunt against administrative abuses and was 'so hardly dealt with' by the council that his 'amazed countenance ... daunted all.' His loss of official favour did not last long: in 1572 he was the council's choice as Speaker of the Commons and five years later he became chief baron of the exchequer. In contrast, the parliamentary attack by James Morice, a royal official, on Archbishop Whitgift of Canterbury in 1593, not only earned him two months of restraint but also proved to be 'a bar against any preferment' by the Queen. Similarly Francis Bacon's injudicious wrecking tactics over the terms of the 1593 subsidy bill wrecked his chances of a career in Elizabeth's service.[24] Even those devotees of

[23] HPT, I, 14, 23–4, 59, 60–5. The figures cited here should not be regarded as sacrosanct. Frequently it is impossible to assess accurately the part which a great man played in the return of a borough member and some of the conclusions in the volumes edited by Hasler are matters of dispute and debate. Nevertheless the evidence is sufficient to confirm the intimate links between personnel of the privy council, Lords and Commons.

[24] Ibid., I, pp. 375–9, 421–4; II, pp. 99–100.

Queen and council, the parliamentary 'men-of-business',[25] could find themselves in disgrace for their indiscretions. The pre-eminent Thomas Norton, for example, paid for the forceful expression of his views in speech and writing with time in the Tower and under house arrest. In particular the Protestant enthusiasm of Norton and other men-of-business sometimes outran their discretion, incurred the Queen's wrath and compelled the council to leave them to suffer awhile, even thought it often sympathized with the views which they expressed. Such men were not 'yes-men', party hacks or fawning courtiers. They were an integral part of the parliamentary mirror image of the loyal, yet independent-tempered men of the governing elite, which managed Elizabethan society under the crown.[26]

Although systematic manipulation of the Commons's membership would have been foreign to the contemporary political mentality, at the same time it would have been irresponsible for the council to sit back and allow the electoral process to lumber to a conclusion without supervision. A certain amount of official organization, surveillance and even direct intervention was deemed necessary. The election of councillors and other royal servants to the Commons was arranged; action was taken to exclude enemies of church and state; and council letters exhorted boroughs to return men with 'understanding and knowledge' of their affairs.[27] Meanwhile the privy council devised a list of parliamentary measures thought fit to pass and, with the assistance of lawyers, drafted them. The vestigial remains of this pre-parliamentary activity include the work of drafting committees appointed in 1559 and 1576, William Cecil's lists of bills to be drawn, drafts of measures promoted by private interests and advanced by individual councillors and especially the preparation of the subsidy bill. One experienced member advised a councillor to have 'the subsidy book, ready written both in paper and parchment' before parliament met. The other item of business to be completed before parliament met was the choice of the Speaker. Theoretically he was freely elected by the house, but, as so often happened, theory and practice differed. For example, on 28 January 1593, three weeks before the opening

---

[25] See below, pp. 57–9.
[26] *CJ*, I, 84–5; Neale, *Parliaments*, I, pp. 218–21, II, pp. 267–76, 309–10; Hartley, *Proceedings*, p. 225; Graves, 'Thomas Norton', p. 33.
[27] A. J. Kempe, *The Loseley Manuscripts* (London, 1836), pp. 242–3; G. R. Elton, *The Tudor Constitution* (Cambridge, 1982), pp. 292–3, 303–5.

ceremonies, Elizabeth and her council named Sir Edward Coke as Speaker. In due course his election by the lower house was 'graciously allowed' by the Queen. Such pre-selection is understandable, because the Speaker's role was crucial to the successful transaction of official business. He controlled the order of business, regulated debate and transmitted royal messages and admonitions to the house. And, as the seats around his chair were reserved for privy councillors, they could direct proceedings by whispered instructions to him.[28]

The first business of a new parliament, before the election of the Speaker, was the lord chancellor's (or lord keeper's) address to the two houses in the Queen's presence. The anomalous nature of his parliamentary position, as spokesman of the house of Lords and voice and orator of the Queen, was more apparent than real. He was premier officer of state, a privy councillor and, first and foremost, a royal servant. Understandably therefore, his speech combined a panegyric on the Queen's virtues and the blessings of her rule with stern admonitions about duty and responsibility and with the reasons for calling parliament couched in nonspecific terms. Once the opening formalities were at an end and the Commons (with conciliar prompting) had chosen its speaker, parliament got down to business. Very soon, absenteeism and the volume of business in the lower house, those perennial parliamentary problems, required the attention of privy councillors. They resorted to various devices to combat these problems. The act of 1515, whereby members wishing to return home during the session required the licence of the Speaker and the house, may have put a brake on early departures, but it did nothing to prevent endemic daily absenteeism. So the statute was supplemented by the imposition of fines (raised from 4d in 1566 to 6d in 1589), the threatened loss of parliamentary wages and especially regular roll calls of the house. There can be little doubt that the privy council, often operating through the Speaker, was responsible for these controls, but its efforts bore meagre fruit and absenteeism continued to plague both the Commons and its committees.[29]

[28] Elton, *Parliament*, pp. 71–4; HMC, 9th Report, p. 373a; V. F. Snow (ed.), *Parliament in Elizabethan England. John Hooker's Order and Usage* (New Haven, 1977), p. 164; BL Harleian MS, 253, ff. 33–35v.

[29] See above, p. 10; P. L. Ward (ed.), *William Lambarde's notes on the procedures and privileges of the House of Commons, 1584* (HMSO, London, 1977), pp. 66–7; *CJ*, I, 76; D'Ewes, p. 439a; Neale, *Commons*, pp. 413–16.

Furthermore, like King Canute, the privy council could not stem the tide, in this case the tide of unofficial bills. It enlisted the aid of the men-of-business, the Speaker, the stern collective voice of the House of Lords and even the Queen in order to ensure preferential treatment for official business. So the Commons was cajoled to set aside private bills or to sort legislation into an order of priority with preference given to commonweal matters. Councillors manoeuvred contentious, time-consuming private measures off the floor of the house and into committee, because they were well aware that, as one of them was advised, 'private bills ever be eagerly followed and make factions.' Furthermore their clients, especially Thomas Norton, were fertile in procedural innovations, all designed to speed up business: for example, regularizing joint conferences with the Lords to iron out differences between the two houses; appointing committees to scrutinize bills on similar or related matters, especially those on cloth; and setting aside afternoon sessions for private bills, thereby allowing more time for public business in the mornings. It must be more than coincidence that most of these procedural improvements were adopted during or after the 1571 parliament when William Cecil, now Lord Burghley, was no longer present to direct affairs personally in the Commons.[30]

Some of these procedural devices and practices proved to be temporary, but two others were more enduring. The most significant (as noted above), was the emergence of the general committee in the parliaments of the period 1593–1601.[31] The other concerned London and was typical of the interplay of Elizabethan politics and economic pressure groups. In 1572 a privy councillor was advised that one way to keep the session short was 'to abridge the things that lengthen the session', above all '[t]he bills of occupation, mysteries and companies and specially the bills of London'. This concern was understandable because London dwarfed all other English cities in its wealth, economic power, diversity of economic activity and therefore in the resultant internal conflicts between rival interests. The parliamentary consequence of this was that competing companies and crafts placed bills (usually in the Commons) to further their own interests, sometimes to the detriment of others. As a result, there were frequent campaigns with curriers ranged against cordwainers, plasterers against painters, white

[30] Graves, 'Management', pp. 14–17, 30–1; Graves, 'Thomas Norton', pp. 24–5; BL Harleian MS 253, f. 34.

[31] See above, p. 48.

bakers against brown bakers and so on. It was in the parliamentary interest of the privy council and in the civic interest of city government that the flow of such measures should be controlled. When, in 1572, the council received a private recommendation to consult the city's members about its bills and, if appropriate, to refer them 'to the Lord Mayor and Aldermen to be considered at London, and so to rid the house thereof', the author was simply trying to plug a loophole in a system of municipal surveillance which already existed. In early Elizabethan London, economic lobbies promoting bills had to present them first to the governing body of mayor and aldermen for scrutiny. Some were approved, a number amended and others rejected. The practice was not watertight and may even have lapsed for a while, but it was vigorously revived in the 1590s, when a special committee of aldermen was empowered to coordinate a legislative programme for the city. Those advices of 1572, obviously written by a Londoner with parliamentary experience, suggest the hand of Thomas Norton. He was the lord mayor's remembrancer (secretary) and as such was the intermediary between council and city. He was also a client of Hatton, Mildmay, Walsingham and, above all, of Burghley. The positive proof of his authorship is wanting but the evidence is strong. Whoever wrote it, he was attempting to accommodate the different but not necessarily conflicting priorities of conciliar management of parliament and aldermanic control of the city.[32]

The councillors' managerial efforts were reinforced by their prestige as the men closest to the monarch. It was natural that members should hang on their informed words, especially if, like William Cecil or Mildmay, their arguments were cogent and supported with carefully marshalled evidence. However, not all councillors were as well received: Sir Francis Knollys probably induced sleep; and the waspish addresses of Sir James Croft irritated, as did the pedagogic manner of Sir Robert Cecil, who

[32] Graves, *Tudor Parliaments*, p. 156; HPT, I, pp. 91–2, 95–6, 99; BL Harleian MS 253, ff. 33v, 34v; Dean, 'Public or Private', pp. 527–9; Archer, pp. 35–7; Neale, *Commons*, pp. 383–6; Dean, 'Bills and Acts', pp. 198–201; Corporation of London RO, Repertories, 15, ff. 177v, 188; ibid., 16, ff. 118v–119, 124–124v, 128–128v, 130, 134, 139–140, 141; ibid., 17, ff. 129v–130, 134v, 141v, 144; ibid., 23, f. 22v; ibid., 24, ff. 133v–134; ibid., 25, f. 275. Professor Elton first identified Norton as the probable author of the 'advices' of 1572 and I am now inclined to agree with him. See Elton, *Parliament*, p. 323 and n. 10.

once lectured the Commons that its conduct was more fit for a grammar school. In any case, no matter how well endowed the councillors were in parliamentary and public relations skills, they were too few to manage parliament on their own. Instead, under the primacy of William Cecil (from 1571 Lord Burghley) they were the prestigious front line of an extensive managerial network which included the speakers and clerks of the two houses. Beyond them, the council was dependent on a loyal, cooperative governing class and, within it, active loyalists whom historians have designated its 'men-of-business'. They did not constitute a formal, organized network, let alone some kind of political party. Their service was grounded simply on personal loyalty to Queen and council and reinforced by bonds of clientage to prominent councillors or their allies, such as Francis, 2nd Earl of Bedford. They served in a variety of ways, in speech, committee business, procedural improvements and the drafting of bills – and usually in the furtherance of conciliar business. One of them – again probably Norton – advised the council to avoid the heavy official hand which could be counterproductive in an assembly of men imbued with self-confidence and a prickly sensitivity. If some important matter had to be raised 'it were well that some other privie of it afore.'

However, the services of the men-of-business did not end there. They also lent their assistance when conciliar policies were at variance with those of the Queen. Especially in the decades before the Spanish war, they frequently rescued the members of the council from a dilemma in which they found themselves. As already observed, councillors were Elizabeth's sworn servants, devoted to her interests, but, at the same time, they sometimes had a different notion as to what her best interests were. Open disobedience to her wishes might result in banishment from court and, even worse, loss of place and profit, especially if they publicly trespassed on forbidden pastures such as church reform, succession and marriage. Therefore they looked to the men-of-business to advance conciliar policies of which the Queen disapproved and to marshal parliamentary pressure when she refused to take positive action on important matters, such as Mary Stuart's fate in 1572. On that occasion Robert Bell, the Speaker, with Norton, Fleetwood, Thomas Dannett and Thomas Digges (all connected with Burghley or Leicester) and other men-of-business worked successfully for the execution of the Duke of Norfolk. However, the frenetic labours of councillors, men-of-business, civil and common lawyers and bishops to get rid of Mary foundered on Elizabeth's obstinacy.[33]

There was infinite variety in the ability and the range of services provided by individual men-of-business in the earlier Elizabethan parliaments. Thomas Norton (MP 1558–81) was a prolific parliamentary draftsman, organizer and persuasive debater, whose fame was such that he was dubbed 'Mr. Norton the parliament Man'. His assertion, that 'all that I have done I did by commandment of the House, and specially of the Queen's Council there, and my chiefest care was in all things to be directed by the Council,' might well have been a watchword for all men-of-business. Although Norton was pre-eminent, he was not unique. And, although he had no outstanding successor, some of the men-of-business who outlived him continued to assist and advance conciliar designs in the Commons: for example, William Fleetwood (active in the house between 1559 and 1589 and serving as a legal assistant in the Lords in 1593); James Dalton (MP 1563–86/7 and 1593); Thomas Digges (MP 1572–81, 84/5), cutting short lengthy debate whenever possible; and three – Richard Onslow, Robert Bell and Christopher Yelverton – who served in the crucial managerial post of Speaker in 1566/7, 1572–6 and 1596/7 respectively. It is true that such men, especially London lawyers, present something of a paradox, because they actively served both the council and their communities. So, in the general interest of the former they worked in the cause of speed and efficiency, whilst at the same time they advanced the particular interests of the latter – especially local bills which were often time-consuming and contentious. Yet, despite this shortcoming, the men-of-business were an integral, perhaps the crucial, element in the privy council's support network throughout much of Elizabeth's reign.[34]

Of course the nature of their services depended on conciliar needs in a particular parliamentary session. In turn these needs were determined by changing circumstances, especially the international situation. So in 1571–2 the challenge was the first political crisis of the reign; and between 1576 and 1587 the related threats of

[33] Graves, 'Thomas Norton', pp. 19, 21, 23, 24–5, 27–35; Graves, 'Management', pp. 17–21, 23–32; Townshend, p. 246; BL Harleian MS 253, ff. 33v–35v.

[34] Graves, 'Thomas Norton', pp. 19–30, 31–2, 34; Graves, 'Management', pp. 19–23, 31–2; HPT, II, p. 38; ibid., III, pp. 86–8; Dean, 'Public or Private?', pp. 529, 532–3, 536–7, 544–6.

Mary Stuart, obstinate English recusants, international Catholicism and Spanish power increasingly demanded parliamentary responses. However, the two sessions of 1584/5 and 1586/7 were the last occasions on which the privy council needed to enlist the aid of its men-of-business in order to coerce the Queen into action – in this case over the fate of Mary Stuart. Thereafter parliaments were summoned primarily to provide continuous taxation in the long war with Spain. Nevertheless, during the 1590s there were disastrous harvests, high bread prices and consequent internal disturbances, the spectre of growing poverty and vagabondage, military stalemate, official corruption and government economies. The last of these encouraged monopolies as a cheap form of royal patronage and raised questions about the misuse of the royal prerogative. The results of such developments were a growing war-weariness and, in 1601, the parliamentary eruption over monopolies at a time when the old generation of experienced councillors had disappeared. Their replacements inherited an extended economic depression and a seemingly endless war. Therefore it is not surprising that, in the parliaments of the period 1593–1601, councillors needed a support network as much as ever.

Throughout the reign the lawyers were prominent within that network. The majority of members in both the Lords and Commons were not trained in the common law. They were not equipped to draft or revise bills in the correct legal language and terminology or to ensure that the contents of those bills did not traverse the principles of common law. Therefore they looked to the lawyers to supply these deficiencies. In the Lords this was no problem because of the formidable presence, advice and skills of the legal assistants.[35] However, it was a more haphazard affair in the Commons. There the available pool of legal expertise depended on the election of lawyers, though it should be added that many boroughs automatically returned their recorders (legal officers). On paper the Elizabethan house was richly provided for, because its lawyer members averaged 17 per cent of the membership, and steadily increased from 12 to 23 per cent. Other members had attended an inn of court and probably carried with them into the lower house some acquaintance both with the law and with the career lawyers who sat alongside them.[36]

[35] See above, p. 49.
[36] HPT, I, pp. 4, 20.

Despite the lawyers' reputation for absenteeism, their growing number was accompanied by the growth of their parliamentary role: in 1601, for example, they were appointed *en bloc* to twenty-four Commons committees. The driving force was often calculated ambition: that an able and loyal parliamentary performance could be the first rung on an ascending ladder of royal service. It worked well enough for Bell, Coke, John Popham and John Puckering, all of whom were Speakers and then moved on to high office. Almost without exception from 1510 onwards the Commons presiding officer was a common lawyer. That was understandable, because the lawyers were expert in legislative and procedural niceties and in oral proceedings. However, there was a subtle change: Elizabeth's was the first Tudor reign in which none of the lawyer Speakers were also privy councillors at the time. Nevertheless they were active in the service of the council, as evinced by Bell's role in the pursuit of Norfolk and Mary Stuart (1572), Popham's partisan conduct (1581), Puckering's abject willingness to please the Queen (1584/5 and 1586/7), Coke's disciplinary regime (1593) and Yelverton's services on Robert Cecil's behalf (1597).[37]

The council too was well served, and with greater continuity from session to session, by other lawyers: not only Norton, but also Dalton, Fleetwood, Thomas Wilbraham and others. However, these earlier Elizabethan men-of-business had one common characteristic. None of them (apart from Bell) were raised to high office in central government, the judiciary, the court or royal household. They remained outside the small, charmed circle of those who formulated policy and activated it – just doers and wheeler-dealers, clients performing in parliament at the request, even behest, of a conciliar patron or the council. They remained 'private' men, who could not be identified publicly as 'official creatures' when contentious issues or conciliar proposals were being aired. Then, between 1581 and 1586/7 there was a managerial watershed. First, Norton died shortly before the 1584 parliament. He had no replacement. Moreover, by then many of the other men-of-business, who had been so busy in the earlier Elizabethan parliaments, had died or retired. Secondly, Mary Stuart was executed during the Christmas recess of 1586/7. Just as Norton's death heralded the passing of the earlier Elizabethan generation of old-style, 'independent'

---

[37] HPT, I, pp. 98 n. 1 (ii), 422–4, 623–4; ibid., III, pp. 235–6, 257–8, 680–1; Elton, *Parliament*, pp. 324–6; Graves, 'Management', pp. 19–20, 24–5, 31–2.

men-of-business, so Mary Stuart's death proved to be the last occasion on which the privy council needed the services of such men in its attempts to coerce the Queen into action.

Certainly there were always men available to serve the council. They included departmental officers and clerks, and the personal assistants of prominent councillors. Such were James Morice, attorney of the court of wards, Thomas Fanshawe, the queen's remembrancer, Robert Beale, clerk of the privy council and the members of the Cecils' secretariat: not only their principal secretaries, Michael Hickes and Henry Maynard, but also Vincent Skinner, John Clapham, Levinius Munck and Simon Willis. However, these men were too easily recognized as official minions, whilst those like Morice and Beale, who chose to walk an independent path, received prompt retribution from the Queen or her ministers.

Instead during the 1580s and 1590s the privy council increasingly conducted its managerial operations through a circle of lawyers who, in contrast to the earlier Elizabethan men-of-business, moved upwards to high office. Edward Coke (1592) and Thomas Fleming (1594) rose via brief tenures of London's recordership after Fleetwood's retirement. Popham (in 1581), Puckering (1584/5 and 1586/7) and Coke again (in 1593) exploited to advantage that trusty rung on the promotion ladder, the Commons Speakership.[38] They were but part of a larger circle of ambitious, upwardly-mobile lawyers, who included Thomas Bromley and Thomas Egerton, both of whom held the great seal during the reign. Yet, in contrast to the extensive support network, which had characterized the earlier Elizabethan parliaments, that circle was not a large one. This narrowing process began in the previous decade, when Bromley, Roger Manwood and Christopher Wray (an ex-Speaker from 1571) became solicitor general, chief baron of the exchequer and chief justice of queen's bench. Gradually members of the circle moved to occupy and virtually monopolize the offices of lord chancellor/lord keeper, master of the rolls, solicitor general and attorney general, and the chief justices of the three great central courts. During the last two decades of Elizabeth's reign, the same names appear repeatedly as occupants of the most important and

---

[38] The relationship between performance and promotion is quite clear. Thomas Snagge and John Croke were unable to keep the Commons in order in 1589 and 1601. The former received no more than the conventional elevation to a Queen's serjeantry, whilst the latter went empty-handed until James I's accession. HPT, I pp. 677–8; ibid., II, 410.

prestigious places in the judiciary: Bromley, Coke, Egerton, Fleming, Popham and Puckering.

So successful were these lawyers that they rose out of the House of Commons to occupy places on the woolsacks in the upper house, as lord chancellor or keeper, the queen's learned counsel, her judges and serjeants. There, without voice (unless called upon to speak) or vote, they provided a learned and professional stiffening to a chamber of amateur legislators. However, it might be assumed that they had also risen out of the mainstream of parliamentary activity, thereby diminishing their managerial value to the privy council. After all, it was the Commons which was so often clogged with bills, and its inefficiency did not abate during the last two decades of the reign. But such an assumption would disregard the very real contribution which the legal assistants made to the efficiency of the House of Lords – and parliamentary efficiency was an important managerial concern. Moreover, some of them were selectively returned to the Commons, either to serve as Speaker or to reinforce the council's managerial team there.[39] As a result there was created a parliamentary network, extending into the privy council and through both chambers, and bonded both by membership of the same profession and common fellowship of the inns of court.

This development was probably a consequence of the most important single event in the history of Elizabethan parliamentary management. The council's managerial techniques were profoundly influenced, even determined, by the placement of the queen's chief advisor. In 1559, 1563 and 1566/7 parliament's focal point was the House of Commons, because that was where William Cecil sat. Then, in 1571, he moved to the upper house as Lord Burghley. No longer could he direct business personally in the inefficient, overburdened lower house, and yet he remained the council's parliamentary supremo. Therefore it is no surprise that, from 1571, the Speaker, the Lords and the Queen applied pressure on the lower house in order to expedite essential business; nor that Burghley received memoranda, diaries, journals and advices on proceedings from the Speaker, clerks, men-of-business and anonymous members.[40]

---

[39] For example, two speakers, Popham (in 1581) and Coke (1593), occupied the office of solicitor general at the time. So did Egerton and Fleming when they sat in the Commons in 1584–6/7 and 1597–1601 respectively. HPT, I, p. 622–4; ibid., II, pp. 80–1, 139; ibid., III, pp. 234–5.

[40] For example, from Fulk Onslow, who was clerk of the Commons from 1571, William Fleetwood (1584/5), possibly Thomas Cromwell (1572–84) and Henry

There was a simultaneous, dramatic growth in the importance of conciliar men-of-business, such as Norton and Fleetwood, Dalton, Dannett and Digges. However, as many of this earlier generation disappeared from parliament in the 1580s, their thinning ranks were reinforced, as we have seen, by members of the Cecils' personal secretariat[41] and Burghley's political heir, Robert Cecil. Apart from Robert, who was appointed to the council in 1591 and so was one of its managers in the parliaments of 1593–1601, none of these men figures prominently in the records of parliamentary proceedings. Perhaps they were inactive, or at least kept a low profile, because they were known to be Cecilian employees and therefore no more than Cecilian mouthpieces. Alternatively, they may have been an intelligence network, reporting regularly to their masters. Such possibilities cannot be transformed into certainties for sheer lack of evidence, but the timing of their first appearances in the Commons is instructive: Vincent Skinner's return when Burghley went to the Lords in 1571 and the election of Robert Cecil, Michael Hickes and Henry Maynard in 1584, just after the death of Thomas Norton, were probably more than coincidences.

It was at about the same time that the council in general, or Burghley in particular, turned increasingly to the circle of ambitious careerist lawyers to advance official objectives in parliament: by serving as Speaker, promoting conciliar designs in the Commons, and rendering assistance to the Lords in its deliberations and legislative activity. The Cecilian secretaries also acted – not often and usually unobtrusively, but nonetheless significantly – on matters which were important to their employers. Skinner sat on committees for the Queen's safety (1581), Mary Stuart (1586/7) and subsidy bills (1589 and 1593); Maynard chaired the subsidy committee in 1601; Hickes drafted a speech to be delivered in the parliament of 1593, in favour of the bill for the relief of maimed soldiers (surely a matter of conciliar concern), and four years later he was a member of the monopolies committee. During the 1590s

---

Jackman (1589), and certainly from a number of anonymous authors in 1571, 1572, 1584/5 and 1586/7; HMC, *The manuscripts of the house of lords*, vol. XI, addenda, 1514–1714 (London, 1962), no. 3186, pp. 6–15; BL Lansdowne MS 41/16, ff. 45–45v; ibid., 55/63, ff. 184–5, Trinity College, Dublin MS 1045, ff. 1–135v; BL Cotton MS Titus F.i, ff. 129–71; Bodleian Library Tanner MS 393, ff. 45–64; BL Lansdowne MS 43/72, ff. 164–75v; BL Harleian MS 7188, ff. 89–103.

[41] See above, p. 59.

Robert Cecil became more active and prominent in public and parliamentary affairs, as the health and energy of his father declined. Hickes was, increasingly, his confidant, whilst Robert's own personal secretaries, Simon Willis and Levinius Munck, were elected to the Commons. By 1601, both his father and his own political rival, the Earl of Essex, were dead. And so the pendulum of parliamentary gravity swung back to the lower house, where the chief minister now sat.[42]

Like any human institution or collection of human beings, the privy council had its share of imperfections. It committed errors of judgement or miscalculations: when, for example, it believed that it could persuade the Queen to marry, name a successor, execute Mary Stuart or improve the conditions of a 'halfly-reformed' church; when in 1571 it sequestered William Strickland and stirred up a hornet's nest of protest in the Commons; when councillors did not collaborate effectively over the subsidy of 1593; and when the council and Queen ignored the ominous parliamentary rumblings about monopolies in 1597.[43] But on the credit side it laboured, with a modicum of success, to ensure that parliaments granted the crown its laws and taxes, and to allow time for at least some private bills to become law. Furthermore, neither the diminishing size of the later Elizabethan privy council, nor its increasingly noble composition, impaired its parliamentary effectiveness. Two other concurrent changes, however, did have that effect. One was the decimation of the earlier Elizabethan privy council. Between 1588 and 1598 the passage of time and the process of ageing removed the Earl of Leicester, Walsingham, Hatton, Knollys and finally Burghley himself from the council board. Their replacements were relatively inexperienced in the arts of parliamentary management. At the same time there was a narrowing of the privy council's once extensive parliamentary support network. During the 1580s and 1590s the old-style 'independent' men-of-business in the Commons virtually disappeared. They were replaced by a much smaller group. As we have seen, it included Cecilian servants, but the most important component consisted of ambitious and successful lawyers, who served in both houses, rose to high judicial offices and

    [42] HPT, I, p. 609; ibid., II, pp. 310–11; ibid, III, p. 39–40, 109, 390–1, 627. Much of the biographical information on pp. 59–61 has been derived from the same work.
    [43] HPT, III, p. 457; Graves, 'Management', pp. 24–9; Neale, *Parliaments*, I, pp. 193–203; ibid., II, pp. 298–312, 352–6.

even became privy councillors. It was a group bonded by common professional association in the law and/or by career obligations to Burghley, Robert Cecil and other councillors. Their considerable legal and legislative skills were an asset to the privy council. This was more than offset, however, by the disadvantage that, by the end of the reign, the conciliar managerial network in the Commons was visibly an official one. When, in 1601, councillors were isolated by the uproar over monopolies, they looked in vain for Nortons and Fleetwoods to stem the floodtide of resentment, for there were none. Their spokesmen, such as Solicitor General Fleming, spoke with an official voice. The privy council was in danger of isolating itself from popular and aggrieved opinion in the lower house. Perhaps it was an ill omen for the future.

3

Parliament and Foreign Policy

WALLACE MacCAFFREY

The reader of this volume might well express some surprise at the inclusion of a chapter dealing with parliament and foreign relations. Surely the conduct of England's relations with her neighbours was firmly and wholly within the control of the Tudor princes. Religion, the succession or other matters might require the involvement of parliament in necessary statutory action, but in dealings with the other powers of Europe the ruler acted by 'our mere will and motion'. The conduct of foreign relations was a matter of state in which neither house would think of intruding. All this was true, but it was not the whole truth. In an age of martial kingship, relations with other princes all too often flared into war. War cost money, money which the monarch could not find in his own coffers and which therefore must come from parliament. Indeed parliament in no small part owed its very existence to the needs of the Plantagenets in financing war against France and Scotland.

In 1571 Lord Keeper Bacon reiterated a long-established principle when he declared that extraordinary expenses required extraordinary income, that is, parliamentary taxation.[1] By then the distinction between ordinary and extraordinary had become blurred, as I shall argue below, but at the beginning of the Tudor era it was quite clear. Extraordinary expenses invariably meant war, a war about to be fought as in the case of the invasions of France in 1475 and 1492, or already under way, for which the bills were coming in. Hence the summons of a parliament coincided with a crisis in foreign affairs, in the recent past or the near future. The assumptions governing the royal request for funds on such occasions were well understood. The money asked for was a free gift,

---

[1] BL Cotton MS Titus I, ff. 123ff; Neale, *Parliaments*, I, p. 186.

but the king was in no doubt that he would receive it. Parliamentary taxation was at once a voluntary act and the performance of due obedience, albeit an obedience limited to a specific occasion.

The rationale behind this seeming paradox was clear enough to contemporaries. It was the ruler's duty to protect his people against external threats or internal disorder, theirs to support him in such actions. Their representatives in parliament did not expect to criticize his judgement in any particular policy but they did expect him to justify his request by showing that it was tied to a specific threat to English security. He did not have to prove his case but he had to make it. Once his spokesman (usually the lord chancellor or keeper) made the royal case, the king could expect a prompt response from parliament although the amount of money and the form of the levy might entail further discussion. This was the set of conventions within which the king had to conduct his relations with other princes and powers. Although the initiatives in foreign relations were wholly in royal hands, the fact that the necessary funds would have to come from his subjects placed implicit limits on those initiatives. What those limits were no one could accurately say. In the hands of a Henry V or Henry VIII they might be widely stretched. Under Edward IV or Henry VII they seemed to contract. How wide or how narrow they might be was determined not only by the ambitions of a particular ruler but also by the circumstances of international relations.

These were the financial limits which parliamentary convention set and within which English kings had to conduct their foreign relations at the end of the fifteenth century. What was the nature of these relations? On what principles did the English monarchs of this era conduct their dealings with their neighbours? They were conceived largely in dynastic terms. From Yorkist times down to the death of Henry VIII they were still deeply affected by the experience of the Hundred Years' War. When war was waged, the enemy was almost always France: the announced goals of war normally the reconquest of the French lands rightfully belonging to the English monarchs. In fact neither Edward nor Henry VII had serious plans for such a reconquest. The expeditions of 1475 and 1492 were essentially blackmailing enterprises for which the rhetoric of reconquest served to justify the demand for money from parliament. The long-term thrust of their policy, particularly of Henry VII, was a wary neutrality, but the rhetoric of foreign relations was still phrased in the traditional claim to the French throne.[2]

When these kings did seek funds from parliament for their projects they were met with cautious reserve. The house haggled over terms and imposed conditions. Money was to go for war purposes only and to be spent within fixed time limits. In both 1475 and 1492 parliamentary provision was inadequate and the war chest had to be filled up from the non-parliamentary source of a benevolence. Underlying this bargaining was the assumption that the campaigns would be of brief duration, no more than a summer or two at most. The accepted mode of parliamentary taxation was the tenth/fifteenth, with a fixed yield of about £30,000. Efforts by both kings to secure a more open-ended tax, based on actual wealth, were defeated by taxpayer recalcitrance.

These circumstances altered fundamentally with the accession of the second Tudor. First of all, this king, unlike his irenic predecessors, hungered after martial glory and hoped to take his place among the renowned captains of the European world. In the course of his reign there would be three costly bouts of warfare, in its first and second decades and again in the 1540s. In each case there was a formal reassertion of Henry's rights in France. Secondly, the crown was successful between 1512 and 1523 in establishing a new mode of taxation, the subsidy. Levied, under new arrangements for assessment and collection, on income from land and the value of goods, it provided a yield at once substantially larger and much more flexible since the incidence could be raised or lowered to produce varying levels of return. The yields of the mid-1520s were roughly double those of the first decade of the century.

A third factor, of quite different character, was the beginning of the great inflation, which steadily pushed up the costs of government, in peace and in war, from about 1530 to the end of the century. These circumstances would in their turn lead to an erosion of the established conventions governing parliamentary taxation. These rested on a distinction between the ordinary and extraordinary needs of the crown. The first would be met out of recurrent, non-parliamentary revenues; the latter would be provided for by parliament. In theory extraordinary income was to be used solely

[2] Charles Ross, *Edward IV* (Berkeley and Los Angeles, 1974), pp. 215–18, 236, 349–50; G. L. Harriss, 'Aids, Loans and Benevolences', *HJ*, 6, (1963), 9; S. B. Chrimes, *Henry VII* (London, 1972), p. 198.

for extraordinary expenditures which were assumed to be military in nature, to be spent on actual or immediately threatening war.

What happened in the course of the sixteenth century, under the pressure of war and inflation, was that exchequer practice changed so that extraordinary revenue was applied to ordinary costs and the old distinction became meaningless.[3] But although the practice of expenditure altered, the theory remained largely unchanged. The grounds on which the crown sought assistance and on which parliament granted it continued to be the traditional ones: the need to cover the shortfall occasioned by defence against external or internal enemies of the crown which could not be met from recurrent revenue. From the mid-1530s the government made a tentative effort to broaden the definition of extraordinary needs to include the overall costs of good government. Had this notion been fully developed the theory of taxation would have shifted from the medieval notion of emergency interventions to one of permanent, sustained support of all governmental activity. Taxes would have ceased to be a medicine administered in moments of fiscal ill health to a steady diet nourishing all the crown's functions. As it was, the theory remained more or less unchanged although, as we shall see, the agreed understanding of extraordinary expenses altered in response to a new set of circumstances. Even before the Spanish war broke out, parliamentary taxation had become a very 'ordinary' feature of English life and government financial operations were posited on the expectation of a regular succession of subsidies whenever parliament was summoned.

The first bout of Henrician warfare, down to 1517, was financed through a series of fiscal experiments which eventuated by 1523 in the perfected machinery of the subsidy. But when war resumed in 1522 Cardinal Wolsey and the King initially took a new tack. Bypassing parliament, they went directly to the country, demanding a loan, to be levied on the new assessment intended for the subsidy. A levy of 10 per cent on land and goods was sought and in spite of much grumbling the government extracted the unprecedented sum of £352,000 from its subjects in 1522 and 1523. Fortified by this success they then asked the 1524 parliament for a subsidy in the staggering amount of £800,000, to be levied at the rate of 4s on the pound. The house reluctantly agreed to a rate of

---

[3] See J. D. Alsop, 'The theory and practice of Tudor taxation,' *EHR*, 97 (1982), 1–30.

2s; between 1524 and 1527 this yielded over £150,000. In 1525, in the wake of French defeat of Pavia, Wolsey attempted a repeat of the 1522 loan, but the hitherto docile taxpaying beast of burden balked and the 'Amicable Loan' foundered on a taxpayers' strike. Nevertheless a statute of 1529 cancelled the King's indebtedness to his creditor subjects; by a stroke of the pen the massive loans of 1522–23 were converted into gifts.[4]

It would be tempting to read into these actions a deliberate move to free the King's hand in the making of war by substituting prerogative taxation for parliamentary consent under the guise of loans. That is probably assuming too much. If Henry had had a more sustained ambition things might have been different, but his goals were basically opportunistic and short term. Thwarted in his schemes for exploiting the disaster of Pavia, his attention soon wandered to the new preoccupation of his marital affairs. In the late 1520s the pressure for war finance faded away, not to be resumed for a decade. Henry had nothing to show for the wars of the 1520s but there were lasting domestic consequences. The barrier of parliamentary reluctance to provide adequately for war had been cracked, if not entirely broken, now that the subsidy was firmly in place.

The decade of the 1530s was a peaceful one but these years witnessed the first efforts of the government to alter altogether the scope and purpose of parliamentary grants by introducing a peace-time levy. In 1534 parliament passed a subsidy act which for the first time was not directly related to actual warfare, past, present or immediately threatening. In the preamble the King's subjects dutifully called to mind his 'wise and politic governance, regiment and rule of this realm' for twenty-five years. Taking into account his 'great industry, labor, pain and travail with the excessive and inestimable charges' sustained in his last war against Scotland, and the costs of forts at Calais and on the Borders as well as the campaign against the Irish rebels, out of 'mere love and obedience' they granted him a subsidy and one tenth/fifteenth. Six years later more money was sought. The rhetoric of the act was much the same as that of its predecessor; thirty-one years of wise government, the abolition of the Roman jurisdiction and the establishment of pure

[4] Harriss, p. 12; F. C. Dietz, *English Government Finance 1485–1558* (London, 1964), pp. 85–88; 94; J. D. Mackie, *The Earlier Tudors* (Oxford, 1952), p. 304; Edward Hall, *Henry VIII* (London, 1904) II, pp. 35–46; George Bernard, *The Amicable Grant* (New York, 1986), *passim*.

religion were cited. The specific charges on the royal means in these six years were listed – the Pilgrimage of Grace, the mobilization of 1539 against threatened invasion, the cost of coastal forts and again Irish expenditures. A subsidy and four tenths/fifteenths were granted.[5]

These preambles quietly but skilfully shift the ground on which 'extraordinary' taxation had been granted. The mention of a Scottish war in the 1534 grant was the merest gesture since no major clash had occurred in more than a decade. The emphasis in both grants fell on costs which were essentially military in character but either preventive as against foreign aggression or suppressive of the internal threats posed by rebellions. Nevertheless there is now at least the implication that subjects owe support to the monarch not only when he is actively defending them against immediate threats to their security but also for the permanent, day-to-day benefits, temporal and spiritual, with which his zealous care for their welfare provides them. These peacetime subsidies point to long-term changes which would not be more fully implemented for another decade or so. In the early 1540s Henry turned once again to military adventures, overseas and in Scotland, and war finance dominated the whole decade. On the continent, jumping eagerly into the Habsburg-Valois struggle, he reasserted his old claims to French sovereignty. In Scotland fortuitous circumstance opened up the real possibility of adding the Scottish kingdom to the Tudor inheritance. This war was to rage on beyond the King's lifetime.

The scale of operations and the scope of royal ambitions in the 1540s went far beyond Henry's earlier wars. An army of unprecedented size was mounted in the French campaign and for the first time since the early years of his reign Henry had something substantial to show for his efforts: the fishing port of Boulogne, which was now added to the March of Calais. Towards Scotland the announced goals were grander – nothing less than the subordination of the smaller kingdom to the larger – but the military effort was initially less extensive. A combination of ruthlessly destructive raids and of diplomatic pressure was counted on to bring the Scots to their knees. Before Henry died a shaky peace had been patched up with France but the Scottish war remained

[5] *SR*, III, pp. 516–24, 812–24; for a discussion of the changing nature of taxation see Elton, *Studies*, III, pp. 216–33; G. L. Harriss, 'Thomas Cromwell's new principle', *EHR*, 93 (1978), 721–38; J. D. Alsop, 'Theory and practice', pp. 14–26.

unsettled, a deadly legacy to the king's successor in power, the Protector Somerset.

This massive war effort entailed correspondingly gigantic costs. The King was less dependent on parliamentary assistance than in the past since he had at his disposal the golden egg of the monastic lands, some two-thirds of which (in capital value) were sold. He also borrowed lavishly at Antwerp and finally he debased the currency, raking in some £367,000 by this operation. Nevertheless, these sources were far from covering the total costs (some £2,134,000 between 1539 and 1547).[6]

The advantages of the subsidy were now fully evident. By lowering the level of incidence from £20 (on both lands and goods) in 1541–2 to £1 in 1544–6, he increased the revenue from a single subsidy handsomely. The 1541 subsidy yielded £95,000; that of 1543 £189,000 and that of 1545 £207,000. The taxpayer contributed on average about £78,000 per annum in the years 1544–7 inclusive. He also contributed £112,000 by a forced loan of 1543 (forgiven by statute in the next parliamentary session) and a benevolence of 1545 (the first since 1491) yielded £119,000. A similar exaction, styled a 'contribution' may have brought in as much again in 1546.[7]

Of this total about three-quarters had come from non-parliamentary sources. What came from the taxpayers' pockets was paid over without any protest, so far as we know. Repayment of the loan of 1542 was remitted by statute in the next parliament; any sums already repaid were to be refunded to the exchequer. The benevolence of 1545 was given retrospective legality by another statute.[8] The contrast with the 1520s is obvious; the reasons for this docility not so easy to find. The King, of course, had greater flexibility because of the liquid resources provided by sales of monastic land and by his readiness to borrow and to debase the currency. These left him free to move without depending so directly upon parliamentary assistance.

Something must be allowed for the weight of royal personality. The Henry of the 1540s was a more fearsome and awe-inspiring figure than he had been twenty years earlier. A king whose sheer

[6] Dietz, *Finance, 1485–1558*, pp. 177, 147.
[7] Roger Schofield, 'Taxation and the political limits of the Tudor State', in *Law and Government under the Tudors*, ed. C. Cross, D. Loades, J.J. Scarisbrick, (Cambridge 1988), pp. 232–34; Dietz, *Finance, 1485–1558*, pp. 164, 166.
[8] *SR* III, pp. 970–71, 1032.

will power had carried through the religious revolution, riding out the storms of popular discontent and crushing all opposition, was too great to be withstood. The rhetoric of the subsidy preambles is an interesting pointer to a new tone in the relation beween crown and parliament and re-emphasizes the claim to extend taxpayers' liability to the whole range of government functions. Earlier preambles had recited the causes of expense, justified the King's actions and rehearsed the ill doings of his rivals of France or Scotland. Recent subsidy acts added a new note by expressing the subjects' gratitude (and their obligations) to a monarch who had laboured so hard and so effectively for their general welfare. But now in the subsidy statute of 1545 a far more obsequious voice is heard. The virtues of the King in providing peace and tranquillity were duly recalled; the war was rather airily justified as one compelled by God, his friends and his own causes.[9] But there then followed an extraordinary bit of highly coloured prose in which his subjects likened themselves to 'the small fishes of the sea [who] in the most tempestuous and strong weather do lie quietly under the rocks and bankside untouched by the scourges of the water'. They ask him to acept in terms almost reminiscent of the Mass, their simple token or gift, freely given, even 'as it pleased the great King Alexander to receive thankfully a cup of water of a poor man by the highway side.' This new tone of submissive humility with its emphasis on the paternal wisdom of the ruler suggests that the obedience his people owe him is as unquestioning as that of dutiful children. Their 'free gift' is in reality no more than what they owe to his beneficent efforts on their behalf. This gift can have no conditions or limits as to its use and is given explicitly in acknowledgement of the benefits bestowed by the benefactor. Whatever hint of a conditional relationship seemed to inhere in earlier arrangements is wiped out.

Nevertheless we should not read too much into this rhetoric or into the submissiveness of the taxpayers of the 1540s. What we are seeing is not a self-conscious programme to substitute prerogative taxation for parliamentary consent; Henry was not a state-builder, systematically encroaching power to the crown, but rather an ageing adventurer, impatient for immediate realization of his ambitions. In any case death cut short all his actions in 1547.

Unwittingly Henry's intervention in Scotland had turned a

[9] Ibid., p. 1019, preamble.

traditional dynastic quarrel which in the past had led to little more than border forays, followed by patched-up truces, into a dangerous struggle in which the security of the realm was at stake. The fortuitous circumstances of the Scottish succession had opened up possibilities of dynastic aggrandizement of the most glittering kind, nothing less than the acquisition of another throne for the house of Tudor. But Henry's bullying diplomacy drove the Scots into the arms of the French and their new king, the ambitious Henry II, became a competitor for the same glittering prize which had tempted the English Henry. The ancient relationships among the English, the French and the Scots were turned topsy-turvy. England, the traditional aggressor against France, was now on the defensive, faced by a formidable French intrusion into the island of Great Britain. In the past Scotland had been regarded by England as an irritating nuisance but hardly a grave danger while the French had treated the northern kingdom as a convenient weapon for distracting English attention. Now direct control of Scotland became a prime goal for both powers.

The consequences of this reversal of power relationships had to be borne by the government of Protector Somerset. Committed by Henry's policy to a strategic goal quite beyond English capability, he floundered helplessly. The policy of a partial occupation of lowland Scotland maximized costs and minimized results. Another £1,386,000[10] went for war purpose in Edward's first few years.

Expenditures continued at a staggering rate but the means to pay for them were hard to find. An interim regime's capacity to raise money was drastically reduced. Lacking the clout of an imperious royal will, it could not resort to prerogative taxation. Indeed it showed itself timid in turning to parliament. There were only two appeals for subsidies in the six and half years of Edward's reign. Together they yielded only £184,000, in contrast to those of 1543 and 1545 which had brought in £396,000. Instead the regime seized chantries and church plate while continuing foreign borrowing and further debasement of the coinage.[11] The first of the two subsidies was levied in 1549; at that point the government could still use the rhetoric of the Henrician years, appealing to its subjects to defend Edward's rights to 'all that was annexed to his imperial crown against enemies who sought to deprive him of them'. It was

[10] Dietz, *Finance, 1485–1558*, p. 182.
[11] Schofield, p. 232.

the last blast of the dynastic trumpet. Neither the Scottish nor the French claim would be asserted again in subsidy preambles.[12]

The second subsidy of 1552 followed the humiliating peace with France of 1550 which left that power firmly established in Scotland. Policies of retrenchment were set on foot but the accumulated debt was enormous. A timorous privy council hesitated to ask for a subsidy, fearing much 'murmuring and grudging' would accompany it. the bellicose preambles of the past were replaced by a dismal catalogue of failure, ascribed to the Somerset regime. The late duke was faulted for his 'inadvised invasions', employment of foreign mercenaries, borrowing abroad and debasement of the coinage. Parliament was now being asked not to back a war of conquest or even to defend the realm, but to pay off the accumulated debts of past war, to bail out a government mired in defeat.[13]

Mary won instant popularity by remitting the subsidy (but not the tenths and fifteenths) granted in the last months of her brother's reign. But she was soon forced to repeat the refrain of his parliament when in 1555 she asked for help to meet 'the great debts wherewith the imperial crown of this realm is charged'.[14] Like Northumberland she sought to restore financial stability by paying off the loans from Antwerp, updating the customs rates and avoiding war. But the war with France into which she was dragged by her husband defeated these good intentions and borrowing at Antwerp resumed. This was followed by a wartime subsidy and forced loans from her subjects, the first of which was partially repaid, the latter not at all.[15]

This was the situation which faced Elizabeth at her accession: an accumulated debt burdened with heavy interest charges, a debased currency and heavy ongoing costs on land and at sea. These circumstances reflected more than mere temporary setbacks. After nearly half a century in which an English king had taken the initiative in wars of aggression against his neighbours with relatively little risk to the basic interests of his own kingdom, the tide had turned and England now and for a generation to come was constantly on the defensive, threatened for a time by French ambitions in Scotland and then later on by the direct assault of a hostile Spain. The whole posture of English foreign policy had to be

[12] *SR* IV (1), pp. 78–93.
[13] *Finance 1485–1558*, p. 199 quoting PRO, SP 12/28/52.
[14] *SR* IV (1), pp. 218, 301–12.
[15] Dietz, *Finance, 1485–1558*, pp. 210–12.

adapted to these new conditions and that in turn led to a new strategy in the crown's financial relations with parliament.

Most immediately the Elizabethan government, having concluded a face-saving peace, set out to restore its financial health by a coherent programme of retrenchment – revaluation of the currency, liquidation of the foreign debt and the mobilization of sufficient resources to cover current costs. Elizabeth and her ministers resolutely turned their backs on the ruinous practices of debasement and the bold but politically risky devices of benevolences or unredeemed loans from subjects. They fixed their eyes on the one positive achievement of Henrician finance, the establishment of the subsidy as the normal mode of taxation. Open-ended, remunerative, reasonably predictable, it had now taken on the settled character of customary practice. More important still it could be made use of because the old distinction beween ordinary expenditure (paid by the crown out of its recurrent income) and extraordinary costs (paid for by the taxpayers) was thoroughly blurred.

We have seen the first stages of this change in the peacetime subsidies of 1536 and 1540 when the causes cited in the preambles were defence-related but when no money was sought for active warfare; in 1552 and 1555 during peacetime the government appealed for money to liquidate the war debts inherited from the preceding reigns. Now under Elizabeth parliament was being asked to construe extraordinary costs in a much broader way so as to include the running costs of foreign relations in a permanently unsettled world. This new approach reflected the European scene, in which 'cold war' would soon break down the old distinction between open conflict and peace. From 1558 to 1585 England had to live in a world of lurking menace, of enduring uncertainty, of suspicion ripening into hostility. The crown now needed support not only on account of occasional collisions of hostile bodies but in the unremitting friction which troubled relations with England's neighbours. The Elizabethan government succeeded in winning the acceptance of parliament and the taxpayers of these new conditions of life. In the twenty-five peacetime years between 1559 and 1585 there were thirteen in which subsidies had to be paid, virtually one out of two. To achieve this end – a routine grant of one subsidy in each successive peacetime parliament – required new tactics and a new posture of the crown in seeking funds from parliament. Elizabeth's approach was evident in the speech of the lord keeper to her first parliament.

She would not, he said, do anything 'to bring any servitude or bondage to her people nor allow any private affection to advance the cause or quarrels with any foreign prince or potentate.'[16] This was, of course aimed at her predecessor, but it also served notice of a policy towards her neighbours, at once pacific and neutral. Such a policy was all the more necessary because of the cost of past war, the 'marvelous decays and wastes of the revenues of the crown, the inestimable consumption of the treasure, levied both of the crown and the subject'. Worse still was 'the incredible sum of money owing at this present and in honor due to be paid and the biting interest that is to be answered for forbearance of this debt'. From this prologue, she now turned to her requests, asking for parliament's assistance in the name of common interest. Taxes were likened to the costs of merchants' insurance, money paid out not for immediate return but as a prudent cover against contingencies. 'This is not a matter of will, no matter of displeasure, no private cause which in times past have been sufficient for princes' pretences (the more pity!) but a matter for the universal weal of this realm, the defense of our country, the preservation of every man, his home and family particularly.' This speech enunciated a foreign policy which was truly national, setting aside all personal or dynastic ambition and calling on the taxpayers to pay for royal enterprises which benefited and protected each subject.

These irenic intentions were to prove difficult to achieve. The intrusion of an alien force in the island could not be long tolerated and when the opportunity to expel the French arose, it had to be seized (even though the army costs alone of the enterprise were some £178,000.)[17] Moreover, the decision of 1559 which made England the foremost Protestant power in Europe also made Elizabeth willy-nilly the protectress to whom continental (and Scottish) Protestant minorities turned for succour. However unwillingly, she could not afford to ignore the pleas of the lords of the Congregation, the Huguenots, or after 1572 the sea beggars. Religious considerations aside, the vulnerability of her kingdom was too great for her to pass up opportunities to check the power of neighbours whose intentions were so suspect. Up to the late 1570s it was France which aroused English fears; this led to the expensive

[16] D'Ewes, pp. 11–14; Hartley, *Proceedings*, pp. 33–9.

[17] *Salis. MSS*, IV, 2 gives a total of £178,000 for 'Leith 1559' while Dietz, *Finance 1558–1640*, pp. 10–11 notes related naval expenses of £106,000 for 1559–60.

Newhaven intervention of 1562–3 as well as the Scottish expeditions of 1560 and 1573, all uncovenanted charges on the English exchequer.

But from the late 1560s it was Spain's policy which aroused new apprehensions. English leaders nervously watched the assertion of firm Spanish control over the seventeen provinces, pressed with increased vigour under Alba; in 1568–9 the rebellion in the north and later the Ridolfi plot revealed a sinister link with Spain; the bull of 1570 outlawed the Queen in the Catholic world, whose secular leader was Philip II.

The spread of this 'cold war' atmosphere was reflected in the crown's dealings with successive parliaments, in the requests for a subsidy with which each parliament met on its arrival at Westminster. In 1563 Lord Keeper Bacon spoke of the foreign enemy abroad[18] and sketched out the French aggression which had compelled the Queen to action in Scotland and at Newhaven emphasizing the entirely reactive and defensive posture of the English crown.

In 1566 Sir Ralph Sadler sounded for the first time in parliament a note to be heard over and over again in the future.[19] War was all about them and the cause of the war religion. England was yet at peace but 'we have heard and we hear daily of secret conspiracies and great confederacies between the Pope, the French King and other princes of the Popish confederacy. As soon as they can settle and establish the Romish religion within their own territories and dominions,' they will attack England (with help from native papists). The conclusion was clear; all must contribute to avert those threats.

In 1571[20] Bacon, reiterating the principle that extraordinary expenses must be met by extraordinary revenues, catalogued those costs – the remains of the foreign debt, the northern rebellion, the foray into Scotland after the death of the Regent Moray and the subduing of Irish rebels. This was not the first mention of Ireland. In 1566[21] Sadler had recited that it was Tudor policy 'to subdue and bring that land to civility and obedience'. The expansion of royal control over all of Ireland, initiated in Cromwell's time, was fast becoming one of recurrent 'extraordinary' expenses which required regular infusions of parliamentary money.

[18] D'Ewes, pp. 69–72; Hartley, *Proceedings*, pp. 80–6.
[19] Hartley, *Proceedings*, pp. 141–4.
[20] D'Ewes, pp. 137–9; Hartley, *Proceedings*, pp. 183–7, 195–7.
[21] Ibid., p. 142.

Through all these parliaments requests for money were matched with repeated reminders of the Queen's economy, and more particularly of her refusal to spend on any purpose except public ones. 'It hath been used in times past that princes pleasures and delights have been commonly followed in matters of charge as things of necessity.' And now because 'the relieving of the realm's necessity is become the prince's pleasure and delight' we should be appropriately grateful.[22] There had been no charge in the past twelve years unless to the weal and profit of the realm. By 1574, in spite of the heavy charges incurred in the successive crises of the 1560s, the foreign debt was wholly liquidated.[23]

By the early 1570s Elizabeth had regularized a relationship in which parliament routinely contributed a single subsidy at each new assembly, the old limitation to wartime having faded away. She could count on this parliamentary cooperation because of her strict economy in domestic expenditure and her cautious, peace-seeking foreign policy. In 1566 Sadler had boasted that the whole world around England 'have been and yet be in arms, in hostility and great garboil. Only we rest here in peace, thanks be to God therefor and the good government of the Queen's Majesty,' while in 1571 Bacon rejoiced in ten years of peace.[24]

The 1570s proved a quieter time. There were only four tax payment years and an average annual charge for the decade of £33,000 (compared with £56,000 in the 1560s). The foreign debt was now cleared away and a surplus building up in the exchequer.[25] It might have seemed a moment when the crown could relax its demand for more money. The meeting of 1576 was in fact the occasion for a whole new tack by the government in its relations with parliament. The chancellor of the exchequer, Sir Walter Mildmay, rose to speak at length.[26] The theme, the need for money, was familiar but the presentation much expanded and the request itself given a new and important twist. He began with Mary's reign, 'a wretched time and wretched ministers' who 'brought hither a strange nation to press our necks against the

[22] D'Ewes, p. 139.

[23] R. B. Outhwaite, 'Studies in Elizabethan government finance: royal borrowing and the sale of Crown lands, 1572–1603', (unpublished PhD thesis, University of Nottingham, 1964), p. 42.

[24] Hartley, *Proceedings*, p. 141.

[25] Outhwaite, 'Studies', p. 42.

[26] Hartley, *Proceedings*, pp. 440–4.

yoke' and involve us in wars which were not our quarrel. From this and from the bondage of papistry the Queen had delivered us. She had moreover established a firm and lasting peace with Scotland, preserved the young King and brought quietness to his realm. She had now delivered the kingdom from the debt which had weighed on it since before the death of Henry VIII. But the future was unclear. The continent had been shaken by great disturbances. 'The tail of these storms which are so bitter and boisterous in other countries may reach us also before they be ended,' especially because of the hatred borne us by the enemies of our religion. We should now be ready to consider 'aforehand the dangers that may come by the malice of enemies and to provide in time how to resist them'. It is parliament's part to fill the royal coffers so that the Queen may be able 'to answer anything that shall be attempted against her and us'. He ended by singing the praises of Elizabeth's fiscal regime. She had just repaid a recent privy seal loan, 'the like whereof was not seen before'. And the Queen never, unlike her predecessors, debased the currency, borrowed abroad on interest or sold land.

The catalogue of recent expenses was familiar, but the weight and the novelty of the speech lay in its request for money against contingent dangers, for prospective expenditure. Hitherto funds had been asked for current expenses or to pay off accumulated debts. Now the Queen was asking for funds to be laid by in case of future emergencies. No particular circumstance was avowed but a clear warning as to the dangers facing the realm was laid out before the house. The Commons were now to finance not only the present and the past but the future as well. The grant was passed, apparently without discussion.

In 1581 Mildmay repeated his performance,[27] focusing on the enmity of Rome, apparent since 1559, enunciated in the bull of 1570 and manifested in the Fitzmaurice invasion of Ireland. But the pope had confederates. 'Note from whence the last invasion of Ireland came, of what country the ships, of what nation the most part of the soldiers were and by whose ministers they received their victual and furniture.' Mildmay went on to name names: 'the Italians and Spaniards pulled out by the ears at Smerwich in Ireland'. The vague threats he spoke of in 1576 were now much more focused in a combination of the pope and the papist princes. His hearers could be assured 'that if their powers be answerable to

[27] Ibid., pp. 502–8.

their wills this realm shall find at this hands all the miseries and extremes they can bring upon it.' The Queen must have ships and men to chastise the Irish rebels and to repress foreign attempts to assist them. The warnings were now more open; indeed there was a 'cold war' already in progress. The MPs were called upon to provide means to oppose any move these thronging enemies might make. The moral was plain; if the English wanted to continue the blessings of peace, they must provide funds for necessary preventive measures. In the past they had been asked to finance war now they were being asked to pay for its prevention, to subsidize not war but foreign policy.

During these years the Queen was in fact pursuing a diplomatic campaign to check the Spanish in the Low Countries by a united Anglo-French front by which she believed she could restore the *status quo ante* in the Netherlands without war. This policy proved a failure and by the time the next parliament met in November 1584 England was poised on the brink of open conflict. The Prince of Orange was dead and the Dutch leadership desperately seeking help. In August 1585 Elizabeth would conclude a treaty of assistance. The subsidy bill had been passed in the previous February 1585.[28] Spain, the pope and the Holy League in France were openly named as enemies. The Queen was spending heavily for the repair of forts, for munitions to be stored up and for an increase in the navy for which parliament would of course bear the charges.

In these three prewar parliaments one sees the fulfilment of the shift which had been taking place for decades past, away from a policy built on a dynastic view of foreign relations to one oriented to national interests, above all the protection of the Protestant regime against enemies at home and abroad. To achieve this an appeal was being made which emphasized the Queen's rejection of any private interest and portrayed her as a sovereign entirely devoted to her role as the protectress of religion and nation. A national myth was being shaped around the image of the Queen as the deliverer of her people from alien bondage and the restorer of pure religion. Entirely peaceful in her intent, she was unjustly assailed by an enemy combining religious hatred with hegemonial ambitions. Her kingdom, the citadel of righteousness, was gratuitously assailed by a sinister international conspiracy. Their taxes would be spent defending not only their protectress but their own lives, their own

[28] D'Ewes, p. 355.

property and their own religion. This expert blend of religious and patriotic themes was highly successful in mobilizing national fervour even before the war began.

How far was Mildmay the spokesman of the Queen and how far of the hawkish members of the council? Her policy of diplomatic action would be sustained by parliamentary backing, but it is at least possible that Mildmay was put forward by those who were pressing for an aggressive role against Spain. This was certainly the case in the next parliament.

When it met in the autumn of 1586 Leicester's expedition was already in the Netherlands and Drake had returned from the West Indies. The first session was devoted to the destruction of the Queen of Scots. Not until the second session in February/March 1587 was a subsidy bill introduced. It was then that a bold effort was made to use parliament to shape foreign policy. Leicester, on his arrival in the Low Countries, had been made general of the States' forces and shortly afterward proclaimed governor general of the provinces, a move which seemed to assert English overlordship. The Queen, enraged at an act which violated a cardinal principle of her foreign policy – that she should add no new territorial acquisition – forced Leicester to resign.

But the activists were not to be so easily tamed and now turned in parliament to another tactic. When the request for supply was to be moved, Hatton, in a long address,[29] traced the war's origins back to Trent where a plan had been hatched 'to extirp Christian religion (which they term heresy)'. To accomplish this a Catholic confederation had been built up, led by Spain but including France and some Italian princes. They had supported the Queen's enemies; most specifically they had sought to set up Mary Stuart in England. Her death had set back their plans but not their determination. Most immediately they aimed at the destruction of the King of Navarre but their next goal was the invasion of England and Ireland for which a great fleet and mighty army were even now preparing. England was countering this impending assault by preparing her own defence but also by assisting the Low Countries. Their fate was tied up with England's. If trade with them were cut off by a Spanish reconquest, England would be choked by an early-day version of the Napoleonic continental system, and an implacable enemy planted directly cross the North Sea, the best

[29] Ibid., p. 408.

possible base for invasion. 'It may not be suffered that a neighbor should grow too strong.'

England was portrayed as a victim and her actions as self-defence. She could not be safe if Spain were 'to bring the Low Countries into a monarchal seat';[30] they must be helped to resist. And there is a hint in Hatton's words that not only a Spanish prince but any foreign prince was an intolerable neighbour; 'He uttered that as though it were not meet another should have it.' Mildmay, taking his cue, rose to propose a subsidy committee. So far the procedure followed a customary pattern. But what came next did not. The committee itself was a weighty one, including Speaker Puckering, Mildmay, Thomas Cecil, Francis Knollys, Francis Bacon and Hatton. Their ensuing deliberations went far beyond the simple proposal for another subsidy. Its novelty lay in the purposes for which the money was to be spent. They boldly canvassed the possibility of the Queen's accepting the sovereignty of the rebel provinces,[31] echoing Hatton's words but carrying his implication a stage further. If a strong prince in the Netherlands were so great a risk both for English commerce and for English safety would it not be better if there were direct English sovereignty? This would ensure continued Dutch resistance and give the English control over any future peace terms.

But would the Queen consent? As a lure to win royal support they proposed a benevolence over and above the regular subsidy if Elizabeth would accept the sovereignty. The two councillors, Mildmay implicitly and Hatton explicitly, gave backing to the proposal. Both Leicester and Walsingham were absent from the court. It is all the more remarkable that Hatton and Mildmay, two councillors not closely associated with the activist party, should have taken the lead. The pressure on the Queen was a very broad-based one.

Exactly what followed is not clear except for one vital fact, the Queen's refusal to approve the plan. Its proponents then scaled down their scheme. The grant of a benevolence but without conditions attached was discussed by both houses; the Lords offered a benevolence of half the subsidy rate (taking a lead from convocations). The Commons probably followed suit.[32] The

---

[30] Ibid., p. 409.

[31] Neale, *Parliaments*, II, pp. 177–83; BL Harleian MS 6845, ff. 30–42.

[32] *LJ*, II, 134, 134–38; Neale, *Parliaments*, II, p. 160; BL Harleian MS 7188, f. 101.

increased funds would at least be an incentive to a vigorous offensive strategy. The Queen refused even this unconditional offer of a lay benevolence. The usual subsidy was granted; the act spoke only of the Queen's need to withstand God's enemy and hers, who sought to suppress the true Christian religion in England and Ireland and of her preparations to withstand invasion.[33] It contained no reference to assistance to the Low Countries. That Elizabeth would have ever accepted the scheme was altogether unlikely since it would have crossed her consistent assertions that she coveted no other prince's lands. She was of course still pursuing a negotiation with Spain (through Parma) and had hopes of a diplomatic settlement which would avoid full-scale war.

The first parliament to meet in the wake of the Armada assembled in February 1589. Mildmay's speech is lost to us except in rough outline but it seems to have followed the pattern of earlier opening orations.[34] Again the purely defensive character of the war was maintained. But the government had something new in mind; they wanted a double subsidy. There was no precedent for such a sum since the invention of the tax and since Elizabeth's accession the single subsidy (with two tenths/fifteenths) had become a fixed pattern. The government's first move was to appoint a much larger and weightier committee, including all the privy councillors in the house, the senior knight from every shire and some forty other members, a body of close to a hundred.[35] After four not very well attended meetings of the committee, Mildmay reported back to the house with a proposal for 'such an extraordinary provision as they thought the present extraordinary occasion of necessity doth require'. But since the grant would be greater than the usual single subsidy of the last thirty years, the preamble was to include a proviso that it should not be a precedent to posterity.[36] It looks very much as if the council had anticipated unwillingness to break with convention and had tried to cover all contingencies by appointing a widely representative committee and by the proviso against repetition. In fact only one solitary voice seems to have been raised in protest, that of a London merchant[37] who urged the

---

[33] SR IV (2), p. 778–92.

[34] Neale, *Parliaments*, II, pp. 204–5, quoting Fitzwilliam of Milton manuscripts, p. 147.

[35] D'Ewes, p. 431.

[36] SR IV (2), pp. 818–34.

[37] Neale, *Parliaments*, II, p. 206; BL Lansdowne MS 55, ff. 180–3, 186–7.

heaviness of such a burden on the husbandman and the artificer. The double subsidy was passed without further ado.

By 1593 the government's financial resources were strained, even with the double subsidy of 1589. Hence the council now proposed to up the levy once again, to an unheard-of triple subsidy. Before the session was a fortnight old the wooing of the house began. A battalion of heavyweights led off, their way paved by the lord keeper Puckering's speech on the opening day.[38] He painted a grim picture of growing menace on all sides; the Spanish were now preparing another armada and had established themselves in Brittany 'a country of more facility to offend us than the Low Countries'. They were also plotting invasion from Scotland, where 'a great part of the nobility be combined in this conspiracy'. The Queen's charge for defence of the realm had exhausted previous subsidies and driven her to sell some of her crown lands. The lesson was there for all to read; subjects must support the Queen, all the more because collection of the former subsidies had been so slack – 'as that the third of the which hath been granted came not to Her Majesty. A great show, a rich grant. A long sum seems to be made but it is hard to be gotten and the sum not great which is paid.'

In the lower house Sir Robert Cecil led off for the council.[39] He echoed the lord keeper's account of encircling menace. Not only Ireland and Scotland but the Hanse cities and Poland were being wooed by the Spanish with hopes of an embargo on English trade. Worst of all they now went about to win France, especially Brittany. He was followed by other councillors. Again a formidable committee, 150 strong, was appointed for the subsidy bill. It included all the privy councillors, all the knights of the shire and an array of court and local luminaries.

Mildmay, bringing in the committee's report did not go beyond proposing another double subsidy.[40] But there were signs of restlessness. Some spokesmen for Essex and the activists urged that a royal army be sent against Spain, that we should not wrestle with him on our own ground but abroad.' Others, including Ralegh, wanted a formal declaration of war, to legalize privateering. Speeches such as these prepared the house for what came next.

It was at this point that the proceedings were shunted on to a

---

[38] D'Ewes, pp. 457–58.

[39] Ibid., pp. 471–4; Cecil's leading off is unusual – possibly because of Fortescue's inexperience. See Dean, 'Bills and Acts', p. 116.

[40] D'Ewes, p. 477.

new course by intervention from the other house. A message arrived from the Lords asking for conference on 'the provision of treasure' against the mighty adversaries of the realm, a subject on which their lordships had expected to hear something before this time. The message, conveyed by Burghley, compared this war with those of Henry VIII where none of the contestants 'did increase in greatness to be dangerous to their enemies'; this struggle was an all-out one, the king of Spain 'not purposing to burn a town in France or England but to conquer all England and Ireland'.[41] The double subsidy of 1589 had yielded £280,000 while the Queen, in the intervening time since the subsidy was granted, had spent £1,030,000. The Lords would not assent to any act for less than three subsidies. They also alleged that the late subsidies were very small and were paid largely by the meaner sort, the richer escaping the burden by ridiculously low assessments. The immediate response of the lower house was one of injured dignity; initiative in taxation lay with them not with the peers.

But apart from this issue there was serious debate about the proposed increase. Sir William More (MP Surrey) with sound historical instinct compared the Queen's position with that of her father in the 1540s. His wars were 'impulsive', that is, offensive, not defensive. He had had the monastic lands to sell and a benevolence to boot. Edward VI had had church plate and chantries, Mary, a loan (which went unredeemed). The Queen, with none of these aids, had repaid her recent loan. Ralegh wanted a royal army in Brittany, to seize that province, and a fleet to lie off the Spanish coast and intercept the Indies trades. The speakers[42] whose words come down to us were largely advocates of the increased subsidy although they acknowledged that the burden would be a heavy one. Several urged that burden be borne by the wealthier sort.

The main objection to the increase came from those who pleaded the country's poverty. None of them is directly quoted in our sources but Bacon, while supporting the subsidy in principle (but extended over a longer payment time), was blunt about the problems it presented.[43] 'The gentlemen must sell their plate and farmers their brass pots ere this will be paid. And for us we are here to search the wounds of the realm and not to stir them over; therefore

[41] BL Lansdowne MS 104, ff. 78–9, 81–2, printed in Strype, *Annals*, IV, pp. 149ff.

[42] D'Ewes, pp. 491–4.

[43] Ibid., p. 493.

not to persuade ourselves of their wealth more than it is.' He warned that the tax would breed discontentment and endanger the Queen's safety. 'And in histories it is to be observed that of all nations the English are not to be subject, base, or taxable.' The subsidy was duly passed again with a proviso it should not constitute a precedent.

The history of this episode is deeply revealing of the limitations within which Elizabeth's wartime government operated. By 1593 the first enthusiasms of the war, the patriotic impulses generated by the Armada, had weakened. Neither the Lisbon voyage of 1589 nor the French expeditions of 1591–3 had prospered, while the burden of annual taxation weighed more heavily than ever. The established conventions of limited taxation began to reassert themselves. The Commons, left to their own devices, were prepared to renew the double subsidy but no more. The bleak account they had from the councillors, even the message that the Queen was selling her patrimony, did not rouse them to greater generosity. Evidently Mildmay felt unable to introduce a bill for more than two subsidies in the Commons; it became necessary to mobilize outside pressure from the Lords, and especially from Burghley, to prod the lower house to an increase in taxation. Even then, it is clear, there was unrest among the members and a genuine concern that continued heavy taxation would breed discontent.

The parliament of 1597 met a year after Cadiz and only a few days after the second Spanish invasion fleet in two years was shattered in the autumnal storms. The tone of the lord keeper's speech was at once strident and defensive.[44] 'Wars heretofore were wont to be made either of ambition or to enlarge dominions or of revenge to quit injuries, but this against us is not so; in this the holy religion of God is to be subdued and the precious life of Her Majesty taken away' (probably a reference to the Lopez plot). To meet the costs of war the Queen had sold lands and although she hears of nothing so unwillingly as aids or subsidies, cannot meet these costs by herself. His peroration reasserted the war to be just, in defence of God's religion and the Queen, 'of our wives, our children, our liberties, lands, lives and whatever we have'. In a later debate, Fortescue[45] reported the Queen had spent treble the sum of the last three subsidies. Bacon followed, warning of new

---

[44] D'Ewes, pp. 524–5.
[45] Neale, *Parliaments*, II, pp. 358–62; *Salis. MSS*, VII, p. 489.

dangers – the approaching Franco-Spanish peace, the capture of Calais, 'that ulcer of Ireland' and the prospect of Spanish revenge for their recent setbacks. He reminded the house that the clamour for 'incursive' war in the first session had been fully met by these voyages. Another triple subsidy (to be paid in three rather than four years) was proposed; one enthusiastic member, Sir Edward Hoby (MP Rochester), called for at least four. The subsidy passed (again with a disclaimer that it should not be a precedent) but one cannot help detecting a note of worry in the council that this second triple levy would meet opposition, hence the echoes of strain in the lord keeper's speech.

The last parliament of the reign (October 1601) met almost at the same moment as the Spanish army landed in Ireland. The lord keeper[46] made much of this, pointing out that the Spaniards had landed not in rebel-held Ulster but in the English-controlled province of Munster – not merely to assist the rebels but to assault the English. Cecil's speech[47] in the lower house painted a broad picture of the European scene. Elizabeth's aid had forced Spain into a humiliating withdrawal from France and overtures for peace had come from the Spanish king. On the other hand he had now thrown 4000 troops into Ireland, which he would reinforce, and was assailing Ostend. The times required a supreme effort by the English but Cecil hinted that, if it were successful, peace might follow. England was willing to accept an honourable peace.

The question of money was dealt with very frankly. The last subsidy was spent by last October, having yielded only £160,000; the Queen since 1597 had spent £300,000; there was a shortfall of £140,000 on the past, plus another £300,000 for Ireland. Fortescue asked for four subsidies. In the debate which followed[48] there was no opposition to the increased tax but much discussion of its incidence on the poorer subject. Cecil's rather smug remark that it was fitting that all, poor as well as rich, should bear the burden alike, brought a tart reminder from Ralegh of the gross under-assessment of the rich. Some, to avoid a precedent, wanted to label the fourth subsidy a benevolence, others a separate act for the extra subsidy. But in the end the old formula was adhered to. The act, acknowledging the candour the councillors had displayed, re-hearsed the grave threat in Ireland, declared parliament's resolve

[46] D'Ewes, p. 599.
[47] Ibid., p. 623.
[48] Ibid., pp. 632–3.

to protect all the rights attached to the imperial crown, and reasserted that this grant was not to be precedent.[49] The history of its collection confirmed the warnings voiced by the more outspoken MPs of recent sessions and very probably the underlying convictions of the council that the country's willingness to bear the burden of the war was rapidly declining. The steady fall in the yield of each annual payment bore mute witness to the taxpaying community's feelings. In 1592–3 the yield was £97,000; in 1603–4 (with the same rates of levy) it was £67,000. In comparison with 1563–4, again with identical rates of charge, the return had fallen from £150,000.[50] Fortunately peace was in the offing; parliament would not meet again until the conclusion of the Treaty of London.

In summary what are we to conclude about parliament's role in the making of Tudor foreign policy? The sovereign's need to obtain war finance from parliamentary sources gave that body great potential but in fact its role was largely inertial. No ruler was ever denied the funds he or she asked for. Nevertheless there were implicit conditions. Extraordinary expense had to be justified and there were implicit limits to the amount of money which would be provided. A regular tug of war between crown and houses, muted but palpable, marked the passage of every subsidy bill.

These conventions put a fairly tight corset on the Yorkists and the first Tudor. Henry VIII lunged heavily against these restraints and would perhaps have broken them altogether. The mid-century financial debauch and its military and strategic consequences pushed his successors into more sober paths. Burdened by accumulated debt and faced by long-term threats to the nation's security, they had to reshape both their foreign policy and their relations with parliament. The customary imperious summons to aid the king to recover his ancient rights in France or Scotland was replaced by an earnest and carefully argued effort to persuade parliament into accepting the need for regular, peacetime taxation in support of national rather than dynastic policies. The convention that the taxpayer paid only for war had to be broadened to cover the costs of an active and sustained foreign policy in an age of great instability. The consequence of these alterations was to draw parliament into something resembling a partnership, very much a junior partnership but a relationship of real cooperation. Parliament

[49] *SR* IV (2), pp. 991–1009.
[50] Schofield, p. 232.

was persuaded to regular peacetime taxation and later to substantial wartime increases in the tax burden on the grounds that the government was acting in behalf of the interests of the whole people, of their lives, property and religion.

The crown on its side, sufficiently but not richly provided for, had to keep its promises; words uttered in parliament must be seen to reflect the real world of action. It meant that the government could count on adequate provision to deal with emergencies, such as the Scottish crises of 1560 and 1572, to put out brush fires such as the 1569 rising, and even to risk a modest intervention in France. But more costly, and open-ended, enterprises such as the proposed intervention in the Low Countries in 1577 were resolutely rejected.

The coming of war changed neither the policy of the regime nor the conventions governing relations with parliament. The rhetoric of the crown's spokesmen on the floor of the house, as war strategy itself, reflected the same insistence on economy and on minimal demands on the subject. The Queen reiterated over and over her entirely defensive aims, insisting that she had no expansionist ambitions, nor did the government's actions belie its words. This was done in the face of fierce pressures, within the council, in the court and at least once in parliament, for resolutely aggressive actions and a victory of conquest. In startling contrast to her continental neighbours the Queen refused to spend more of her resources or those of her subjects than the barest needs of security required. The short-term result was a war which, practically speaking, left no debt behind it.

There were many considerations which led to this economy of effort. The basic facts of England's inferiority in wealth and population, the temperamental disposition of the Queen, the considered convictions of her most trusted councillors, all entered into the making of policy. But underneath these considerations lay the deeply ingrained political habits of this society, shared by rulers and subjects alike, which set undefined but ultimately unbreachable barriers to the crown's expenditure. That calculation powerfully shaped all government thought and action.

The long-term consequences were of the first importance. The posture assumed by the crown through the long period of tension, leading ultimately to war, powerfully modified its relations with parliament. In return for regular infusions of tax funds the crown had implicitly acknowledged, first, that relations with other states must be governed by needs and interests which were those of the whole nation, not of the sovereign alone or of the dynasty. Secondly there was now a raised expectation that the crown should in conducting foreign relations give a much larger share of its confidence to MPs and even – although this was much less conscious – secure their tacit consent. The consequence of this shift of expectations would be brought home fully and painfully two decades later when the Stuart kings sought to play a major role in continental affairs.

4

Parliament and Taxation

J. D. ALSOP

The transfer of money from subjects to ruler was one very tangible area of interaction between members of society and the early modern state. The increasing requirement for extraordinary assistance within sixteenth-century government finance brought stresses and modifications to the circumstances and role of parliamentary support during the long reign of Elizabeth I. The transfer of wealth could be harmonious or disruptive. It could be the occasion for disagreement or the cause of political disagreement. The significance of direct taxation as a political topic for historians depends very much upon the nature of the interaction. As is well known, the passage of supply legislation was a regular feature of parliamentary affairs. The monarch's representatives requested, and were granted, direct lay taxation in all except one (1572) of the thirteen sessions of Elizabeth's ten parliaments. From 1559 the standard grant involved two fifteenths and tenths for every full subsidy (varied only in 1566 when a single fifteenth and tenth accompanied the partial subsidy), and during the war years after 1588 multiple grants became routine. The subject has provided fertile ground for scholarly debate among historians, but has all too frequently been misunderstood.

The analysis of Elizabethan tax statutes and debates has long been conducted within the traditional portrayal of Tudor parliamentary history which emphasized polarization and confrontation, obstructing an accurate understanding of the Elizabethan experience.[1] So long as conflict was a central theme of historical scholarship, the question as to why in financial topics the monarch

[1] For example, Neale, *Parliaments*, I, pp. 123, 136–64; ibid., II, pp. 68, 205–7, 298–312, 358–62, 411–16.

and two houses of parliament functioned harmoniously with a minimum of friction was never seriously addressed. Instead, attention was focused upon the exceptional instances of disagreement, magnifying their importance, distorting the context, and in general searching for obscure hints of obstructionism and opposition wherever possible. Even those scholars who adhere to the basic premise of cooperation and attempted consensus frequently express partial reservations when it comes to the theme of parliamentary taxation. Michael Graves has portrayed the Commons as characterized by at times grudging acceptance of taxation, capable of resistance and requiring careful handling.[2] Geoffrey Elton has suggested that the Commons did not 'automatically regard all taxation with the bigoted irresponsibility too readily ascribed to them by some historians' but went on to imply that cooperation depended upon royal demonstration that the purposes were sound, and more recently stated 'the business of getting the subsidy through was always and obviously a delicate one.' He elsewhere repeated the belief that any attempt to enlarge the size of the grant was certain to rouse the Commons, yet correctly noted that all Elizabethan actions were successful and the bills almost invariably passed readily.[3] The notion of an aroused House of Commons which accepts increased taxation without known complaint raises the question as to the relationship between evidence and historical interpretation. Historians customarily assume that requests for taxation must necessarily have been unpopular with both the members of the Commons and the general population. One does not need to invent a non-materialistic, patriotic nation of parliamentarians and taxpayers, eager to take the words of the subsidy preambles at face value by surrendering their lives and estates in aid of the Queen, in order to demonstrate that the Elizabethan period possessed a system of parliamentary taxation which reduced friction to an absolute minimum, even in the face of unprecedented multiple subsidy grants.

Parliamentary taxation was heavier over a longer period of years

---

[2] M. A. R. Graves, *Elizabethan Parliaments, 1559–1601* (London and New York, 1987), pp. 4, 5, 11, 16, 60; *idem, The Tudor Parliaments: Crown, Lords and Commons, 1485–1603* (London and New York, 1985), p. 145.

[3] G. R. Elton, 'Tudor Government: The Points of Contact. I. Parliament', *Transactions of the Royal Historical Society*, 5th ser. XXIV (1974), 190; *idem*, 'Parliament', in *The Reign of Elizabeth I*, ed. Christopher Haigh (London, 1984), p. 93; *idem, Parliament*, pp. 155–6, 159–63.

under Elizabeth than was true for the earlier Tudors. In the twenty-six years prior to 1585 parliaments approved six subsidies and eleven fifteenths and tenths, and thus subjected the laity to twenty-four separate collections spread over twelve calendar years. Over the remaining nineteen years parliaments granted fourteen subsidies and twenty-eight fifteenths and tenths. From 1588 until 1605 taxes were payable in the exchequer every single year, sometimes on as many as four occasions and in theory at up to three times the customary annual amounts. The crisis of 1588 was followed by the introduction for the first time in the statutes of a double subsidy. The last time this had been attempted by the crown, in 1558 following the loss of Calais, negotiations reduced the request by one-half.[4] The session of 1593 introduced the reality of a triple subsidy along with the appeal 'Wee most humblie beseeche your most excellent Majestie ... that this which wee have nowe doon ... be not drawn a President for the tymes to come.' The following session of 1597 witnessed another triple subsidy and an identical, word-for-word appeal. Finally, in 1601 the government requested and received four subsidies; instead of a plea against future repetitions the preamble simply noted that there was no precedent for such a grant 'because noe Age either hath or can produce the like president of so much happines under any Princes Reigne.'[5] Wartime parliamentary taxation certainly did not match the increasing costs of extensive military activity, but even allowing for declining yields and inflation, annual receipts between 1588 and 1603 were higher than at any other time in the century with the exception of 1541–7.[6] Peacetime taxation was not unprecedented, nevertheless, it was still fairly novel and, as Professor Elton has noted, the regularity by which theoretically extraordinary assistance for an emergency was levied demonstrates the disjunction

[4] Jennifer Loach, *Parliament and the Crown in the Reign of Mary Tudor* (Oxford, 1986), pp. 160–1; 4 and 5 Philip and Mary, c. 11; PRO, SP 11/12, ff. 66–9.

[5] *SR*, IV, pp. 867, 938, 992.

[6] Approximate average annual receipts from parliamentary lay taxation were £93, 285 in the period 1541–7, and £104,056 for 1588–1603. Calculated from: Roger S. Schofield, 'Parliamentary Lay Taxation, 1485–1547' (Cambridge University PhD dissertation, 1963), tables 40, i, ii, as corrected for 1547 in James D. Alsop, 'The Exchequer of Receipt in the Reign of Edward VI' (Cambridge University PhD dissertation, 1978), pp. 225, 228; Frederick C. Dietz, *The Exchequer in Elizabeth's Reign* (Northampton, Mass., 1923), pp. 86–9; *idem*, *The Receipts and Issues of the Exchequer During the Reigns of James I and Charles I* (Northampton, Mass., 1928), p. 136.

between theory and reality. William Harrison, although presenting a case against clerical taxation and including special pleading, was certainly under no illusions:[7]

Seldom also are they [the clergy] without the compass of a subsidy, for if they be one year clear from this payment, a thing not often seen of late years, they are like in the next to hear of another grant; so that I say again, they are seldom without the limit of a subsidy.

The same could be said, with no greater exaggeration, for the laity.

In accounting for the apparent generosity of the Commons, recent studies have generally viewed the parliamentary process as a more or less civilized tug of war in which government representatives or agents in parliament worked strenuously to convince the members of the necessity for taxation, and/or strove simply to 'manage' effectively an unruly and precocious assembly containing a fair share of thin-skinned principle-hunters.[8] Thus, the issue of taxation has been firmly placed within what is rapidly emerging as the new orthodoxy for Tudor parliaments. In spite of the considerable merits and accuracy of the general interpretation, danger exists with any attempt to embrace all aspects of the parliamentary experience – in this case taxation – within a single, appealingly straightforward explanation. There exists, in fact, remarkably little evidence of any need to convince the Commons of the legitimacy of crown requests, or much reason to believe subsidy bills required a special degree of management beyond that routinely required to steer any measure through the house. Indeed, reasons can readily be advanced as to why the bills frequently necessitated less than the normal attentiveness of parliamentary managers.

Taxation could be either the reason for political conflict, or the opportunity to express or win conflicts arising elsewhere in the political process. Previous scholarship has sufficiently demonstrated how the notion of no supply without redress of grievances was foreign to the sixteenth century. The introduction of a subsidy bill was rarely the occasion for political manoeuvring.[9] The only clear case of this during Elizabeth's reign, as will be seen, involved

[7] Elton, *Parliament*, p. 154; J. D. Alsop, 'The Theory and Practice of Tudor Taxation', *EHR*, XCVII (1982), 1–30; William Harrison, *The Description of England*, ed. Georges Edelen (Ithaca, 1968), p. 30.

[8] Elton, *Parliament*, pp. 151–74; Graves, *Elizabethan Parliaments*, passim.

[9] Elton, 'Parliament', pp. 92–3; Elton, 'Points of Contact', pp. 190–1; Schofield, 'Parliamentary Lay Taxation', pp. 11–14.

the exceptional session of 1566. Professor Elton has continued the speculation that the politics of the succession issue figured in the delay of the 1563 bill. The second reading on 9 February was followed, unusually, by debates on 10 and 13 February: 'and though perhaps (there is no evidence to that effect) some tactics concerning the petition for the succession may have been involved, the only thing we know to have caused trouble was the oath demanded of the commissioners for the assessment.' Since Professor Elton went on to demonstrate his belief that the oath was a serious concern in this session, there really is no reason to invoke the possibility that members of the Commons either cynically exploited the need for money in order to exert pressure upon the Queen, or vented their frustration at the lack of movement on the succession.[10] The known evidence adequately accounts for the delay.

The 1571 parliament has also been misinterpreted by some commentators. The initial speech by Robert Newdigate introducing the topic of taxation immediately led to a debate on sundry abuses and concerns, followed by the establishment of a committee for motions of griefs and petitions. The problems identified at that initial debate included one topic directly involving the subsidy (the abuse of collectors who retained receipts for their own use as much as one year after collection) as well as broader concerns (licences issued under letters patent, informers, the embezzlement of funds by royal officials, abuses of purveyors, the respite of homage, the exchequer writ *quo titulo ingressus est* and ecclesiastical affairs).[11] We now know that it would be incorrect to consider this an example of redress of grievances tied to supply.[12] The introduction of a committee on grievances was in all likelihood the initiative of the crown managers in the Commons who desired to minimize the disruption which multiple, ill-considered motions would entail. The movers of the initial motions were instructed to collect notes on their concerns and present these for consideration in the framing of bills in the committee.[13] The main intention appears to have been to salvage a productive session free of 'nuisance' bills, and perhaps

[10] Elton, *Parliament*, pp. 161–2; *CJ*, I, 65–6. Sir John Neale's account also assumed, without evidence or argument, that politics delayed the subsidy bill: II, pp. 123–5.

[11] *CJ*, I, 83; Hartley, *Proceedings*, pp. 202–3, 245.

[12] Sheila Lambert, 'Procedure in the House of Commons in the Early Stuart Period', *EHR*, XCV (1980), 759–60; Elton, 'Parliament', p. 93.

[13] *CJ*, I, 83.

as well to delay or modify contentious legislation in committee. We possess no evidence that anyone – managers, the protestors or whoever – believed the subsidy was itself in danger, or that it was tied to consideration of grievances. The original outburst was quite simply the result of an unforeseen occurrence. Newdigate's speech on 7 April, the fourth working day of the parliament, appears to have been unexpected and unsolicited.[14] The Commons Journal notes that he made a motion to offer a subsidy, unasked. The two private accounts of this parliament agree that the speech was unpopular; the anonymous diarist reported 'which speech was not liked of by the House' and John Hooker noted it 'was mich myslyked'.[15] These were exceptional comments for Elizabethan taxation requests. Lord Keeper Bacon in the traditional opening speech had already provided a fulsome commentary on the necessity for sufficient provision for the crown and state, so the introduction of the customary subsidy motion could not have been unexpected.[16] The substance of Newdigate's speech is unknown, but it could well be that it was disliked not because taxation was unpopular but due to the fact that the speaker was acting out of turn. After all, the single element in the speech which the anonymous diarist saw fit to repeat was Newdigate's statement he believed it proper to offer a subsidy before it was required. The attempt by Sir Francis Knollys, the senior privy councillor in the house, to regain control with a lengthy speech was unsuccessful, and at least six members spoke in the following wide-ranging debate. It is certainly of significance that the introduction of the subsidy proposal in 1571 triggered a

[14] Professor Elton has stated Newdigate spoke at the behest of the council, and therefore placed him among the council's 'men-of-business' in the Commons (*Parliament*, pp. 101–2, 159, 165–7). This appears to be based solely upon Elton's belief that prior to 1576 the theme of supply was purposely introduced in the Commons by a private member acting under direction (ibid., pp. 157–8; Elton, 'Parliament', pp. 92–3). I do not adhere to this notion; it certainly was not followed in the preceding 1566 session. Newdigate himself was reported to have begun his speech 'that where on of the causes for calling of the parliament (and perhapps the cheefest) was for a subsedie, hee thought it not amisse to make offer of a subsedie before it should bee required': Hartley, *Proceedings*, p. 202. Dr Graves argues Newdigate was acting upon his own initiative and proved an embarrassment to the council: M. A. R. Graves, 'The Management of the Elizabethan House of Commons: The Council's "Men-Of-Business"', *Parliamentary History*, II (1983), 19. Newdigate's character has been termed 'quarrelsome': HPT, III, p. 129.

[15] Hartley, *Proceedings*, pp. 202, 245.

[16] Ibid., pp. 183–7, 195–7.

substantial debate on grievances. It is also noteworthy that, unlike some tense Jacobean debates, members did not argue along the lines that if the crown reformed the abuses within its own administration it would have no need for taxation. Rather, most speakers went to some lengths to state that relief was justified; the reformation of abuses would simply expedite collection.[17] Three days later, on 10 April, when Sir Francis Knollys reported on the subsidy committee's deliberations, the journal noted that the articles 'were well liked', and the bill passed its readings on 21 and 24 April and 8 May without difficulty.[18]

The 1571 session provides little support for the belief that the introduction of a tax measure was the occasion for political stratagems. Professor Elton is correct in stating that the way was open for any member who wished to raise a grievance, and thus supply was always a potential occasion for trouble.[19] What must be added is that in Elizabethan parliaments that potential was very rarely realized. Sir John Neale believed he had located an example of 'the classical strategy of linking supply with redress of grievances' for 1585, but the evidence cited simply shows an awareness on the part of one member of the traditional reciprocity and good will expected, and frequently achieved. Or again, for the 1601 parliament, Professor Neale interpreted the refusal of the house to permit the reading of the subsidy bill during the monopolies debate as the open adoption of the 'classical strategy of linking redress of grievances with supply – irresistible against a poverty-stricken government'. Yet this incident demonstrated no such connection and no threat to the tax measure. If contemporaries had actually believed in the doctrine of redress of grievances before supply it

---

[17] Ibid., pp. 202–3. For testy Jacobean observations: *Proceedings in Parliament 1610*, ed. Elizabeth Read Foster (2 vols, New Haven and London, 1966), II, pp. 402–3; *Parliamentary Debates in 1610*, ed. Samuel R. Gardiner (London, 1862), pp. 10–12, 135–6, 144–5.

[18] The only issue mentioned in the Journal was the addition on 27 April of the exemption for the residents of Romney Marsh, following the example of the 1563 act. The time taken to move the bill through the Commons was a consequence of the volume of business in this parliament, and not of deliberate obstruction. On 21 April, after conference with the Lords, it was found necessary to urge the members to spend their time proceeding with the necessary measures for the commonwealth rather than private concerns. The former included both the subsidy bill and measures to alleviate several of the grievances expressed on 7 April. *CJ*, I, 85–8; Elton, *Parliament*, p. 167.

[19] Elton, *Parliament*, p. 155.

would have been asinine folly to place the unprecedented four subsidies on the agenda when the debate over monopolies was at its height. Beginning the day with a bill which would take hours merely to read out was in fact a good way to divert the attention of the house, and it is presumably for this reason that members were opposed and called instead for the report from the committee considering monopolies. Even within Professor Neale's reading of the documents, one could not possibly maintain that the Commons intended to delay discussion of taxation until the Queen responded favourably on monopolies.[20] It took, thus, a truly exceptional occurrence to provoke a debate on grievances linked in any fashion to taxation. The explanation is not simply that the privy councillors and their agents provided effective management.[21] As well, the mind set which bound redress, or even expression, of grievances to the subsidy debate simply was not an attribute of the normal Elizabethan member.

The 1566 session itself has been dealt with at length in a fashion which demonstrates the limitations of any exploitation of the subsidy bill for tactical purposes.[22] A concerted effort to solve the succession issue orchestrated in parliament by privy councillors could never have been pushed to the limit whereby taxation would have been refused. Any pressure exerted was a bluff – and one which ultimately failed. Moreover, the connection between supply and succession was not as substantial as Sir John Neale believed.[23] The events of 1566 constitute as much an illustration of a very confused session as they do a case of the deliberate (unsuccessful) attempt to use the subsidy for the extraction of political concessions. In all the hot words and challenges to the Queen's authority, the threat to withhold supply was rarely, if ever, made.[24] More indicative of the spirit of the assembly was the anonymous speech 'touching the nominacion of a successor to the Crowne'.

[20] Neale, *Parliaments*, II, pp. 68, 384, 416. At most, his evidence for 1601 suggests the house intended to resolve the issue as to how it intended to *proceed* (by petition or by bill) on monopolies before turning to the subsidy. These, with the 1566 session, constitute Professor Neale's evidence for the theory. For other sessions, such as 1576, he found it necessary to explain the lack of any attempts in terms of exceptional pliancy (*Parliaments*, II, p. 349).

[21] Elton, *Parliament*, p. 159.

[22] Ibid., pp. 162–5, 364–74.

[23] Neale, *Parliaments*, II, p. 139 and *passim*.

[24] Neale's only evidence for such a threat derives from the unverifiable report of the French ambassador: ibid., p. 137.

This argued that both supply and the settlement should proceed. For all his criticism of the Queen and her councillors, the speaker urged progress on the subsidy in order to secure Elizabeth's good will: the tax was a carrot, not a stick.[25] Molyneux's motion of 18 October to move forward on both topics 'was very well allowed of the House'.[26] Indeed, the only clear evidence of the subsidy being used as a weapon is the hostile statement by Sir Ralph Sadler in his response to Molyneux's speech. Sadler argued against bargaining or covenanting with the Queen, 'as who [i.e. Molyneux?] wolde say, if her Majeste will graunte us the one we will the more willingly graunte the other.'[27] The interpretation of Molyneux's action as an organized attempt to withhold supply until Elizabeth agreed to name a successor,[28] is without adequate foundation. Sadler's opposition was to an explicit deal; even then, he interpreted the opposite point of view as one which would then 'more willingly graunte' taxation. Where is the threat to withhold a grant, and why have historians argued, mistakenly, that taxation came close to being refused entirely in this session? Of course, a sceptic may well argue that caution prevented debaters from speaking their minds openly; expressions of willingness to proceed with the subsidy were necessary but constituted empty rhetoric. Yet, in order to be effective the audience as well as the speaker would have had to be able to decode the hidden message. The only way the historian can detect successful doublespeak is when the actions of the participants ran counter to their stated intentions. We cannot determine that members of the 1566 parliament contradicted their own words and deliberately attempted to delay supply. It remains possible that some viewed taxation as an explicit weapon in this session, but if so we as yet lack a clear demonstration of this turn of mind.

Taxation was rarely the occasion for disagreement; but was it ever the cause of disagreement? The answer must be: far less commonly than scholars have hitherto believed. I know of no

[25] PRO, SP 46/166, f. 9v (printed in Hartley, *Proceedings*, pp. 129–39).

[26] *CJ*, I, 74.

[27] *Proceedings*, p. 143. If Dr Hartley's suggestion is correct (as appears likely) and the anonymous speech quoted earlier is in fact the text of Molyneux's motion (ibid., pp. 119–20), then Sadler was apparently misrepresenting Molyneux's position.

[28] Neale, *Parliaments*, II, pp. 137–9; see also the biography of John Molyneux by M. R. Pickering in HPT, III, p. 61.

unequivocal evidence that any member of the Elizabethan Commons, let alone the house as a whole, ever attempted to refuse a
request for taxation. The crown's case, even when weakly made
and inconsistent with the niceties of constitutional theory, was
always accepted. The extant evidence demonstrates the topics
under debate (when debates occurred) were limited to subsidiary
issues which did not question or modify parliament's perceived
obligation to provide supply whenever it was requested, normally
at the rates suggested or demanded by the Crown.

   Historians have assumed that since taxation was central to the
summoning of virtually every parliament, the subsidy legislation
was necessarily somewhere near to the heart of parliamentary
proceedings. It was a very important topic considered carefully and
extensively by all those involved in the process, either on its own
merits or else as a pawn in another endeavour. What happens,
however, if one develops the concept of parliamentary taxation
during the Elizabethan age as a subject which contained a fairly
high degree of ritual and formalism, in which little of substance was
actually contested so long as all parties kept within, or close to, the
traditional framework? The assumption of centrality must disappear.
This actually dovetails nicely with the current historiographical
emphasis upon parliament as a forum where private interests could
achieve realization of their own priorities. The granting of taxation
which was rapidly becoming routine was not at the forefront of
attention for any substantial number of parliamentarians, or one
suspects the majority of their contemporaries within the nation at
large. Professor Cope, for example, has demonstrated how during
the 1630s supply was far from the centre of the early Stuart
perception of parliament. Professor Elton has remarked on the
consistent failure of all Elizabethan commentators on parliament to
devote more than casual attention to the theme of supply, and
comments: '... the way in which one of the most constant preoccupations of any meeting of Parliament is passed over by the
commentators remains striking – and a warning against equating
their comment too readily with the truth and whole truth.' This
really begs the question as to why even the writers attempting
systematic descriptions merely 'slip the matter of money in very
casually'. The suggested explanation – that no one was inclined to
remind his readers of an unpleasant topic – by itself hardly seems
sufficient. The conclusion appears obvious: if Elizabethans consist-
ently wrote about the institution in a manner which appears

strange to historians it is because their perception of that assembly differs from our own.[29]

In respect to procedure, the initial statement indicating royal necessity was made by the lord keeper or lord chancellor in the opening address to a new parliament. Fairly early in each session reference to the need for supply was raised in the Commons. This generally led to some discussion, followed by the establishment of a house committee which, at least in theory, prepared the specific terms of the grant. These 'articles' were then reported to the Commons. Following general approval, the elaborate bill was presented for the three readings in the Commons and subsequently the three readings in the Lords. Our knowledge of tax debates, derived from the Commons Journal and private diaries, is incomplete, but every indication is that bills only occasionally received fulsome discussion. Frequently very little debate was recorded. Passage in the House of Lords was invariably a formality, taking on average three or four days without comment.[30] Within the Commons, third reading was itself a formality. Debate was exceedingly rare. In 1585 when a member attempted to insert a proviso he was informed that for the third reading of the engrossed bill a motion 'was far out of season'.[31] Serious interventions were infrequent even at first and second readings. The bill for the subsidy and fifteenth and tenth was a highly complex and protracted document, but throughout the reign the overwhelming majority of the clauses were repeated verbatim in every grant. After the reading of the subsidy bill had continued for almost two hours in 1585 the Speaker of the Commons brought it to a premature end by stating that for lengthy safeguarding clauses members should refer to the previous act, because they were taken word for word from it.[32]

The aspects routinely considered or altered were restricted to the preamble, the amounts and the timing of the taxation. Pre-session planning was a regular feature of the legislation. This does not imply the government anticipated opposition; even when much was

---

[29] Ester S. Cope, 'Public Images of Parliament During Its Absence', *Legislative Studies Quarterly*, VII (1982), 221–34; Elton, *Parliament*, p. 25; Lambert, 'Procedure in the House', p. 760.

[30] The Lords could take the initiative for an alteration upon petition, as in respect to the Welsh mises in 1559, but this was unusual. *LJ*, I, 549 and *passim*; ibid., II, *passim*.

[31] Dean, 'Bills and Acts', p. 120; Neale, *Parliaments*, II, pp. 56–7.

[32] BL Lansdowne MS 43, f. 167.

pro forma, a bill of this magnitude depended for speedy passage upon effective organization. Thus, in 1572 an anonymous experienced member urged upon a privy councillor the advantages of thorough preparation. His advice – that the bill should be ready prior to the session 'both in paper and parchment' – required in advance not only the paper draft but also the engrossed bill, normally created after second reading when the final form was fairly certain. As Graves has noted, the implications of such advice are astounding. The government could undertake such action only if parliamentary approval of taxation was a mere formality, with no amendments or meaningful opposition anticipated.[33] We do not know whether this advice was ever followed during the reign. At the very least, the fact that a member could indulge in such thoughts is of some significance. What is certain is that the Commons's role in initiating and deliberating on supply came very close to being a constitutional fiction under Elizabeth. Privy councillors always prepared the terms of the grant, even if the bill was not actually written out beforehand.[34] They expected no opposition,[35] and were generally proved correct.

Parliamentary amendments or provisos were infrequent for Elizabethan supply legislation. This can be contrasted with the substantial numbers of alterations to the bills of the first half of the century.[36] The standard, traditional form of the bills by the Queen's accession neither necessitated nor encouraged alterations. Most proposals were minor in terms of the overall taxation: an unsuccessful attempt to have recusants pay double rates like aliens (1585); a proviso to exempt the inhabitants of Romney Marsh (1563, 1571); the establishment of double rates for native-born children of aliens when they received lands or goods from their parents merely to escape parental double rating (1581).[37] Since the report out of committee on the articles invariably received common assent in the house, any intention by one or more members to refuse or alter substantially the government's predetermined plans

[33] BL Harleian MS 253, ff. 34v–35v; Graves, 'Management of Elizabethan Commons', pp. 16, 33; Elton, 'Parliament', pp. 90–2.

[34] Elton, *Parliament*, pp. 157, 159–68; Dean, 'Bills and Acts', pp. 114–40.

[35] BL Harleian MS 74, f. 305, Lansdowne MS 60, f. 142v, 102, f. 20v; Elton, *Parliament*, p. 161; Wallace MacCaffrey, *Queen Elizabeth and the Making of Policy, 1572–1558* (Princeton, 1981), p. 470.

[36] Schofield, 'Parliamentary Lay Taxation', pp. 45–50.

[37] Neale, *Parliaments*, II, pp. 56–7; *CJ*, I, 66, 86; *SR*, IV, 478, 698; BL Lansdowne MS 43, f. 166v; D'Ewes, pp. 412, 496.

for taxation (should they have wished to do so) was unlikely to be successful after this point. Professor Elton's arguments that serious and successful opposition to taxation took place after second reading in 1563 and throughout the 1566 session are unconvincing.[38] A successful challenge really needed to come earlier, either at the initial debate or in committee. Both were unlikely.

The initial debate was intended solely to establish the necessity for supply. If this could be confirmed, the creation of a committee to consider relief was in practice automatic, and the tasks of discussion and recommending amounts and timing fell to the committee. Francis Bacon stated in 1597:

... it shall not be fit for me to enter into or to insist upon secrets either of her Majesty's coffers or of her counsel. ... Neither will I now at this time put the case of this realm of England too precisely how it standeth with the subject in point of payments to the Crown: though ... never subjects were partakers of greater freedom and ease ... which now I reserve to mention ... because speech in the House is fit to persuade the general point, and *particularity is more proper and seasonable for the committee.*[39]

Establishing a case for necessity was relatively easy, even during peacetime when the orthodox doctrine of extraordinary need was stretched to the very limit without known complaint.[40] Perhaps in some instances (for example in the post-Armada 1589 session) the case was so self-evident that detailed exposition was unnecessary, but at other times the evidence presented by those who spoke in favour of supply would have convinced only a house already well intentioned and ready to accept taxation. In 1566 Privy Councillor

---

[38] Elton, *Parliament*, pp. 160–5. I examine the 1566 evidence in 'Re-interpreting the Elizabethan Commons: The Parliamentary Session of 1566' (*Journal of British Studies*, 1990, forthcoming). As for 1563, the belief that the debate over the assessors' oath (not – as is incorrectly stated – the commissioners' oath) represented a struggle between a government determined to reform subsidy assessments and an unreceptive Commons is entirely speculative. Given Elizabethan preoccupations, several days could well be devoted to the issue of oath-taking without this necessarily being confrontational. The question of the relative effectiveness of the oath versus the fiscal penalty introduced in its place, and the evolving nature of this clause in subsidy acts between 1563 and 1576 have not yet been studied.

[39] *The Works of Francis Bacon*, ed. James Spedding, Robert Ellis and Douglas Heath (14 vols, London, 1858–74; reprint Stuttgart, 1961–3), IX, pp. 85–6 (emphasis mine).

[40] Alsop, 'Theory and Practice of Taxation', pp. 1–30; Alsop, 'Innovation in Tudor Taxation', *EHR*, XCIX (1984), 83–93.

Sir Ralph Sadler portrayed the necessity as self-evident: 'I shall not nede to use any persuasions to move or persuade you thereunto: in dede, I will not go about to persuade you, the causes of themselfes are sufficient to persuade you ....'[41] The verbose and well-tuned speeches were invariably present, of course. But were these intended to inform and/or convince, or were they set pieces in an expected ritual? Sir William Cecil blissfully made the same item do double duty in his 1563 and 1566 speeches; Sir Walter Mildmay's speeches in 1576, 1581, 1585, 1587 and 1589 are all of a piece, so close in tone and substance that scholars have disagreed upon some datings.[42] Most commentators opined that the conciliar speeches were learned; none indicate they swayed a hitherto unconvinced audience. In 1571 the anonymous diarist bluntly dismissed Sir Francis Knollys's oration (the second in the debate and the first by a councillor) as 'a longe needeles discourse'.[43] It was needless simply because there was no contest, no opposition and no doubt as to the outcome.

Serious deliberation depended upon a degree of informed knowledge. For most members we have no method of determining either their interests in, or knowledge of, crown finance. Many were without doubt well informed on the economic conditions of their localities. However, barring sustained poverty, economics were not central to the constitutional issue, which was to establish the nature of the sovereign's necessity. The extent of national deprivation could well influence the debate (primarily as a factor in the determination of timing for taxation) but it could not resolve the issue of the Queen's need. Those likely to be best informed were the members holding places in the privy council, the revenue courts, and the disbursing agencies of government. Many favourable comments, as might be expected, came from these members. Rarely, though, did the administration provide financial information within the house to buttress its argument for royal need, nor do we know of any requests from burgesses for similar material. The series of speeches on supply by Sir Walter Mildmay between 1576 and 1589 have been praised as coherent expositions of policy.

---

[41] Hartley, *Proceedings*, p. 143, and see also pp. 184, 495.

[42] Elton, *Parliament*, p. 163; *CJ*, I, 63, 74; Hartley, *Proceedings*, pp. 440–4, 502–8; Neale, *Parliaments*, II, pp. 54–7, 204–5; BL Lansdowne MS 43, f. 171v. For comments on ritualism: Bacon, *Works*, IX, p. 85; Hartley, *Proceedings*, pp. 85, 184; Elton, *Parliament*, p. 168.

[43] Hartley, *Proceedings*, p. 202.

However, they are not developed expositions of demonstrated fiscal necessity. Essentially the speeches are requests for trust: Mildmay used his position as a privy councillor and chancellor and under-treasurer of the exchequer to affirm that the Queen required relief: 'I assure you as I am an honest man'.[44] As late as the 1590s Mildmay's successor Sir John Fortescue was repeating these senti-ments, and, indeed, we know of only two instances when any effort was made to provide some knowledge of financial affairs. In 1601 the preamble for the unprecedented grant of four subsidies and eight fifteenths and tenths reported 'in this tyme of our advised and mature deliberacon we have sufficiently perceaved howe greate and inestimable Charges your Majestie hath susteyned many years.' When parliament first granted an unprecedented three subsidies and six fifteenths and tenths in 1593 more financial information than normal was made available by Fortescue. However, even then, the perfunctory nature of Fortescue's intervention was re-vealed by the numerous generalities and the exaggerated, fanciful data. Among other claims, Fortescue asserted that at Elizabeth's accession in 1558 the crown had been indebted to the tune of £4,000,000, and that at present the expenses of the Queen's household were less than those of any preceding monarch. Some superior evidence may actually have reached the Commons in this session from Lord Treasurer Burghley, by way of the joint confer-ences with the Lords, but it played little role in the final outcome.[45]

The learned orations provided assurances rather than informa-tion. Even then, how many were actually assured, or cared to be assured? For new parliaments the lord keeper or lord chancellor

[44] MacCaffrey, *Making of Policy*, pp. 483–5; idem, 'Parliament: The Eliza-bethan Experience', in *Tudor Rule and Revolution*, ed. D.J. Guth and J.W. McKenna (Cambridge, 1982), pp. 139–41; Hartley, *Proceedings*, pp. 443, 506; BL Lansdowne MS 43, f. 171v.

[45] *SR*, IV, pp. 991–2; BL Cotton MS Titus Fii, f. 58; D'Ewes, pp. 473, 482, 485, 492–3; PRO, SP 12/244, f. 105-v. The true debt in 1558 is estimated at less than £200,000. The average annual expenditure in the cofferer's responsibility for the decade 1581–90 was over £57,000, which was the highest average hitherto experienced (compare average expenditure of less than £15,000 in Henry VII's final years, or less than £43,000 in the 1540s). The fact that household expenditure was running at unprecedented levels was well known to the administration at the time. Frederick C. Dietz, *English Public Finance 1558–1641* (New York and London, 1932; reprint 1964), p. 7, PRO, E 101/413–31, *passim*, E 351/1795–1816; BL Lansdowne MS 1, ff. 112–13, 147–8, 2, ff. 79–80, 96–7, 3, f. 124, 4, ff. 17–19, 21, ff. 127–8, 34, ff. 48–54; Additional MS 27,449, ff. 1–2.

commented at length, albeit in generalities, during the opening ceremonies and within the Commons privy councillors usually spoke on supply early in the session. We know that attendance could be low at the start of a session, and proceedings were often disorganized and noisy. Freshmen members, who were always numerous, possessed only the vaguest notions of elementary parliamentary procedures.[46] At the opening of the 1584–5 parliament, William Fleetwood lamented the lack of order and noted that of those present only seven or eight had previously sat in the Commons. Thus, almost all members missed the lord chancellor's speech because they were being sworn while he spoke. Similarly, during the 1581 session exceptionally meagre attendance and the delay in administering the oath to new members likely limited the impact of Mildmay's oration on supply.[47] In 1601 a burgess claimed that he and many of his colleagues were forcibly kept out of the upper house during the lord keeper's address. If the experiences of 1586 and 1593 were representative, even when in attendance parliamentarians – thrusting and in disarray – could well go through the opening proceedings without hearing the contents of the speeches.[48]

In theory the committee stage was central to the development of a parliamentary grant. In practice most issues of substance normally had already been decided elsewhere. Although Bacon's comment of 1597 indicates a belief that the committee would move beyond the general issue and address the particulars of the crown's necessity, our knowledge of committee proceedings suggests that, with the possible exceptions of 1593 and 1601, discussions were no better informed than in the house. Royal necessity was already accepted and was not an issue for debate.[49] The task of the committee was to

---

[46] HPT, I, pp. 67–100; Graves, 'Management of Elizabethan Commons', pp. 16–17; idem, *Elizabethan Parliaments*, p. 66.

[47] In 1581 the new members could not be sworn on 16 January because a lord steward had not been appointed; they were eventually sworn on 18 January, the same day Mildmay introduced the issue of supply. *CJ*, I, 62, 82, 94, 115; A. F. Pollard and M. Blatcher (eds), 'Hayward Townshend's Journals. I. The Parliament of 1597/8', *BIHR*, XII (1934–5), 4–5; BL Lansdowne MS 41, f. 45.

[48] J. E. Neale (ed.), 'The Lord Keeper's Speech to the Parliament of 1592/3', *EHR*, XXXI (1916), 129; Pollard and Blatcher, 'Townshend's Journals', pp. 5, 9; D'Ewes, pp. 593, 623; BL Stowe MS 362, f. 66v. For difficulty in hearing even in the subsidy committee of 1601: Neale, *Parliaments*, II, p. 412.

[49] This is readily apparent from the descriptions of the committee and its functions, and the documents produced by the committees: *CJ*, I, 53, 63, 74, 104;

compose the articles specifying the form, rates and timing of the taxation. The committee varied in membership from a low of twenty-four in 1559 to a high of approximately 140 in 1597, and invariably included all privy councillors in the Commons as well as a number of lower-level officials. The membership tended to be more experienced than the house as a whole, but even during the earlier period of small committees included some novices.[50] The movement towards large committees has been explained as a government initiative.[51] At all times the conciliar element appears to have dominated the committees, whether through assertiveness in discussions or by prearrangement of plans. Our knowledge of events within committees is limited. Nevertheless, there exists no evidence that this stage constituted a free and fulsome exploration of alternatives for supply prior to the spontaneous composition of common articles. What do exist are numerous indications that the members were customarily presented with a more or less complete proposal. Disagreement would require open confrontation, and at

---

Hartley, *Proceedings*, p. 208; D'Ewes, p. 409; BL Lansdowne MS 55, f. 185; Harleian MS 75, f. 211–v; PRO, SP 12/40, ff. 190–1v; 107, ff. 73–4; Hatfield House MS 89/82–3.

[50] The membership figures are: 1559 – 24, 1563 – 38, 1566 – 48, 1571 – 36, 1576 – 29, 1581 – 62, 1585 – 90, 1586 – 127, 1589 – 80, 1593 – *c*. 136, 1597 – *c*. 140, 1601 – 103. *CJ*, I, 53, 64–5, 74, 83, 104, 119–20; Dean, 'Bills and Acts', p. 117. For the 1571 committee, twelve were in their first parliament (33 per cent), twelve were in their second or third, and twelve were in their fourth to ninth – for an average previous participation of 2.25 parliaments. For the 1576 parliament, four were in their first parliament (14 per cent), thirteen in their second or third, and twelve in their fourth to ninth – for an average previous participation of 2.86 parliaments. Turnover was substantial: in 1576, excluding the privy councillors, only four members had been on the 1571 committee, even though many others still sat in the house. Sources: *CJ*, I, 83, 104; HPT, *passim*.

[51] Lambert, 'Procedure in the House', p. 761. For a negative critique of Neale's political explanation of the size of the 1589 committee (*Parliaments*, II, p. 205), see Dean, 'Bills and Acts', p. 117. Since the 1589 committee was in fact smaller than the two previous committees, it is not reasonable to argue, as Neale does, that an exceptionally large body was chosen because the government intended to confront parliament with the extraordinary demand of two subsidies and thus encouraged a substantial section of the house to air their fears and misgivings in committee rather than attack the proposal in the Commons. The single most important factor influencing the size of the committees was the decision (apparently first made in 1585) to include automatically the first knight of every shire and burgess of every city; in 1597 all knights of the shires and city representatives were included: BL Lansdowne MS 43, f. 171; D'Ewes, pp. 356, 409, 431, 557, 624; Hatfield House MS 57/24.

most the committee tinkered with the details rather than determined the essence of the grant. In 1559, 1566, 1576 and 1585, for example, the committee met merely once on each occasion. In 1559 and 1585 the committee made its report to the house on the very day following its creation; in 1576 the treasurer of the household, who reported in the Commons on behalf of the committee, stated that at the meeting the members did *assent* to the articles.[52] The direction of the committee and the responsibility to report were in almost all instances the tasks of privy councillors. In 1566 Sir William Cecil held a membership list, noted attendance and the agreed articles and reported to the house. In 1601 Sir William Knollys, comptroller of the household, held a list of members and Sir Robert Cecil made the report. In 1581 Sir Walter Mildmay and the conciliar agent Thomas Norton dominated the committee, with the latter drafting the articles. In 1571, 1576 and 1581 the treasurer of the household, Sir Francis Knollys, reported to the house; in 1585, 1589, 1593 and 1597 this function was performed by the chancellor and undertreasurer of the exchequer (Mildmay followed by Fortescue).[53]

Realistically, the functions of the supply committee were *pro forma* as long as Tudor taxation retained its established features. In particular, prior to 1587 little discussion or amendment appears to have occurred in committee. The articles composed in 1576 simply recorded the by then customary recommendation for one subsidy and two fifteenths and tenths, at standard rates and timing (identical to the preceding 1571 tax), and concluded by stating all provisions and exemptions of the 1571 act were to pertain to the new bill.[54] The rough notes composed during the committee meeting in 1566 suggest only a single item was altered during the course of the afternoon: the timing of the subsidy of two shillings and eight pence payable upon goods was amended slightly to the benefit of taxpayers. Low attendance can serve as a good indication of formalized proceedings. In 1566 close to half the membership

[52] *CJ*, I, 53–4, 63–4, 105; D'Ewes, p. 356; PRO, SP 12/40, f. 190.

[53] Direction was apparently entrusted in 1559 to Sir Thomas Parry, treasurer of the household, and in 1563 to Sir Edward Rogers, comptroller of the household. Elton, *Parliament*, p. 164; Dean, 'Bills and Acts', pp. 117–18; M. A. R. Graves, 'Thomas Norton, the Parliament Man: an Elizabethan M.P., 1559–1581', *HJ*, 23 (1980), 31–2; *CJ*, I, 53, 64, 75, 84, 105, 192; D'Ewes, pp. 356, 433–4, 477, 496, 559, 631; BL Harleian MS 74, f. 305, 75, f. 211; PRO, SP 12/40, ff. 190–1v.

[54] PRO, SP 12/107, ff. 73–4.

was absent.[55] We possess no evidence that the Elizabethan committees ever discussed the body of the bill, apart from the exceptional circumstances of the protracted 1593 deliberations, and only partial indications that they debated the preamble.[56] The very routine nature of the committee deliberations offers an explanation why some obvious alterations (for example the proviso for Romney Marsh in 1571) were introduced much later following second reading. The committee was unused to tampering with the body of the legislation. Later in the reign when escalating military expenditure demonstrated the inadequacy of standard grants, the committee stage could become more animated. In 1589, when first considering a double subsidy, the committee met four times, although Mildmay also noted that albeit the greater part of the committee was present, 'diuers of them did not giue that attendance therein which soe great and waighty a Cause doth require.' Robert Cecil's report on the committee acceptance of four subsidies in 1601 indicates both a high level of attendance and a vigorous debate. As well, the indications are that in 1593, 1597 and 1601 the councillors did not have the precise articles prepared in advance of the first meeting of the committee, albeit the crown as always possessed definite expectations.[57] This could have encouraged committee discussions, and in 1593 and 1597 at least necessitated a subsequent meeting.

Closer attention to the deliberations of 1601, within the committee and in the house, clarifies the character of parliamentary supply when under the stress of rising demands. This examination provides no support for the theory that any attempt to increase taxation was certain to anger the Commons. On the contrary, the evidence suggests a generally responsive and indulgent Commons throughout the multiple grants of 1589, 1593, 1597 and 1601. On 3 November 1601 Sir Robert Cecil introduced the topic of aid. He purported to summarize briefly the lord keeper's oration for the benefit of those who had not been in attendance, but in fact he

[55] Professor Elton is incorrect in citing the details of the 1566 committee evidence (*Parliament*, p. 164n.; PRO, SP 12/40, ff. 190–1v), but his general position, that a) Cecil's notes demonstrate little was altered during the discussion, and b) the marks in the margin of the membership list denote attendance, appears reasonable and is accepted here.

[56] Elton, *Parliament*, p. 155; Dean, 'Bills and Acts', pp. 118–19, 121–6; D'Ewes, p. 496.

[57] BL Harleian MS 74, f. 305, 75, f. 211v; D'Ewes, pp. 471–4, 477–8, 559–60, 629–31.

spoke at great length on his own initiative, focusing upon military dangers. Supply was evidently a readily apparent requirement, for – as the diarist reported – when 'hee fell to perswade vs, because newe occasions were offered of consultacons, to be provideinge in provision of meanes for our owne deffence' Cecil's comments were limited to a few passing sentences. The most noteworthy one consisted of: 'He showed that Treasure must be the meanes ffor Treasure is the Synnowes of Warre.' The speech was followed by a motion from Sir George More for a committee. Debate was non-existent. The final word still went to Cecil, who stated openly that Sir Robert Wroth had offered one hundred pounds per annum towards the maintenance of the wars. The cryptic comment was presumably intended to encourage generosity.[58] When the committee met for its single session on the afternoon of 7 November, it sat in silence awaiting the customary conciliar lead. Sir Walter Ralegh, captain of the guard and steward of the Duchy of Cornwall, in the event began the discussion with the suggestion that the Queen's necessity was greater now than it had been at the time of the previous parliament, when three subsidies had been granted. The notion that more than three subsidies and six fifteenths and tenths were required met with universal acceptance; not a single member spoke against this either in committee or subsequently in the house. Cecil himself stated that if the committee had agreed upon the manner of taxation as speedily it did the matter (the approximate level of supply) then the business would have been concluded in an hour's time.

The debate centred around the topic of how best to provide the level of aid required by the government with the least inconvenience. No discussion ensued for the by now virtually standard three subsidies; the 'extraordinary' tax received all the attention. Because of the necessity for substantial assistance before the start of the 1602 campaign season, everyone agreed this would be assessed and paid first. The two problems which delayed the conclusion were both relatively minor, produced little friction and were easily overcome. Some members desired either a full or partial exemption from this extraordinary tax of those rated at the lower end of the subsidy scales.[59] The strategy which emerged as the official

[58] Cecil's speech is reported in BL Stowe MS 362, ff. 66v–70.
[59] Depending upon the speaker, this could have benefited merely those assessed on one pound for lands and three pounds for personality (the lowest rates), those on three pounds and five pounds, respectively, or all subsidymen below four pounds for lands and six pounds for personality.

position – stated in turn by Cecil, Fortescue, Knollys, Secretary of State John Herbert, Thomas Hesketh and Thomas Harris – entailed the payment, in a single instalment for each, of a full subsidy and two fifteenths and tenths at the customary levels with no special exemptions. One member, Edward Phelips, argued for heavier taxation, equivalent to one and one-half subsidies, but subsequently altered his position. Cecil reported in the Commons that his view prevailed with 'the most voices'. Exemptions, he said, would reduce the monetary value of the tax and breed dissension, suspicions of partiality and confusion amongst taxpayers. The other concern arose from the exceptional size of the request, with a desire to avoid the precedent of four subsidies and eight fifteenths and tenths. Several speakers urged that the extraordinary component be termed a contribution and enacted in a separate statute. Cecil reported that four subsidies 'was said to bee subjecte to great mistakinge because on our tyme it would bee said a great Innovation,' but at length on the 'more voices' the committee resolved to go by 'the old name of a subsidy'. This same objection was subsequently easily overcome in the Commons when raised by Sir Robert Wroth, and the ensuing preamble to the act did not even request, as in 1593 and 1597, that the multiple grant not serve as a precedent. Timing of the grant was not an issue at any stage. The 'routine' three-quarters of the entire taxation was due to be paid in essentially half the time customary prior to 1593 but by 1601 this evoked no controversy whatsoever. As for the exceptional component, even the members who spoke in favour of exemptions and/ or a separate statute urged speedier collection than the eventual act specified.[60]

The subsidy debates of 1593 were similar, in that agreement to the then unprecedented three subsidies and six fifteenths and tenths was never seriously in doubt once the government's intentions became clear. The lengthy debates arose in part out of the peculiar method by which the crown made known its requirements, through a joint conference between Lords and Commons, in part as a consequence of the numerous methods proposed for the taxation, and finally because of serious reservations over the timing of the subsidies. The discussions were extensive and must have proved exasperating for councillors who were attempting to maintain

---

[60] BL Harleian MS 75, f. 211–v; Stowe MS 359, ff. 278–9; Hatfield House MS 89/82–3; D'Ewes, pp. 523–33.

a legislative schedule, but in the end only one feature of Lord Treasurer Burghley's initial demand was altered. Sir Robert Cecil agreed to spread payment over four years instead of the original three (and amidst suggestions for the customary six), with the heaviest burden falling in the first two years. Even the critics accepted that the necessity was manifestly obvious and the collections should proceed as quickly as was reasonably possible.[61] Overall, the documentary evidence for the reign is straightforward. So long as the crown was content with the Elizabethan 'standard' parliamentary grant enacted up to 1589 approval came very close to being routine. Extremely few features of the acts were ever altered. From 1589 until 1601 unprecedented demands provided scope, not for opposition, but rather for reiteration of stock remedies and innovative suggestions. Most interested parliamentarians restricted their favoured notions to the new portion of the grant, and these new components rapidly became accepted as normal and unquestioned. The fresh vigour in the subsidy debates did not simply represent attempts to undercut or derail governmental plans for tax increases. If they were that, then they constitute almost total, abject failures. In fact, innovative proposals first made a noticeable impression upon the discussions in 1587, when without royal pressure or approval some members engaged in a wide-ranging debate on novel tax methods designed to support an aggressive foreign policy.[62]

In 1625 a member of the Commons stated that it was conventional not to put supply to the question 'till it be sure to be granted'. In 1606 an earlier representative reported to the house James's observation when discussion on a third subsidy was protracted:

... he knoweth you are so wise as to conceiue, that yf the noyse of more doubtes, debates, and contradictions, should now continew but a few dayes longer, not onely the value of that addition which is desyred would be lessened by the forme of giuinge; but much of the estimation would be impayred of those subsidies whereof by your honest gratuities, you haue already put his Majestie into possession.

---

[61] A fulsome examination of this session would be worthwhile, not least in explaining why Burghley's wide-ranging thoughts for increasing the yields of the subsidy and fifteenth and tenth were – despite some discussion – never pursued to a conclusion. D'Ewes, pp. 471–99; BL Cotton MS Titus Fii. f. 58; Bacon, *Works*, VIII, pp. 223, 233–4; PRO, SP 12/244, ff. 104–5, 165–6; 'Dean, 'Bills and Acts', pp. 137–8, 141–2.

[62] BL Harleian MS 7188, ff. 89v–102; MacCaffrey, *Making of Policy*, pp. 488–9.

These statements were far from disinterested observations, yet presumably the speakers believed they would strike a responsive cord within their contemporaries.[63]

The traditional values revealed by the comments can help explain why so little opposition was apparent within Elizabethan parliaments. Two sixteenth-century illustrations, one from prior to Elizabeth's accession and another from the latter portion of the reign, are instructive for the relationship of form and substance within parliamentary subsidy grants. In January 1558 the Marian regime engineered the exceptional joint committee recommendation for two subsidies and two fifteenths and tenths, payable in two years. The contemporary account of the parliamentary process surviving amongst the state papers noted that when this recommendation was reported to the house, the Commons 'with one voyce and mynde condestained and agreed'. Never – so it was said – was aid given with so hearty and loving a will. The final statute, of course, provided for one subsidy and one fifteenth and tenth payable within a year. Behind-the-scenes negotiations, couched in appropriate terms of deference, the good of the commonweal and readiness to provide the second half of the supply in the next session of parliament effectively circumvented the government's intentions. The language of consensus remained intact even in the midst of substantial conflict.[64] Thirty-one years later the Elizabethan Commons was faced for the first time with a very similar recommendation: two subsidies and four fifteenths and tenths, payable in four years. The parliamentary record indicates a smooth passage, and indeed we have no reason to disbelieve the sources. Supply was granted precisely as requested. But second reading was followed by a highly unusual event. A lone member gave voice to heartfelt arguments against the proposal.[65] He spoke not in anger – of necessity even in opposition he employed the language of cooperation and consensus. The arguments were acute, yet the target was not really the administration and he made no criticism of conciliar

[63] *Debates in the House of Commons in 1625*, ed. S. R. Gardiner (London, 1873), p. 114; Conrad Russell, *Parliaments and English Politics 1621–1629* (Oxford, 1979), p. 250; PRO SP 14/19, f. 108v.

[64] PRO, SP 11/12, ff. 66–9; Loach, *Parliament and the Crown*, pp. 160–1; 4 and 5 Philip and Mary, c. 11.

[65] BL Lansdowne MS 55, ff. 180–3v, 186v–7. On the basis of the handwriting, Neale attributed this speech to Henry Jackman: Neale, *Parliaments*, II, pp. 206–8; HPT, II, p. 371. The timing of the speech is fixed by the author's notice that the bill had already been engrossed.

management or manipulation. Rather, the prevailing concern was the lack of serious consideration devoted to the taxation by the Commons. It had, one might say, gone through 'on the nod'. Why, after consideration by 'a great grave and wise committee' and 'so general and current a consent' by the house, did he venture to speak, so presumptious and foolhearty, at such an unseasonable time? Because to date the arguments and debate were shallow and unconvincing. In all conscience he could not give his personal consent to the final passage of the bill and if he did not speak up at this juncture he must be forever silent. The portrayal of a vexed conscience seeking relief is convincing, if only because as a political ploy the interruption at such a late stage would have been futile. The speaker accepted without question the customary single subsidy. The double grant, however, was neither necessary nor to the benefit of the nation. The Commons had heard that the tax was necessary because of the imminent danger to the entire realm.[66] He dismissed out of hand that often repeated assertion of late Tudor subsidy justifications, and argued that if the crisis point was expected within a year then the requirement for a second subsidy, which would not begin to be collected before 1592, remained unsubstantiated. A voluntary benevolence would be more appropriate. We possess simply the speaker's perception that his concerns were unique in the house, though of certainty no member followed the lead. Was debate in the Elizabethan Commons really so formalized that only a maverick burgess at the last possible moment, with obvious reluctance and trepidation, could ask the searching questions which informed evaluation and agreement required?[67]

The recognition that a substantial proportion of what took place in parliament during the passage of the customary form of taxation was ritualistic raises important issues, not all of which can be explored at this juncture. In respect to the politics of parliamentary

[66] BL Lansdowne MS 55, ff. 181–2; Harleian MS 74, f. 305v. The emphasis upon the immediate threat of invasion derived from Burghley himself: BL Lansdowne MS 104, ff. 62–4v; 60, ff. 142–3.

[67] Professor Neale maintained that other members could well have expressed similar misgivings in committee, but this assumption was premised upon the mistaken interpretation of that committee (above, note 51). Neale elsewhere noted the bill caused no trouble (*Parliaments*, II, pp. 205–7). See also the profuse apology of 28 February by several members for suggesting that the bill was moving so speedily through the Commons that other worthwhile legislation might be endangered by an early dissolution: D'Ewes, pp. 440–1.

taxation, however, it can produce a challenge to the portrayal of a generally harmonious Elizabethan environment free of tension. Perhaps the harmony already well established was superficial and mere show, while beneath this calm surface there existed the turmoil of fiscal resentment and unresolved grievances. It remains the prerogative of any scholar unconvinced by this present examination to demonstrate the existence of such opposition. That would prove to be a difficult, if not impossible, task. The Elizabethan period is devoid of the evidence of tension-laden tax negotiations which do exist for some parliaments prior to 1559 and after 1603. In all instances apart from 1566 the Elizabethan regime acquired the level of taxation which it requested, and due to the particular character of the 1566 session the reduced grant in that year cannot serve to demonstrate opposition or resentment. Undoubtedly the Commons did not uniformly speak with a single enthusiastic voice. A maverick, though, constituted no threat, and venturesome members were mainly an inconvenience, as frequently in advance of government intentions as grudgingly bringing up the rear. The overwhelming majority of members of the Commons simply accepted the crown's lead.

For direct taxation, parliament did not function primarily as a forum where the political nation could discuss problems and their solutions. The social problems of parliamentary supply and the unreality of assessments were aired but never resolved. Meanwhile the related contemporary issues of prerogative taxation were barely raised at all (and with extreme rarity during the subsidy debates themselves).[68] Dr Dean has observed that many participants in the later Elizabethan discussions utilized the debate on supply as an opportunity to demonstrate loyalty.[69] The politics of parliamentary taxation were to a considerable extent formalized. Indeed, within a short space of time some developments of recent origin were transformed into the orthodoxy of 'ancient custom'. It was only with the jaundiced perspective, or possibly self-interested assertions, of a parliamentary manager that Francis Bacon could portray to James I in 1615 the circumstances of supply under the former Queen in his famous statement: 'in whose reign things were so well settled and disposed, as if she demanded anything it was

[68] For example: BL Lansdowne MS 43, f. 167, 55, f. 182; Harleian MS 7188, f. 102; D'Ewes, p. 494.
[69] Dean, 'Bills and Acts', p. 119.

seldom denied, and if she pretended any it was never inquired'.[70] Agreement did not spring out of thin air. Relevant considerations can range from the prevailing mind set, through pragmatic fears of retribution, to the materialistic benefits of the current practices for all parties involved in the political process. To suggest that the crucial factor involved in ready and unquestioning acceptance of crown proposals was effective management, was to ignore the real presence of common ground, the strength of good will, the pattern of deference and the absence of meaningful opposition. Perhaps the search for obscure hints of obstructionism, opportunism and opposition can now be abandoned, in favour of more fruitful lines of enquiry.

[70] Bacon, *Works*, XII, p. 177.

The author wishes to acknowledge the financial assistance of the Social Sciences and Humanities Research Council of Canada in the preparation of this study.

5

Religion in Parliament

N. L. JONES

The Tudor parliaments and religion are inextricably intertwined. From the Reformation Parliament to the enthused Protestantism of the Edwardian parliaments, from the restoration of Catholicism in Mary's parliaments to the enactment of the Elizabethan settlement and the Puritan drive of the 1580s, regulation of religion by statute was an important parliamentary activity.

The use of parliament to reform religion is central to the story of the institution and the history of the Reformation in England, but too often major religious legislation is all that is noticed by scholars. Even worse, those same scholars are often too obsessed with charting the theological doctrine contained in legislation to notice the larger part religion played in parliament or to understand the reasons why parliament became a context for religious debate. A window on the mental world of the legislators, parliament's contact with religious issues was much broader than is usually recognized. Therefore it behoves us to consider the way religious perceptions shaped the behaviour of legislators as well as the way parliament shaped religion.

Religion is found in parliament because parliament was the supreme legislator, the only court in the land capable of resolving any issue and able to make laws binding on all subjects of the crown. It was for this reason that the Reformation began and was continued through parliamentary statute, and it was for this reason that anyone wishing to alter the church had to seek parliament's approval. The legal necessity of employing parliament brought several types of religious legislation before the two houses. Anyone wishing to reform the institution of the church, or the faith of the English, had to have parliamentary sanction. Therefore a number of different kinds of reforming legislation were introduced. Broadly, these can be classified as bills for reform emanating from the government; bills for reform emanating from official church channels; and bills for reform introduced from unofficial quarters.

The government bills for reform included things like the Acts of Uniformity and Supremacy, while the church bills include ones like the 'alphabetical' reforms that dealt with discipline that appeared in 1566. The unofficial proposals for ecclesiastical reform are harder to track, but include attempts like the 'bill and book' movements of 1581 and 1586. All of these share the assumption that parliament and only parliament had the legal power to impose religious change on the nation. Not even the bishops could alter the way the church was organized and run without parliamentary approval.

The bills for reform and those concerning ecclesiastical property had an obvious connection with the established church. They dealt with issues of worship, discipline and structure. Another variety of bills reflected the influence of religion without concerning itself with the way the Church of England managed its flock. Preeminent among these are the bills aimed at the religious enemies of the state, such as the acts against treason that made Catholicism a crime or the bill against the heretical Family of Love.

Less obvious, but highly informative, are the bills which attempted to legislate upon a religious premise. Contemporary concepts of right and wrong were based upon biblical ethics and the Aquinian notion of natural law as a form of revelation, so it comes as no surprise to find legislators outlawing things explicitly forbidden by God and condemning unnatural acts. The Act against Usury of 1571 presents us with a classic case of the use of religious norms to define an offence, as do bills concerning sodomy, witchcraft, sorcery, perjury and many other things. In the area of private bills, too, we can see religious attitudes being brought to bear, as when market days were moved to a day other than Sunday.

Last but not least are attempts made to use the machinery of the church to deal with secular problems. The classic example of this involvement of parliament with the church is the Elizabethan poor law. The statute of 1563 enforced Christian charity by imposing the duty of collecting poor relief on the churchwardens, making the parish a unit of secular administration.

Most government-sponsored reform legislation appeared in the parliament of 1559, the first of the reign. Elizabeth wished to re-establish the monarch's supremacy over the church, to reintroduce

Protestantism to her realm and to recover revenues Mary had returned to the spirituality. To do these things she needed parliamentary sanction, so that a significant portion of parliament's time in 1559 was taken up with the struggle over the religious settlement. Fighting a rearguard action, the Catholic bishops in the Lords, allying with lay peers, nearly stopped the bill for uniformity of religion and gutted the bill for supremacy. The fighting and the fear over the shape of the religious settlement flushed several unofficial bills for religious toleration before Elizabeth, through minor concessions and the strategic arrest of some of the bishops, scraped together a bare majority for the passage of the act of uniformity. The supremacy and the acts dissolving the monasteries and returning first fruits and tenths to the crown passed easily, in keeping with the laity's greed for church property.

The story of the passage of the Elizabethan settlement is the best-known piece of Elizabethan parliamentary history and needs not be rehearsed here. However, it is necessary to recap the contents of the act of uniformity passed in 1559 if we are to understand later attempts at religious reform.[1] Requiring that all worship conform to the Book of Common Prayer of 1552, changed slightly to make it more palatable to Catholics but indubitably Protestant, the act specified that ornaments in the church and the dress of its clergy were to be as they had been in 1549 until the Queen saw fit to change them. That she never did, apparently believing that the 1559 statutes had settled religion for good, deeply offended those who sought to complete the half-way reformation of the English church, described by Bishop Jewel as 'leaden mediocrity'.

The clerical battle over vestments that would result from the enforcement of the ornaments rubric in the 1560s would underscore the major fault of the 1559 settlement. It did not establish a new church discipline to match the Protestant prayerbook. Nor did it reform the ecclesiastical hierarchy. Now liturgically Protestant, the English church retained its Catholic organization and the Catholic canon law. It did not know exactly what it believed or what behaviour was expected of its employees or its flock. The failure of the Queen to provide these things in 1559 led to the next round of religious legislation, a round lasting through the sessions of 1563,

---

[1] See my *Faith by Statute. Parliament and the Settlement of Religion 1559* (London, 1982), for a detailed account of religious legislation in that parliament.

1566 and 1571 as the clerical hierarchy sought to remedy the deficiencies of the settlement.

The responsibility for religion in England was shared by the crown and the clergy, and it was the bishops and the representatives of the clergy, meeting in convocation in 1563, who drafted legislation to complete the restoration of Protestantism. Dubbed the 'alphabetical bills' for religion, they were produced by ecclesiastical administrators and theologians who believed they were charged with creating a more efficient and theologically accurate church. They had yet to learn that the Queen considered religion her prerogative – and that she liked it just the way it was.

In a number of working papers prepared in convocation the leaders of the church defined its problems and outlined solutions. In particular, a document known as 'General Notes of Matters to be Moved by the Clergy in the Next Parliament and Synod' outlined four kinds of problems to be addressed. The first was the need for an established form of doctrine. The second dealt with the need for conformity in rites, while the third section was devoted to ecclesiastical laws and discipline. The last portion focused on the need to enhance small livings. From all these sections, as well as from the recommendations prepared by various bishops and others, there were born parliamentary bills in 1563 and 1566.[2]

Most of the recommendations coming out of convocation did not reach parliament in 1563 because of the lack of time, but some did. For instance, that year saw the passage of the act for the due execution of the writ *de excommunicato capiendo*, intended to aid the enforcement of sanctions against persons excommunicated by the church courts. The bill rested on the fact that the maintenance of the authority of the church courts was a concern of parliament and the crown:

Forasmuche as in these our dayes divers subiects of this realme and other the quenes maiesties dominions, are grown into such licence and contempt of the lawes ecclesiasticall ... that onlesse yt were for feare of the temporall sworde and power they wold altogether despise and neglect the same ... [which are] often tymes slowly and negligently executed, by reason that the writte de excommunicato capiendo, being directed to the sheriff ... is either not executed at all, or els so slowly, that thexecution of justice therby is letted or delayed, and the partie excommunicate therby encouraged to contynewe and persiste in wilfull and obstinate contumacy

<hr />

[2] William Haugaard, *Elizabeth and the English Reformation* (Cambridge, 1970) treats this convocation in detail.

... whereby the corrections and censures of the church do endure in great contempte, and are lyke dayly to growe into more, unless some speedy remedy be provided in that behalf.

The proposal went on to petition parliament for a law requiring that writs of excommunication be sent to all sheriffs and other officials in the sinner's neighbourhood. All of these would be empowered to apprehend and incarcerate the unrepentant individual, without bail, until he submitted to the church court.[3]

Acting on this advice someone, probably a bishop, introduced a bill into the Lords calling for the due execution of the writs. Dressed in legal niceties, it followed the convocation proposal to the letter. Passing the Lords without objection, it hit an important snag in the Commons. There the members were reluctant to grant such powers to secular officials without the clear definition of excommunicable offences. Once it was amended to their satisfaction they passed it, too.[4]

This statute born in convocation succeeded in 1563; most of its sisters had to wait until 1566, when the clerk of the Commons, recognizing them as part of a slate of church reform bills, alphabetized them. Bill A contained the Thirty-Nine Articles passed by convocation to create doctrinal uniformity, making it clear what Anglicans believed. Bills B through F dealt with various aspects of clerical discipline. Prepared by convocation under the leadership of the bishops – though they denied it when they discovered how angry the introduction of the bills made the Queen – these were the church's reform programme.

In 1566 Elizabeth stopped these bills dead, angered that she had not been consulted before their introduction, insisting that regulation of the church was her prerogative as supreme governor. In 1571, however, five of the alphabetical bills were reintroduced, though only bill A passed, making the Thirty-Nine Articles the legal faith of the English.[5]

---

[3] Corpus Christi College, Cambridge, MS 121, ff. 280, 380–3.

[4] HLRO, Lords MS Journals, IV, ff. 110, 118. Commons MS Journals, I, ff. 250v, 251–v; 5 Elizabeth, OA 26; 5 Elizabeth I, c. 23.

[5] The history of these bills has often been sketched, but interpretations differ and none is complete. Neale, *Parliaments*, I, pp. 165–76; 191–207, portrays their introduction and the divisions over them as part of a puritan plot. This is patently wrong. Elton, *Parliament*, pp. 199–214 is much briefer but more accurate. No one has followed the linkages between convocation and parliament from 1562/3 through to 1571.

The year 1571 is a turning point in the history of bills for religion in parliament. The 1559 parliament had been a time of official government bills for religion; the 1560s had been dominated by official church bills; the failure of most of those bills in 1571 forced the impetus for reform into the hands of unofficial enthusiasts who were no longer content to await reform from the top. It was the beginning of the puritan movement in parliament.

Professor Sir John Neale's two-volume history of the Elizabethan parliaments was in large part built around the story of how puritanism had given birth to the modern House of Commons, so that he traced the religious legislation with great care. Today scholars are less willing to believe in the importance of the puritans in parliament as a formative force, but there can be no doubt that men who desired a more thorough reformation tried to use parliament to get it. Their attempts dominate the story of religion in parliament in the sessions of the 1570s and 1580s. Though they never succeeded in their efforts, they stand as a testimony to the general conviction that parliament had the right and responsibility to control religion in England.

In 1571 William Strickland, an enthusiastic friend of reformed religion, made two attempts at reform, neither of which seem to have had official sanction (though he may have had encouragement from high places). At the beginning of the session he made a 'longe discourse, tendinge to the remembraunce of Gode's goodness in giveinge to us the light of his word, together with [the] gratious disposition of her Majestie', God's instrument of reform. The gist of it was that it would be good if the English church would publish its beliefs and purify the Book of Common Prayer. It was, he said,

drawne very neere to the sinceritie of the truth, yet are there somethinges inserted more superstitious or erronious then in soe highe matters bee tollerable, as namely, in the ministracion of the sacrament of baptisme, the signe of the crosse be made with some ceremonies, and the ministracion of the sacrament by women in tyme of extremitie . . .

Furthermore there were abuses in the Church of England that needed reform. Known papists had great livings, true preachers of the word had none and the court of faculties was corrupt, allowing pluralism and the presentation of children to ecclesiastical livings. He ended with a call for the house to appoint a committee to meet with the bishops 'for consideracion and reformation of the matters'.

The Commons responded by creating a committee of twenty-one to consult the bishops.[6]

The Commons committee met once and sent in the alphabetical bills for religion, but that did not satisfy Strickland. In frustration he introduced his own bill for reform of the Book of Common Prayer. The anonymous diary of 1571 summarized its effects:

first, for takinge away of copes, surplesses, etc.; then for the needeless confirmacion of children (as he tearmed it), the childishe askinge of questions of the children at baptisme, the kneelinge at the communion, the ministracion of the sacramentes in private houses, the givinge of a ringe at marriage, and such like, that without these matters the booke might bee established.

The reaction to the bill was mixed. The privy councillors present attacked Strickland's motion as contrary to the Queen's prerogative and a derogation of her authority as supreme head [sic]: 'what secrett cause or other scrupelositie there may bee in princes, it is not for all sortes to knowe.' Tristram Pistor took Strickland's side, delivering an eloquent speech on a *contemptu mundi* theme, insisting that the salvation of souls was more important than any terrestrial affairs and urging the members to seek the kingdom of God first.[7]

In the end it was ordered that the Queen be informed of the bill before it proceeded any further, with the result that it stopped dead in its tracks. A few days later the clerk of the Commons prepared for Lord Burghley a list of the bills in the House and their progress. A 'bill for reformacion of certeyne things in the boke of comon prayer once redd' appears there, but, beside it, 'strycken' has been written in Burghley's hand. Then in the list of bills not read the same entry is crossed out.[8]

That, however, did not mean that those who sought further reform (which included men of all Protestant stripes) gave up on using parliament to achieve it. In 1572 two divines who favoured reform and presbyterian ecclesiology wrote the *Admonitions to Parliament*, demanding that parliament see to it that the word was properly preached, the sacraments sincerely administered and the church properly disciplined. Attacking episcopal government as

[6] Hartley, *Proceedings*, I, pp. 200–1. N. L. Jones, An Elizabethan Bill for the Reformation of the Ecclesiastical Law, *Parliamentary History* 4 (1985), 180–2.

[7] Hartley, I, 220–2.

[8] SP 12/77, f. 111v.

popish, it called for the abolition of the medieval church structure and its replacement with a government composed equally of ministers, elders and deacons (not by a supreme governor and her archbishops). Another pamphlet called on parliament to expunge all popish remnants from the prayerbook, the church courts and clerical costume. The *Admonitions* mark the beginning of what can truly be called a puritan movement in parliament.

The authors of the *Admonitions* coordinated their efforts with men in the Commons who introduced a bill 'concerning dispensations for rites and ceremonies' which attacked the act of uniformity for retaining too many false ceremonies. Worse, the act was hindering the exercise of true religion because some bishops were suppressing the prophesyings in its name. Therefore it should be altered to 'extende onelie to such as shall saie anie papisticall service ... and to forbeare the wearing of such attire as limyted by the said former statute'.[9]

Engrossed without opposition on the second reading, it was committed on the third reading, an unusual move. The committee produced a new bill with a less offensive preamble, but left its substance intact. The Queen, jealous of her control over religion, intervened at this point and stopped its progress. In future, she ordered, no 'bill of religion sholde be admitted into the House onlesse conference and allowance of the bisshoppes therin were first had.'[10]

The rebuff the reformers received in 1572 taught them circumspection. In 1576 and 1581 the Commons were content to petition the Queen for the correction of ecclesiastical abuses rather than proceedings by legislation.[11] However, the 1584–5 and 1586–7 sessions saw renewed attempts to secure reformed worship by legislative fiat.

In 1584 Dr Peter Turner introduced a bill, framed by 'certain godly and learned ministers', that began the 'bill and book' campaign. It would have replaced the Book of Common Prayer of 1552 with a new book, the *Form of Prayers*, a Genevan liturgy. In addition it would have restructured the church government, changing from an episcopal to a presbyterian form, though without abolishing the episcopate. The reading of Turner's bill and book

---

[9] Hartley, *Proceedings*, I, p. 359.

[10] Ibid., p. 330.

[11] Ibid., pp. 445–7, 510–21. Elton, *Parliament*, pp. 214–16. Neale, *Parliaments*, I, pp. 287–304, 349–53, 398–404.

was prevented by the privy councillors in the house, who turned the members' attention to three petitions for 'the liberty of Godly Preachers, and to exercise and continue their Ministries, and also for the speedy supply of able and sufficient men into divers places now destitute and void of the ordinary means of Salvation'. These were turned into a single petition begging for a better educated and disciplined ministry and sent to the Lords for their reaction. They, in turn, consulted the Queen, and in the end Lord Burghley and Archbishop Whitgift delivered an answer. Burghley's was that those reforms that were needed were being seen to, and that the others were unfit for consideration, disturbing the church. Whitgift's answer was more caustic and less politic, offending many members. Thus the bill and book, and the petition, came to nothing.[12]

There was a new attempt to get a bill and book through parliament in 1586. Sponsored this time by Anthony Cope, it echoed the previous attempts at reform, complaining of the ignorance and ill-discipline of the clergy; it petitioned that all laws concerning church government should be repealed and a new prayerbook established. Once more the leadership of the house tried to prevent its reading, the Speaker informing Cope that 'her Majesty before this time had commanded the House not to meddle with this matter, and that her Majesty had promised to take order in those Causes.' The house, however, wanted the bill read and the Speaker had ordered the clerk to begin when a motion was made to stop it. This sparked a debate which lasted until the Commons adjourned for the day.

The next day the Queen sent for the bill and book, with the upshot that Cope and those who spoke in favour of reading the bill were imprisoned in the Tower. Their imprisonment raised questions about the liberties of the house. Peter Wentworth demanded to know if the parliament was not

a place for any Member of the same here assembled freely and without controllment of any person or danger of Laws by Bill or speech to utter any griefs of this Commonwealth whatsoever touching the service of God, the safety of the Prince and this Noble Realm.
Whether that great honour may be done unto God, and benefit unto the Prince and State without free speech in this Council, which may be done with it.

[12] D'Ewes, pp. 339, 340, 344, 349, 357–60. Neale, *Parliaments*, II, pp. 62–6.

His speech and motions for the liberty of the imprisoned members prompted Vice-Chamberlain Christopher Hatton, Chancellor of the Exchequer Walter Mildmay and Solicitor General Thomas Egerton to put the members in their place by a series of speeches demonstrating the legal ineptitude of Cope's bill and the danger it posed to the state and church.[13] Chastened, the Commons dealt no more with wholesale religious reform in that session, or in any of the later sessions of Elizabeth's reign. There would be future attacks on pluralities and ignorant and non-preaching clergy, but no more attempts to remake the Church of England.

The reform of the church was an important part of parliament's responsibility, but after 1559 neither the leaders of the church nor private members were successful in getting wholesale reform bills made into law. The Queen was too jealous of her prerogative, too afraid of religious dissension, to permit parliament to meddle in religion. It tried and failed on many occasions, leading to what might be described as a constitutional conundrum. One of the reasons statute law became the law of the land in England was the way the Reformation Parliament was used to create a law higher than the church's, conferring on Henry VIII the title of 'supreme head of the church'. As English monarchs seesawed between religions, parliament's approval was sought for each change. By the 1560s many members of the parliament believed that they, as members of parliament, had a responsibility to God for the maintenance of true religion. The fact that the Queen refused to permit the exercise of that responsibility frustrated and puzzled them, and it took most of the reign, and some nasty confrontations with their sovereign, before the Commons learned that they were not to meddle with religion.

One result was the internalization of puritanism, as those who wished to create a better reformed church abandoned their attempts to impose their model of reform from the top and began to work to achieve it from below. At the same time, the puritan campaigns of the 1570s and 1580s hardened many against them, widening the religious division in the nation, making consensus more and more difficult to obtain and maintain. Another result was the creation of a dissenting theology which placed individual conscience above human law. If the law could not be made to conform to God's will, then godly people were not always to be

---

[13] D'Ewes, pp. 410–12. Neale, *Parliaments*, II, pp. 148–65.

bound to the state. This frightened those who still believed that hierarchy was divinely dictated and essential to stability. As the Queen said in her proclamation against the Marprelate tracts in 1589, those who thought like Turner and Cope 'bring in a monstrous and apparent dangerous innovation within her dominions and countries of all manner ecclesiastical government now in use, and to the abridging, or rather to the overthrow of her highness' lawful prerogative allowed by God's law and established by the laws of the realm ....'[14]

A third result was a shift in the way the making of law was understood. If religious belief could not be used as the ground upon which all good laws were established; if men could not agree on what God willed in order to make the commonwealth prosper, there had to be a new way of rationalizing law. By the end of Elizabeth's reign these factors were coming together to create a new, secular approach to lawmaking and a division between those who would still hold the state to God's law and those who sought compromise by separating the spiritual and temporal spheres.[15]

Any bill for change in the church might be stopped by the Queen if she deemed it a threat to her prerogative, but not all bills for reform were radical bills. Many of them reflected the desire of members to correct ecclesiastical abuses, strengthening the established church. For instance, the same day in 1571 that Strickland proposed changing the Book of Common Prayer it was moved that the archbishop of Canterbury's court of faculties be reformed.

The bill was introduced on the floor by Mr Carleton, 'who exhibited a bill into the House against lycenses, dispensations, faculties and rescriptes to bee by the archbusshoppe of canterbury graunted contrary to the word of god, and for the reversinge of the statute made in the 25 Henry 8, by which statute the Bushoppe of Canterbury is made as it were a pope ...'[16] Created to handle cases

---

[14] P. L. Hughes and J. F. Larkin (eds), *Tudor Royal Proclamations* (New Haven, 1969), III, p. 34.

[15] The idea that the disputes over religion in the Elizabethan parliaments led to constitutional change has been generally ignored by recent historians in the aftermath of the discrediting of Neale's ideas about a puritan party in the early part of the reign. Nonetheless, we must be aware that even though religious conflict was not as important as Neale believed, it did exist and it did reflect the ideals of the members. Patrick Collinson has reminded us of this in his 'Puritans, Men of Business, and Elizabethan Parliaments', *Parliamentary History* 7, 2 (1988), 187–211.

[16] Hartley, *Proceedings*, I, p. 222.

that had formerly been appealed to the pope, the court of faculties was disliked by most serious reformers because it seemed to encourage simony, nonresidence, plurality and a number of other offences – the very things alphabetical bills B-G were designed to halt – and to represent Catholic laxness.

In 1570 Archbishop Parker, under attack for rejecting the presentation of a fourteen-year-old to a prebend, told William Cecil 'I write *coram Deo in amaritudine animae meae* ... I have a long time offered in convocation to my brethren to procure the dispatchment of this offensive court. I have signified the same to your honours. For I have more grief thereby than gain, and I would it were wholly suppressed, as reason and statute would bear withal ...'[17] The authors of the *Admonition to Parliament* would have been delighted if Parker had carried out the dissolution of the court they described as 'the filthy quavemire and poisoned plash of all the abominations that do infect the whole realm', but Parker did not abolish it, leaving it to bother his successor, Edmund Grindal.[18] Thus it would seem that all Protestant opinion was firmly in favour of Carleton's bill, for it was apparent that the court had to be reformed by statute if its abuses were to be ended.[19] Moreover, there is no evidence that the Queen intervened to stop the bill, yet it failed.

Its death was not caused by religious opposition; it was caused by legal quibbles. Laudable as its ends might be, the bill was unworkable, as the lawyers were quick to point out. As drafted the bill said that the court of faculties should do nothing contrary to the will of God, a principle which was good in theology, but bad in law and reason.[20] Eminent men of law rose to explain why it would not work. Serjeant Manwood said:

The meaninge of the lawe hee approved, but how farr the same might stretch hee knewe not, and therefore hee thought requisite that there should bee a perticuler declaracion of the greifes and what the abuses were which are intended to growe by these lycenses, for to conclude without knowledge and in a generality it were overmuch obsurd.

---

[17] John Bruce (ed.), *The Correspondence of Matthew Parker* (Cambridge, 1853), p. 363.

[18] Patrick Collinson, *Archbishop Grindal 1519–1583* (Berkeley, 1980), pp. 228–9.

[19] John Daeley, 'Pluralism in the Diocese of Canterbury during the Administration of Matthew Parker', *Journal of Ecclesiastical History* 18 (1967), 37.

[20] The text of the bill survives. SP 12/27/ff. 223–5.

Serjeant Lovelace went further. Making clear his agreement with Manwood, he pointed out that the only way to know that a bishop had made a dispensation contrary to the Word of God was for the person receiving it to admit it in a secular court, a thing which he thought highly unlikely.[21]

In the end the bill was committed, rewritten, introduced as a new bill and passed by the Commons. In the Lords it was committed to Archbishop Parker and a group of legal specialists three days before the session ended. It died with the dissolution, killed by the delays needed to give it a workable legal framework.

Supported by many, this bill against the court of faculties lacked legal precision, with the result that no matter how much they liked the bill in principle the members could not accept it as written. Their care in making it into a law which could be understood and enforced was not unusual, a point that emphasizes the fact that the members of parliament were there to make workable law, even when God was concerned.

Many bills touching the church appeared in parliament because ecclesiastical property and power were regulated by secular law. Affecting the way the church operated, they had little to do with theology and a great deal to do with money. In 1559, for instance, the ownership of ecclesiastical property was a major issue. The crown was in the process of taking back the lands Mary had returned to the church, dissolving the new monasteries and assuring itself of the income from vacant sees as well as the right to exchange property with bishops – usually to their detriment.[22] Inspired by the same spirit, the laity were rushing to assert their claims to ecclesiastical property and to settle disputes over ownership born from the religious confusion of the 1550s.[23] An act of parliament was the only certain way to gain clear legal title to some of the properties granted and regranted by Edwardian and Marian bishops. Later in the reign there were many other bills concerning ecclesiastical property and the enforcement of secular law against ecclesiastical privilege. The numerous bills for uniting parishes and enhancing church livings are examples of these, as are bills like the 1566 'bill to avoid sanctuaries for debt'.

Another chapter in the struggle between ecclesiastical authority

---

[21] Hartley, *Proceedings*, I, pp. 222–3.

[22] Jones, *Faith by Statute*, pp. 160–8.

[23] N. L. Jones, 'Profiting from Religious Reform: The Land Rush of 1559', *Historical Journal* 22 (1979), 279–94.

and secular authority that had been raging throughout the later Middle Ages, the bill would have made it impossible for a person to claim sanctuary for debt in a sanctuary church. In the last parliament of Mary's reign a similar attempt had been made, but it was blocked by Abbot Feckenham, who defended Westminster's right to be a sanctuary by coming personally into the Commons to present his titles.[24] In 1566 the Protestant dean of Westminster did exactly the same thing. He 'making his oration for the sanctuary, alleged divers grants of King Lucius, and other Christian kings; and Mr. Plouden, of his Councel, alleged the grant for sanctuary there, by King Edward, five hundred years past ... with great resaon in law, and chronicles ...'.[25] The master of the rolls was asked to certify the force of the law that made sanctuaries legal, and, in the end, the bill was defeated in a division of the Commons, sixty for and seventy-seven against.[26] Bills of this sort continually remind us that the legal right to property was as sacred for many as theology. Although all the members of the 1566 parliament were sworn Protestants it did not mean that they would overturn a legal right that had outlived its theological usefulness.

If ecclesiastical rights and property could be regulated by parliament, the machinery and property of the church could also be appropriated for the common good. The church had always performed social services for the community, and in England the parish had become the basic unit of poor relief before the Reformation. However, as the numbers of destitute people increased in the mid-sixteenth century, it became apparent that purely local efforts at poor relief were not working well enough to alleviate the problem. The upshot of this was the adoption in parliament of a compulsory poor rate. Under the terms of the act for the relief of the poor of 1563 every parish was to have collectors of alms, working under the direction of the churchwardens. It was ordered that the collectors 'when the people are at the Churche in Dyvine Service, shall gentelly aske and demaunde of every Man and Woman what they of their Charitee wilbee contented to gyve weekly towardes the Relief of the Poor.'

The exhortation of Christians to charity was not new; what was new was the order that anyone refusing to contribute was to be reported to the bishop or his ordinary. If spiritual sanctions failed

[24] D. M. Loades, *The Reign of Mary Tudor* (London, 1979), pp. 449–50.
[25] *CJ*, I, 74.
[26] *CJ*, I, 79.

to persuade him to make a charitable gift, he was to be remanded to the next general session of the justices and imprisoned for further refusals. Collectors who failed to gather these alms could be fined ten pounds, and churchwardens who colluded with them were in mercy for twenty pounds.[27]

In the poor law we have an example of the union of the machinery of church and state to solve a social problem, a union that was seen as natural by many Elizabethans. With the spiritual and temporal swords united in the person of their monarch it was assumed that church and state should work together toward their common ends. The state should help to make the world more Christian and the church should help to strengthen the state.

Elizabethans were believing, if confused, Christians and much of their legislation was inspired by religion. In the early Elizabethan years it was not uncommon for a preamble to observe, as the 1563 perjury statute does, that the offence was committed 'to the high displeasure of God'.[28] Elizabethans accepted, as their forebears had, that some things should be illegal because God said they were, and that things condemned by God ought to be condemned by people. The result was that many statutes were rationalized by focusing religious opinion on what, to us, seem to be secular problems. A textbook example of this is the 1571 act against usury.

Since the fall of Rome Christian theologians had been condemning lending with certain interest as a sin. In St Luke's gospel Christ had ordered his followers to 'lend freely, expecting nothing in return', while in many places in the Old Testament God had forbidden lending at interest. Aquinas had explained the divine reasoning behind these condemnations in terms of the unnaturalness of interest, an explanation that was used in canon law to create a working definition of usury. For late medieval lawyers, then, usury meant breaking the law of God and the law of nature by contracting for certain interest without assuming any of the borrower's risk.[29]

The church courts had punished usurers for centuries, but in the late fifteenth century parliament saw fit to make usury a crime

[27] 5 Elizabeth 1, c. 3.

[28] 5 Elizabeth 1, c. 14.1.

[29] For a lengthy explanation of this see John T. Noonan, *The Scholastic Analysis of Usury* (Cambridge, Mass., 1957). For a detailed study of the Act, 13 Elizabeth I, c. 8, see my *God and the Moneylenders. Usury and Law in Early Modern England* (Oxford, 1989).

against the state as well. In Henry VII's reign two statutes introduced the canonical definition of usury into statute law, forbidding lending at interest on secular pains. In 1545 parliament repealed the ban and, in the name of better enforcement through regulated toleration, made the legal rate 10 per cent.[30] Edward VI's last parliament reversed that law, on the grounds that 'usurie is by the worde of God utterly prohibited, as vyce most odyous and detestable, as in dyvers places of the hollie Scripture it is evydent ....'[31]

After this statute was enacted in 1552, several attempts were made to get parliament to change the usury law, but it was not altered until 1571. In that year a long debate erupted that allows us to glimpse the way religion influenced the perceptions of Elizabethan lawmakers. For them secular law had to correlate with God's law, and the way one understood God determined the way one voted on issues like usury.

At the heart of the 1571 debate over usury was a legal conundrum whose resolution would determine how parliament ought to decide the question. In English law a distinction had always been made between actions which are *malum in se*, evil in themselves, and *mala prohibita*, things not inherently evil but which may be regulated in the common interest. If usury was explicitly forbidden by God, and therefore *malum in se*, parliament must prohibit it. If usury was not explicitly forbidden by God it was subject to the whim of the lawmakers and political expedience.

This legal distinction focused the debate on God's word and how strictly it should be a model for statute law. In turn this led to a series of questions about usury, framed here by Lord Burghley:

1 whether it be agaynst nature or not
2 whether it be forbydden by gods worde or no
3 whether it be a iudiciall or morall lawe
4 whether it be wholy forbidden or but where it is used with the poore
5 whether, if it be not unlawfull by gods lawe, yet it be convenient to prohibitt it by mans lawe.[32]

The Commons tried to answer these questions. Conservatives, drawing on Aquinian definitions, were determined to prove that

---

[30] 3 Henry VII, c. 5; 11 Henry VII, c. 8; 35 Henry VIII, c. 9.
[31] 5 & 6 Edward VI, c. 20.
[32] BL Lansdowne 101/24, 26.

usury was always wrong and damnable, for, as Aristotle said, interest was unnatural and, as Augustine had observed, 'to take but a cuppe of wine' in interest 'is usury and damnable'.[33]

Their opponents drew on another stream of scholastic thought, taking their proofs from the Tübingen nominalists like Conrad Summenhardt and Gabriel Biel and their Protestant descendants, Charles du Moulin and Martin Bucer. Arguing that usury only occurred when a loan 'bit' a borrower (a distinction that turned around the latest humanist philological scholarship), they argued against the mechanical, contractual definition used in the canon law. For them the sin of usury only occurred when the lender knowingly oppressed the borrower; when the borrower and lender were in charity with one another there was no sin. In short, it was the lender's evil intent that created the crime. Since, however, men were incapable of knowing the true intent of a loan, interest should be allowed so long as it was not socially damaging. As the Queen's Latin secretary said, 'to take reasonable or soe that both parties might doe good was not hatefull' and therefore not repugnant to the word of God.[34]

Those who favoured redefining usury to include only loans made with evil intent found allies in a third school of thought, the legal pragmatists. These men thought it was pointless to worry about whether God had explicitly forbidden something. The question was, could a total prohibition be enforced? If it could not then man's law could not be expected to conform perfectly with God's law. Serjeant Lovelace insisted that 'to prohibite the ill of covetousnes in generalitie were vayne, voyd and frivolous, since that the speech and act it selfe is indefinite … and therefore as utterly vaine it were to prohibitte it in vayne wordes of a generality.'[35]

In the end the usury bill, redrafted and amended by the bishops, was a compromise between various camps, with the conservatives winning a paper victory. In the original bill all interest under 10 per cent was to have been tolerated but in the act no interest was legal, though a distinction was made between petty usury (under 10 per cent) and grand usury (over 10 per cent). Many more teeth were put into the law, too, such as the nullification of usurious contracts. Strikingly, no one in the debate thought it necessary to discuss the economic effects of the law.

[33] Hartley, *Proceedings*, I, p. 232.
[34] Ibid., I, p. 231.
[35] Ibid., I, pp. 234–5.

The story of the usury act demonstrates the importance of religion as an influence in parliament, but that influence was not overtly theological. Although the members were operating under religious assumptions drawn from various branches of scholasticism and humanism, they were disagreeing over the interpretive technique to be applied while sharing the belief that legislation should be directed by God's word. The arbiter between the conflicting schools of interpretation was the English legal tradition.

The moral is that whenever we ask about religion in parliament we should be prepared to seek it in places where it is not obvious. Tudor men cared about religion and had been steeped in its categories, so their religious ideals appear in nearly every piece of legislation they crafted. For an Elizabethan to leave God out of the solution to a question was nearly unthinkable. Difficulty arose only when they disagreed about God's will.

If most parliamentarians of the early Elizabethan period were still using scholastic analysis to solve secular questions with theological insights, they were nonetheless Protestants. After 1563 Catholics were prevented from sitting in the Commons and it became an exclusively Protestant body. Many of its members did not understand what that meant theologically, and many who did dissented from the formulation of the Thirty-Nine Articles, but they did know who the enemies of their faith and state were. The religious hatred that marks the post-Reformation period became part of the political glue that held the Elizabethan state together.

Robustly fearing and hating Catholics, the members of both houses of parliament enthusiastically supported legislation that would curb them and protect their Queen. In 1563, for instance, parliament enacted a treason law aimed at anyone who upheld the authority of the pope. The Queen did not like the new legislation and it was seldom enforced, but the revolt of the northern earls in 1569 provoked another round of anti-Catholic legislation in the parliament of 1571.

That year the council sent two treason bills to parliament, both aimed at finding and stopping propapal activity. Another, the bill for coming to church, would have empowered the ecclesiastical authorities to force everyone to attend church once a quarter and to commune by the Anglican rite once a year, separating the Anglican sheep from the Catholic goats.

The introduction of this bill caused a furore. The Commons were under the impression that it was an unofficial bill (though it was drafted by Edmund Grindal, Bishop of London),[36] allowing them more room for reaction than if it had been sponsored by the council. At any rate, the resistance to it had nothing to do with Catholics – everyone was agreed they were bad – and everything to do with the legal problems such a bill raised. Some disliked it because it was flawed in its construction: Sir Owen Hopton feared that leaving enforcement to the churchwardens would be pointless, they 'beinge simple men and fearinge to offend, would rather incurre the daunger of periurie then displease some of their neighbours.'[37] Others apparently objected to the handling of such a matter by the Commons, for William Fleetwood was moved to point out that 'princes in their parliamentes have made ecclesiasticall lawes and constitucions such as these.'[38]

The legal objections were joined to other concerns. Several wished that no exceptions should be made for gentlemen 'in their private oratories', and Thomas Snagge, who wanted a new, better reformed prayerbook, raised the issue of whether or not attending a service that did not exactly conform to the Book of Common Prayer would make one punishable under the law. He feared that services where 'a sermon and some other prayers as the minister should thinke good in place' of the prayerbook would be accounted the legal equivalent of a Catholic mass.[39]

Others attacked the provision that everyone should receive the Eucharist once a year. Though it was proper to force people to go to church, it was 'not convenient to enforce consciences', for all the doctors agreed that 'noe lawes may make a good man fitt to receave that greate misterie but God above.' Though resting directly upon the central Protestant tenet of solafidianism, several members attacked this observation. William Strickland, whose puritan conscience brooked no sympathy for sensitive Catholic consciences

shewed the practice and doings of the Pope, the banishment of the Arians; that the sword of the prince for lacke of lawe must not bee tyed; the Isralites hee sayd were constrayned to receave the Passover; and finally hee concluded it was noe straitninge of their consciences, but a chardge or losse of their goodes, if they could not vouchsafe to bee as they should bee, good men and Christians.[40]

---

[36] Elton, *Parliament*, p. 201.
[37] Hartley, *Proceedings*, I, p. 202.
[38] Ibid.
[39] Ibid., p. 205.
[40] Ibid., p. 206.

Despite the legal and theological doubts the bill raised, it passed in both houses only to be vetoed by the Queen. The bishops begged her to permit its reintroduction in 1572, but she deflected them. In 1576 it was brought into the upper house, but was quickly killed, probably by a message from the palace.[41] As late as the parliament of 1601 the members were seeking ways to enforce church attendance, forcing recusant Catholics to reveal themselves so they could be punished.[42]

The bill for coming to church underscores one of the religious realities of the age: to be Protestant was to be first and foremost anti-Catholic. Since the crown, Lords, and Commons were agreed on the danger Catholic ideology and armies presented to the kingdom anti-Catholic legislation makes up the single largest body of bills and acts concerning religion. Despite the Queen's reluctance to enforce harsh laws against recusants, parliament enthusiastically enacted them, especially in the 1570s and 1580s when the revolt of the northern earls, the Duke of Norfolk's treason, the ongoing crisis over Mary, Queen of Scots, the appearance of Jesuits and seminary priests in the land and the Spanish threat kept the Catholic menace before everyone's eyes. One of the peaks of the anti-Catholic reaction came in the parliament of 1581 when the act to retain the queen's majesty's subjects in their due obedience was passed. It was the most severe statute ever enacted against the pope's followers and began a period of persecution, but as passed it was gentle in comparison with the original bill. Lords and Commons had united in their support for extreme penalties, only to have the Queen force them to modify its harshest provisions.[43] The moral is that when we think of religion in Elizabethan parliaments we must be careful to remember the powerful nationalistic feelings it evoked as well as the ecclesiological disputes it caused. The members might fight over God's will among themselves, but they all agree God was not a Roman Catholic and most suspected that a Catholic was not a good Englishman.

When we speak of religion in parliament in Elizabeth's reign we are really speaking of a number of distinct but interrelated things. Most visibly religious are the bills which would have changed worship and church discipline, whether they came from the

[41] Elton, *Parliaments*, p. 202.

[42] Neale, *Parliaments*, II, pp. 396–404. Kenneth L. Parker, *The English Sabbath* (Cambridge, 1988), pp. 72–82, 121–8.

[43] Neale, *Parliaments*, I, pp. 382–91.

council, the convocation, or private members inspired by religious conviction. Bills from the council and convocation dominate the group until the 1570s, after which private initiatives correspond to the rise of the puritan movement.

Proposals concerning the church but which are atheological make up another set of bills. These sought to make use of the church's machinery to achieve some desirable secular end or to make the church provide some social good that people thought it ought to provide. Bills of this sort tended to be well intentioned, unlike those which sought to strip the church of its property. The regulation of property rights was a power of parliament, and changes in the way leases were held and property bestowed could be imposed on the church by parliament, a fact that neither the crown nor private individuals were slow to notice.

More difficult to detect but very important are the influences religion had on the way legislation was conceived and discussed. Assumptions about right and wrong, about the relationship between human law and God's law, and conflicting definitions of sin and the state's duty to prevent it all shaped parliamentary activity. Over the length of the reign conflicting religious ideals created more and more tension in parliament as members sought to make the state conform to their particular image of God's will.

Much less subtle, religion's influence on members' attitudes toward national security is very visible. The defence of the monarch and her nation were identical with the defence of Protestantism, making members willing to persecute their neighbours to make them into good Christian English people. Only the Queen's reluctance to persecute Catholics tempered parliament's enthusiasm for ferreting out and punishing the enemies of the supreme governor of the Church of England.

Given that religion and religiosity deeply influenced the bills introduced in parliament, the reaction of members to these bills tells us something else about the ways they conceived parliament's relationship to religion. Whenever we catch an echo of the debates they confirm that parliament was in the business of making law. Through law religion could be reformed, but the formal nature of statute law and the necessity of creating enforceable statutes tempered the members' religious enthusiasm. No matter how much they might approve in principle of a proposal inspired by religion or affecting religion, few of them would let it pass until the demands of the law gods had been met.

Parliament dealt with the church because it was the supreme legislator, capable even of changing the nation's religion and believing itself charged with the responsibility to safeguard the faith. For that same reason anything and everything parliament did was informed by religious feeling.

6

Parliament and Locality*

D. M. DEAN

Whereas there is no doubt as to why Elizabeth and her ministers saw fit to call a meeting of parliament, the hopes and aspirations of those sending MPs to Westminster are much more difficult to ascertain. The history of Elizabethan parliaments has consequently been largely written from the perspective of the centre, drawing upon state papers, parliamentary journals and the papers of privy councillors such as William Cecil, Lord Burghley's collection, the Lansdowne Manuscripts in the British Library. This essay seeks to add to our understanding of Elizabeth's parliaments by shifting the focus to the boroughs and counties which selected men to represent them in parliament. By examining in particular their legislative concerns and activities, something closer to the contemporary perception of parliament can be reached. In order to set this in its proper perspective, however, something must first be said of what privy councillors sought to obtain from a meeting of the 'hiest, cheefest and greatest Court' of England and how they viewed the 'Knights, Citizens and Burgesses' who 'represented the Commons of the whole Realm'.[1]

So far as the privy council was concerned the main reason for calling parliament was to secure parliamentary subsidies. Writs for

* An earlier version of this paper was read to the Conference of Australasian Historians of Medieval and Early Modern Europe, Auckland, New Zealand, September 1987, a paper which had benefited from the comments of Dr Pauline Croft. My attendance at that conference and further research into local archives upon which this paper is based has been generously supported by the British Academy. I would like to especially thank the staff of the record offices whose manuscripts are cited here and the Clerk of the Skinners' Company of London for assisting with the records in their keeping.

[1] Vernon F. Snow (ed.), *Parliament in Elizabethan England, John Hooker's Order and Usage* (New Haven and London, 1977), pp. 181–2.

elections and summons to peers were frequently drawn up as the last of the taxes voted in the previous parliament entered the exchequer. Only on rare occasions, as with the Elizabethan settlement of 1559 or the problem of Mary, Queen of Scots in 1572 and 1586–7, did matters other than subsidies cause parliaments to be called.[2] Each parliament also provided the privy council with the opportunity to get important and necessary laws onto the statute book and every Elizabethan session saw measures initiated by the government pass both houses, escape the royal veto and join the large number of laws to be enforced by royal officials.[3] Besides subsidies and necessary laws, Elizabethan councillors had little doubt as to the opportunities offered when the governing class of the realm was brought together in a parliament. The many rituals of a parliamentary session, from the colourful procession and fulsome speeches by the lord chancellor or lord keeper at the opening, to elaborate procedural practices such as those MPs who voted against a successful bill carrying it out of the chamber and then returning it, and the final closing speech by the Speaker, were intended to reveal the harmony of the body politic. The sessions of 1572 and 1586–7 served to demonstrate to the Queen, no less than the Catholic princes of Europe, that the Protestant ruling class of England would not suffer the treasonous activities of the Scottish Queen. In 1584–5 the governing class in parliament openly declared its solidarity in meeting the Catholic threat and its commitment to preserve the safety of their sovereign. Grants of parliamentary subsidies gave members the opportunity to declare publicly their support for their Queen and her council. Such gatherings of the lay peers, bishops, knights of the shires, burgesses and citizens of the boroughs also provided the government with the opportunity to consult with those responsible for collecting taxes,

[2] Even in 1586–7, when Vice-Chamberlain Sir Christopher Hatton told the Commons that they had been gathered together to determine Mary's fate and not to make laws or grant a subsidy, he added 'albeit if neede soe required the same were convenient enough to bee donne', D'Ewes, p. 393. He repeated this eleven days later, p. 403.

[3] Around 40 per cent of Elizabethan statutes seem to have had an official origin, and this despite the belief of some privy councillors and officials that there were already too many laws in existence, D. M. Dean, 'Enacting Clauses and Legislative Initiative, 1584–1601', *BIHR* 57 (1984) 141; BL Lansdowne MS 43/72, f. 171; D'Ewes, p. 345. On initiatives see Elton, *Parliament*, pp. 62–87 and Dean, 'Bills and Acts', pp. 95–110.

mustering troops and enforcing law and order. Parliaments were unique in bringing together the political elite of Elizabethan England to consider possible remedies to social problems, solutions to economic difficulties or the means to curtail irregularities in the law. A parliamentary session thus played a vital role in the ability of the Tudor state to function.[4]

It was for this reason that the privy council was concerned to ensure that the 'best and fittest' men sat in the Commons, for it was in the lower house that the counties and boroughs of the realm were represented. In the well-known debate over the residency of burgesses in 1571 one of the most experienced of Elizabethan parliament men and self-confessed servant of the council, Thomas Norton, explained that 'any thing mighte bee obiected to the imperfeccion of the parliamentes, which may seeme to bee scant sufficient by reason of the choyce made by burroughes, for the most part, of strangers, not burgesses.' As one member asked,

Howe may her Majestie or howe may this court knowe the state of her frontiers, or who shall make report of the portes, or howe every quarter, shiere or countrey is in state? Wee who nether have seene Barwicke or St Michaelle's Mount can but blindlie guesse at them, albeit wee looke on the mapps that come from thence, or letters of instruccions sent from thence: some one whom observacion, experience and due consideracion of that countrey hath taught can more perfectly open what shall in question thereof growe, and more effectually reason thereuppon, then the skillful-lest otherwise whatsoever. And that they shoulde bee the very inhabitors of the severall counties of this kingdome who should bee here in tymes certaine imployed, doubtles it was the true meaninge of the auncient kings and our forfathers who first began and established this court might bee founde.

There was no doubt, he concluded, that there were 'none soe fitt for every countrey as those who knowe the same'.[5]

Throughout the reign the government reiterated the need for

---

[4] It thus forms one of Professor Elton's three 'points of contact' between the crown and the governing class of the realm, G. R. Elton, *Studies*, III, p. 3–21.

[5] Hartley, *Proceedings*, pp. 225–7. A similar point was made in 1601 by a Derbyshire knight who declared, in drawing attention to the 'inequalitye' of weights and measures 'no man but knows it' he told the lower house, 'who knows the State of his Country', D'Ewes, p. 662. On Norton see M. A. R. Graves, 'Thomas Norton, The Parliament Man: An Elizabethan M.P., 1559–1581', *HJ* 23, 1 (1980), 17–35.

towns to elect men of local experience. After the grave economic crises of the mid-1590s, and following its overreaction to a relatively minor disturbance in Oxfordshire, the privy council wrote to towns in August 1597 insisting that they avoid choosing burgesses 'unmeet and un-acquainted with the state of borough named thereto'.[6] In some cases they need not have bothered, for many Elizabethan boroughs had resolved to elect only men with strong local connections. Gloucester made such a ruling during Mary's reign, threatening all freemen and burgesses who voted for a person who was not free of the town, or a burgess or recorder, with loss of their status. In 1584, when Robert Dudley, Earl of Leicester, sought the nomination of one of their MPs, he was told that only those sworn to the franchise of the city could be elected.[7] The Cinque Ports made such a ruling in 1572, as did Canterbury in 1581, although those supporting unqualified candidates there suffered only a 20 shilling fine.[8] Warwick had similar resolutions. In the election dispute of 1586 one of the arguments used against the candidacy of Job Throckmorton was that he would have no real interest in the needs of the town. His supporters countered by pointing out that his father, Clement Throckmorton, 'was not only a good freeholder in the towne and dwelled ther and kept house there many yeres.' Moreover, an earlier MP had had to be sworne into his burgess-ship before election, and this is what was done in Throckmorton's case.[9] When Rye chose the nonresident Sampson Leonard as their MP in 1597, they noted that he would have to come to Rye and take his oath as freeman 'otherwyse this electyon concernyng him to be voyde'; he was later let off because of his lameness and 'great affairs' and 'upon his faithfull promys by his letters for our good'.[10] His was a frequent promise by nonresident representatives of the boroughs. In 1593 the city of Lincoln selected a local gentleman, Charles Dymoke, because he had 'allways showed himself very

---

[6] *APC*, XXVII, pp. 361–2. The letter was minuted in Gloucester and Warwick, and probably elsewhere, Gloucester RO, GBR B2/1, f. 164; Warwickshire RO, Black Book of Warwick, f. 267v. Of related interest is the November 1596 proclamation stressing the residency of the gentry in their counties, P. L. Hughes and J. F. Larkin (eds) *Tudor Royal Proclamations* (3 vols, New Haven, 1964–9), III, pp. 169–72.

[7] Gloucestershire RO, GBR B2/1, ff. 57v–58, 189v.

[8] Kent Archives Office (Maidstone), CP/B2, f. 3; Canterbury Cathedral, City and Diocesan RO, AC3, f. 28.

[9] Warwickshire RO, Black Book of Warwick, ff. 238v–242v.

[10] East Sussex RO, Rye Ms. 1/6, ff. 183v, 184.

courteous to the citizens and promised to attempt in parliament any thing that may be beneficial to this corporation'.[11]

Lincoln may also have been persuaded to choose Dymoke because he had promised not to ask them 'for any burgess money'. The expenses of maintaining two burgesses in parliament, especially given the frequency of parliamentary sessions in the last three decades of Elizabeth's reign, must have encouraged many boroughs to allow a patron to nominate one, and even both, of their MPs. Indeed, it has been estimated that only one-quarter of Elizabethan boroughs regularly returned residents.[12] As Reading noted when they recorded the election of Robert Devereux, Earl of Essex, as their high steward, he was to have the nomination of one MP 'so that suche Burgesse be not chardgeable to this Boroughe for his service or diett'.[13] However, it should not be assumed that such nominees failed to represent the locality properly for, as we shall see later in this paper, the patronage and support of such men could have important advantages. Such is implicit in Sir Thomas Heneage's letter to Salisbury's officials in 1593: selecting his candidate would 'ease the towne of half your charge and make me beholding unto you'.[14] As Ambrose Dudley, Earl of Warwick, promised the townsmen of Warwick in 1570, his nominee would be 'veary forward in th'advauncement of any thing that may tend to the common profit and commoditie of your towne'.[15]

Yet Warwick provides a good example of a town which did not entirely regard the calling of parliament with enthusiasm. The earl's nominee for the parliament of 1571 sat with a local man, John Fisher, who had attempted to get out of the job but was persuaded by the flattery of the townsmen who claimed they had 'great cause to chose and appoynt a faithfull and trustie man'. Despite such declarations, Fisher experienced great frustration at the hands of his townsmen. He attended parliament between the last day of March until the nineteenth day of May

---

[11] HMC, *14th Report, Appendix Pt. VIII*, p. 74. On the rivalry between the Dymokes and the Clintons in late sixteenth-century Lincolnshire see H. Hajzcyk, 'The Church in Lincolnshire, c. 1595–1640 (unpublished Cambridge PhD dissertation, 1980), pp. 322–30. I am grateful to Dr John Adamson for this reference.

[12] HPT, I, p. 58.

[13] Berkshire RO, R/Acl/1/1, p. 616.

[14] HMC, *Various Collections, Volume IV*, p. 230.

[15] Warwickshire RO, Black Book of Warwick, ff. 31–31v.

In all which tyme neither the said Bailief nor principall Burgessis did neither send or wryte to the said Burgeisses or either of them although the same John Fisher had from tyme to tyme addressed letters to the said Bailief and Burgeisses with such advertisementes as he might ... but all in vayne for he culd never receive any aunswer by writing or woord of any his letters from the said Bailiff which grounded in the said John no litle discuragement of his service.

The business 'thought by the said John a cause of great Joye encoraged him oftener to write' was the success of the Earl of Leicester in getting a statute for the building of his famous hospital in Warwick, a matter which Warwick's MPs were surely entitled to believe should have met with some greater support from the town than appears to have been shown.[16]

It is thus clear that while some of the ruling elites in the boroughs shared the privy councillors' concern to have burgesses in parliament who were truly representative of the boroughs for which they sat, others saw such representation almost as a burden. Despite being the third largest city in the country, and one whose status was recognized in parliament by the privilege of sitting close to the Speaker in the Commons, York's authorities seemed very reluctant to use their status to secure legislation.[17] The town's instructions to their MPs always included extra-parliamentary matters. In 1562, for example, they were not only to obtain a revision of the statute of apprentices, but also to pursue the confirmation of the charter, secure exemption from the payment of the subsidy and inform one of the privy councillors that her Majesty's chantry lands in York were much decayed. In 1584–5 the two MPs had much to do besides lobbying in parliament for the revising of the statute concerning apprentices, restricting the selling of rabbit skins, extending the power of York's Goldsmiths' and Saddlers' Companies and obtaining greater freedom to import salted fish. Their main activity was to secure a lease of royal chantry lands and to deal with the matter of concealed lands in the town, about which the corporation had solicited the comptroller of the royal household, Sir James Croft. After the Christmas recess, York's authorities added another extra-parliamentary matter to the MPs' shopping list: they were to secure the help of Henry Cheke (a member of the council of the

---

[16] Warwickshire RO, Black Book of Warwick, ff. 31–31v, 32.
[17] Snow (ed.), *Hooker's Order and Usage*, pp. 163–4.

north) to find 'a grave, learned and godlie man' to fill the vacancy of town preacher.[18]

York's parliamentary activity was remarkably unsuccessful. Its attempts to revise apprentice regulations – to secure 'such lyke proviso concernyng thacte ageynst takyng of apprentices, for the Citie of Yorke as is for London and Norwiche' – appear with regular montony in the MPs' instructions from the second session of the reign (1562) to the seventh (1586–7) and the matter of importing salted fish from 1581 until the end of the reign. As Professor Elton has suggested, it seems that York's early efforts suffered from lack of experience and financial conservatism.[19] Indeed, after Gregory Paycock and Hugh Graves, York's MPs for 1572, had reported the session's business to the corporation they remarked

as towchynge certayne articles latly devised by theis presens for the common weale of this Citie, whiche the said Burgesses had up with theym to putt into the Parliament they shewed that the chardges about sewte of any one thyng for a Citie wold stand in xx[li] and more whiche they durst not attempt to doo withowte further consent of this howse.[20]

There are even indications that York's aldermen and burgesses felt that full parliamentary representation was not always necessary. In 1566 it was decided to send only one MP, since the other had recently been elected mayor, and in 1575, although the corporation decided that one MP would be sufficient, the other declared, with a due sense of priority, that he would 'goe uppe to the said Parlyament for that he hath certaine other busynesse ther that he must needs goe'.[21] It was only towards the end of Elizabeth's reign that York developed something approaching a lobbying campaign.

Other towns also viewed the sending up of MPs to Westminster and London as an opportunity for getting other business done. In 1584–5 Rye's members may well have spent as much time dealing with a dispute over concealed lands as on parliamentary business and certainly one of them took the opportunity to buy a new drum for the musters. In 1593 they were to take out time to discuss work

[18] A. Raine (ed.), *York Civic Records* (Yorkshire Archaeological Society, Record Series), vol. 6, pp. 49, 50–1; vol. 8, pp. 81–2, 85–90, 91–2.

[19] Elton, *Parliament*, p. 85, n. 122.

[20] *York Civic Records*, vol. 7, p. 51.

[21] Ibid., vol. 6, pp. 117–18; vol. 7, p. 114.

to be done on the haven with an Italian engineer in London, a task for which they would be paid extra.[22] Early in the next reign Bristol was using its MPs to pursue disputes with the government over purveyance while they attended parliament.[23]

Yet it is important not to exaggerate boroughs' lack of enthusiasm over parliament, nor to assume that simply because they made the most of their opportunities in having representatives in London and Westminster that they did not take parliament itself seriously. The real test of borough and county involvement in parliamentary assemblies is the extent to which they pursued legislation on the behalf of their locality, or sought to secure the defeat of unfavourable measures. In some Elizabethan sessions such bills comprised one-third of the bills introduced, although they regularly made up only one-fifth of the statutes. Yet, even if the odds were against such private bills becoming acts, temporal and spiritual peers, no less than the knights, citizens and burgesses who sat in the Commons, were keen to promote them. Indeed, they did so with such enthusiasm that experienced Elizabethan parliament men offered advice as to how the numbers could be reduced and both houses adopted procedures designed to limit the time spent on private business.[24] It is the purpose of the remainder of this essay to examine the general nature of this local legislation, to explore the ways and means such bills were promoted and to set these measures in both their parliamentary and extra-parliamentary context.

One of the major legislative concerns of towns and corporations was to secure endowments to schools and hospitals by obtaining an act of parliament. One such statute concerned the school of Tonbridge, Kent, established by Sir Andrew Judd, a local man who became a prominent London merchant, a leading member of the Skinners Company and eventually lord mayor. Completed during Mary's reign, the school was endowed by Judd with properties worth £1,786 and the Skinners Company of London were made trustees. Unfortunately, Judd died before the conveyances were complete and the whole businss was assigned to another skinner and citizen of London, Henry Fisher. It was

[22] East Sussex RO, Rye MS 1/5, ff. 51v, 53v, 276–7; MS 60/9, f. 229.

[23] Bristol RO 04264/1, p. 107.

[24] On the nature of private bills and the attempts to control their number see my 'Public or Private? London, Leather and Legislation in Elizabethan England', *HJ* 31 (1988), 525–7.

Fisher's son, Andrew, who gave the school and the company difficulty by laying claim to the endowments and going so far as to forge documents which provided that after sixty years the property would come to him as a legacy. In 1572 the Skinners secured an act of parliament confirming Judd's original intentions but in order to prevent Fisher from asserting his claim before the courts the company introduced a bill in 1589 confirming both the school's royal charter and the earlier statute. Amended and debated in both houses, the bill's passage was eased by Fisher's appearance giving his consent and the company's records attest to much negotiation before the parliament.[25] They also reveal the considerable expense involved in promoting such bills.[26]

Such measures made secure the ownership of property; others enabled towns to bear such authority. As Gloucester's legal counsel told the town in 1586, their charter did not allow them to 'meddle' in the property of orphans and an act of parliament was needed.[27] Property belonging to the almshouse in Lambourne, Buckinghamshire, was threatened because the original grant involved maintaining a chantry priest and someone contended it was made invalid by the Edwardian statute dissolving chantries; a Lords bill confirmed the grant. Schools like Sevenoaks in Kent, colleges like Queen's in Oxford and Clare and Sidney Sussex in Cambridge and hospitals like Eastbridge in Canterbury, Christ's in Durham, Queen Elizabeth's in Bristol and Leicester's in Warwick all needed statutory confirmation of this sort.[28]

Towns also sought acts of parliament to give them the ability, by establishing the right, to collect funds for road, bridge and harbour repair. Colchester sought legislative authority to levy two pence on

---

[25] For a history of the school see S. Rivington, *The History of Tonbridge School From its Foundation in 1553 to the Present Day* (London, 1869). According to Elton, the original act of 1572 is missing but survives on the parliament roll as item 16, *Parliament*, p. 274, n. 286. The 1589 act and proceedings are found in HLRO, 31 Elizabeth, OA 24; PRO, SP 12/223/6; D'Ewes, pp. 437, 439, 443, 447, 451. The Skinners' activities are recorded in the company's court books: Skinners' Company, London, Court Book I, 1551–1617, ff. 44v, 50, 52, 52v; Book II, 1577–1617, f. 176v.

[26] Skinners' Company, Renter Wardens' Receipts and Payments 1564–1596, entries for 1588, 1589, 1592/3. For an account of costs incurred by other London companies in pursuing legislation see my article in the *HJ* cited in n. 24 above.

[27] Gloucestershire RO, GBR B3/1, f. 103v.

[28] HLRO, 27 Elizabeth, OA 31, 32; 31 Elizabeth, OA 20; 35 Elizabeth, OA 16 and 39 Elizabeth, OA 41.

all ships unloading goods in 1593, but the bill failed because the committee 'could not conveniently agree to such conclusion in the same as might satisfie the inhabitantes of the said Towne'.[29] New Windsor in Berkshire, Newark in Nottinghamshire and Aylesbury in Buckinghamshire were more successful in providing the means to repair their roads. In the case of Newark, the measure began in the upper house and was supported by Lord Rutland; when the legal assistants carried the bill down to the Commons Rutland used the opportunity to urge personally the bill's expedition in the lower house.[30]

Port towns like Plymouth, Dover, Lyme Regis and Orford secured acts for their havens, and others, such as Rye and New Romney, tried to do so.[31] Orford secured an act in 1584–5 which restricted the size of fishing nets in an attempt to protect small fry and, by preserving its fishing, preserve its haven. The 1584–5 statute had received much support in the Commons, provoking an emotional speech by the Aldeburgh MP John Foxe: 'The country people', he told the house, 'have come in when the fishing tyme is with dung cartes and have caryed them full awaye with young frye to fede their swyne and dong their groundes – it hath grieved my hart to see it.' William Fleetwood, Recorder of London, had professed himself amazed at the size of the nets allowed: 'Did ever any man', he exclaimed, 'see such a shamfull one as it is?' Such would not be allowed in the Thames and he warned that, by tradition, those MPs who spoke against the commonwealth were to wear a halter for a day. Given such persuasive arguments the bill passed both houses easily. Yet Orford soon realized that it had made a mistake: the poor had suffered and the number of fry had still declined. The town's authorities had concluded that it was the number of boats, not the size of the nets, that had been the problem. Despite the privy council's express orders not to spend

[29] HLRO, MP 1586–92; D'Ewes, pp. 505, 512; BL Cotton MS Fii, ff. 66v–67, 78. Colchester had also resolved to promote a bill in 1584–5 'for the amendement of the haven and channel' and in 1580 for the uniting of certain benefices, Essex RO (Colchester), D/Y 2/7, p. 13; Colchester Assembly Book 1576–1599, ff. 22v, 36. However, on both occasions they appear to have had second thoughts; none appears in the records of these sessions, although the loss of the Commons' journal for the second half of the reign prohibits certainty in this matter.

[30] HLRO, 27 Elizabeth, OA 34, 36; 39 Elizabeth, OA 40; D'Ewes, p. 340.

[31] SR, IV, pp. 728–9, 811, 729; East Sussex RO, Rye MS 1/4, f. 232v; 1/5, f. 51v; 1/7, f. 385v; Kent Archives Office (Maidstone), NR/CPc 25. The Original Act for Lyme Regis is missing but the paper bill survives in HLRO, MP, 1582–5.

time on private bills (because the session had been called to deal with the Scottish Queen), Orford's authorities were determined that their bill 'for sprats and smelts' had to pass. For this purpose they selected as their MP William Downing, a Suffolk man married to the widow of a Yarmouth merchant and now a London lawyer. He told the town's authorities, 'I will willingly attend the parliament to do eny good that maye lye in me as concernynge your towne it self for I holde my self as one of you. I will performe the best office that I can. I praie you take order that I maie have good instruccions and some bodie to solicite, as nede shall require.' He did well; the bill got through both houses only to be vetoed.[32] But, as Sir Edward Coke later commented in his *Institutes*, good bills seldom die and this one passed in the next parliament.[33]

The remaining measures related to or promoted by towns concerned a variety of matters from the confirming of statutes merchant to Exeter, Lincoln and Nottingham and locating quarter sessions in north Wales and Northumberland to saving herrings off Yarmouth's coast, regulating malt production in Norwich and producing coals in Newcastle.[34] As noted earlier, Lincoln selected a local gentleman, Charles Dymoke, in 1593 on his promise to pursue the town's interests in parliament. His relative, Sir Edward, had been very active in pursuing a bill in 1589 which exempted Lincoln from existing restrictions on buying and selling wool. With Charles, he was put to good use again in 1593; they succeeded in obtaining a statute confirming Henrician letters patent pertaining to impropriations belonging to certain parsonages in the town.[35] A different matter was pursued by Caernarfon's burgesses in 1584–5. They promoted a bill transferring all quarter sessions, hitherto shared between Conwy and Caernarfon, to Caernarfon alone. Conwy,

---

[32] Suffolk RO, EE5/8/60 (6 October 1586) and EE5/2/2, ff. 45v–46v;*SR*, IV, p. 729; HLRO, 31 Elizabeth, OA 17; *LJ*, ii, 93, 97, 134, 135; BL Lansdowne MS 43/72, f. 173; BL Harleian MS 7188, ff. 89v, 99v; D'Ewes, pp. 364, 393, 395, 395–6, 398, 403, 412, 413. Fleetwood may have recalled the unsuccessful 1566 bill to remove illegal nets from the Thames; in the end an act of common council dealt with the matter, Elton, *Parliament*, p. 234.

[33] Sir Edward Coke, *The Fourth Part of the Institutes of the Laws of England* (London, 1681), p. 32.

[34] The variety is revealed in Elton, *Parliament*, pp. 223–62, 273–5, 316–18 and Dean, 'Bills and Acts', pp. 198–225. For Norwich's bill on malt see Norfolk RO, 16/C/5, f. 53.

[35] HLRO, 31 Elizabeth, OA 21; 35 Elizabeth, OA 15; D'Ewes, pp. 444, 446, 448, 497, 501.

with no MPs in the lower house, proved unable even to obtain a copy of the bill from the clerk of the Commons and eventually wrote to Lord Treasurer William Cecil, Lord Burghley, for help. He seems to have persuaded the Queen to veto the measure.[36]

Yet lacking MPs did not prohibit some towns securing legislation. As Robert Tittler points out, in the first seven sessions of Elizabeth's reign a higher percentage of bills promoted by towns without franchises became statutes than those promoted by towns with MPs.[37] Small communities could and did mount intensive lobbying campaigns. In 1597–8 the small Suffolk port of Lowestoft ran into trouble in the lower house when its supporters were accused of having 'openlie in the howse canvassed for voices and procured councillors to speake on their behalf'. This activity related to the special privileges enjoyed by Great Yarmouth over the herring industry on the East Anglian coast, privileges which were much resented by Suffolk fishermen. By the 1590s the matter was heard before two judges of the Queen's Bench and a privy councillor, Sir John Fortescue; after several attempts at resolution the judges suggested that parliament would be the best place to settle the matter.[38]

Lowestoft's strategy involved two bills: the first proposed to repeal part of Yarmouth's charter while the second provided for a conclusive measuring and demarcating of the Norfolk port's jurisdiction. Both ended up in committees dominated by East Anglians and interested officials, although somewhat weighted in Lowestoft's favour. A large number of the papers relating to the committee's proceedings survive in both Yarmouth and Lowestoft. Affidavits were drawn up on the quantity of herring and its markets; lists of arguments under the headings 'Yarmouth defendant, Lowestoft complainant' were prepared. In the house, Yarmouth's MPs John Felton and Henry Hobart drew attention to Yarmouth's considerable

---

[36] *LJ*, ii, 71, 72; Trinity College, Dublin MS 1045, ff. 77, 78, 81v; D'Ewes, p. 342; PRO, SP 12/176/49.

[37] R. Tittler, 'Elizabethan Towns and the "Points of Contact": Parliament' in *Interest Groups and Legislative Activity in Elizabeth's Parliaments*, ed. N. Jones and D. Dean, a special issue of *Parliamentary History*, 8, 2 (November 1989), 275–88.

[38] Norfolk RO, Y C19/4, ff. 246, 247, 248v; Y C36/7/13, 14; *APC*, XXV, pp. 400–3, 404; XXVI, pp. 66–7; Edmund Gillingwater, *Historical Account of the Auncient Town of Lowestoft in the County of Suffolk* (London, 1790), pp. 148–9. This dispute is the subject of my 'Parliament, Privy Council and Local Politics in Elizabethan England: The Yarmouth-Lowestoft Fishing Dispute', forthcoming in *Albion*.

contributions to the English merchant fleet and warned that the assault on the port's privileges 'is a fayre warninge to all other men for their libertyes (the case beinge Comon with all other cities and townes) for if these be thus shrifted and shaken so may others bee.' Lowestoft's records show that £120 was paid out for lobbying in support of the two measures. However, the committee considering the measuring bill was unable to agree on the action to be taken and Henry Hobart, after much consultation with Lord Admiral Nottingham, spoke firmly against the bill on its third reading. Even then Lowestoft's supporters secured a division and it lost by only eighteen votes; the charter bill lapsed in committee.[39]

Although Yarmouth was able to defeat Lowestoft's challenge to its privileges, Lowestoft had proved able to secure some favourable conciliar decisions before the parliament met and succeeded in getting a bill as far as the third reading in the Commons despite the fact that the town had no official representatives there. Lowestoft's inhabitants organized a sophisticated lobbying campaign; besides the burgesses of Orford and Ipswich, and the support of the knights of the shire, they were able to call upon east Suffolk's connections with the court and central administration as well as the support of some privy councillors.[40]

The dispute between Yarmouth and Lowestoft reveals another dimension to local legislation: the use of statute as a means of solving matters of contention between two towns. In 1576 Bristol sent letters to Lord Burghley, the Earl of Leicester and Chief Justice Manwood protesting about a bill put into parliament by Gloucester which removed itself from Bristol's jurisdiction over the landing of goods in the Severn. This measure had passed the upper house, despite Leicester's apparent support for Bristol (he was later given a gift of wine for soliciting Burghley on the matter and 'for his favor and furtherance that he shewyd therein'); Gloucester enjoyed Burghley's support and their records contain many papers of

---

[39] D'Ewes, pp. 562, 565–6, 567, 586, 587, 591, 594; BL Stowe MS 362, ff. 17v–18; Norfolk RO, Y C36/7/5, 7, 16; Y C19/4, f. 279; Gillingwater, pp. 149–50.

[40] Among the councillors whose voices Lowestoft was accused of procuring may well have been Sir John Fortescue, a major beneficiary of duchy lands in Suffolk and the patron of George Waldegrave for one of the Sudbury seats in 1597–8, and Thomas Sackville, Lord Buckhurst, the patron of the Suffolk men appointed to implement the judges' decisions prior to the calling of the 1597–8 parliament, HPT, I, pp. 609–10; II, pp. 148–51 and Diarmaid MacCulloch, *Suffolk and the Tudors: Politics and Religion in An English Country 1500–1600* (Oxford, 1986), pp. 212–13, 243.

arguments for and against establishing a customs house there. As in the Yarmouth-Lowestoft dispute, parliament was only a temporary arena.[41]

Schools and hospitals, bridges and havens, fishing and trading rights were not the only concern of towns: religion mattered too. In 1580–1 Exeter promoted a measure which provided for the uniting of several small churches in order to create a large parish church. The bill affected the interests of the bishop and the dean and chapter, and it was opposed by Bishop John Woolton who had the measure copied into the Act Book together with a letter sent to his 'procuratores' in parliament. This instructed them as to the best means of defeating the measure in the Commons. If unable to defeat the bill outright, they were to get it amended. They should propose that the responsibility for the new church be removed from the citizens to a commission; that provisions had to be made to prevent the selling of church goods and lands for purposes other than the new living. To persuade this, Woolton told the recipient, 'you maie not sticke or feare to notifie (the house) the colde charitie of this people towardes their pastors who lately by the Instigacion of some good men interteyning a preacher to Catechyse their youth and instructe themselves could not be indused to intertaine him with a simple stipende and certen but only for one yere and no more.'[42]

A later bishop, William Cotton, opposed an almost identical bill in 1601. In the Commons one of his servants claimed its promoter wanted the lands in order to build a privy. This speaker was roundly condemned by the Devon man, now a prominent London lawyer, Richard Martin, who urged a committal and who also criticized John Hele, one of Exeter's MPs and their recorder, for his absence. Hele may have felt it prudent to absent himself, for the previous day he had declared, during the subsidy debate, 'I do marvel much that the House will stand upon granting of a subsidy or the time of payment when all we have is her Majesty's and she may lawfully at her pleasure take it from us', at which speech the house had hissed and hummed. Martin declared that he wished Hele, who had yesterday 'soe much Flattered his Prince' was now present to do 'his Countrye good servyce'. Indeed, when Exeter's

[41] Bristol RO, 04026/10, pp. 87, 88, 92, 93, 96; Gloucestershire RO, GBR B2/1, ff. 79, 84v–105.

[42] Devon RO, Bishop of Exeter, Act Book I, pp. 155–63, 164–6. Elton, *Parliaments*, pp. 69–70, notes a bill of this sort in 1563 but not in 1581.

authorities wrote to Sir Robert Cecil in favour of the churches bill they informed him that their other member, John Howell, was the person to consult with, not Hele; Martin's father was one of the signatories. Internal squabblings aside, Exeter failed to get the bill past the committee stage, as in 1580–1, a success for the bishop.[43]

Turning from towns to the sorts of measures which concerned a shire or group of shires (but no more than three, according to the Speaker's ruling of 1607),[44] it is the cloth industry which dominates the field. Devon and Cornwall, Somerset, Wiltshire and Gloucestershire cloths were constantly the subject of bills, especially the production of plunkets and kerseys. There were also measures regulating the size and weight of the lighter cloths of Sussex, Surrey and Kent, a few for Essex and one or two for northern cloth. Fen drainage in East Anglia and marsh drainage in Kent gave rise to a number of controversial bills, especially towards the end of the reign; earlier, but equally controversial, were those bills attempting to preserve timber supplies from the encroachment of iron mills in Surrey, Sussex and Kent.[45]

For these sorts of measures it is much more difficult to establish who promoted them and why. However, borough assembly minute books, audited accounts and letters sometimes allow insights into the countrywide activities of their rulers. In 1563 Exeter's MPs, Geoffrey Tothill and Thomas Williams, worked hard to secure several measures for the town. They had been instructed to initiate bills concerning the charter of the orphans, repealing the custom of gavelkind as used in the town, limiting apprenticeships, renewing the statutes merchant of the staple, and general measures concerning the mending of highways and poor relief. Tothill reported back that they had put two bills forward, one on churches and the other concerning the relief of orphans; a third proposal, on apprentices, was unnecessary because the master of the rolls had already initiated a government bill on the matter. Tothill noted that it was not wise to introduce both bills to the lower house in case the Commons 'wold nott be best contentyd with too bylles for our private Cyttye' and so the orphans bill was to begin in the Commons and the other in the Lords; by doing so they would also

[43] BL Egerton MS 2222, f. 29v; BL Stowe MS 362, f. 94v; D'Ewes, p. 633; PRO, SP 12/282/49, 50; Salis. MSS, XII, p. 499.
[44] CJ, i, 388.
[45] See Elton, Parliament, pp. 223–62, 273–5, 316–18 and Dean, 'Bills and Acts', pp. 198–225.

save time. In all of this manoeuvring Tothill had one great advantage over many burgesses and citizens: Williams had been elected Speaker; thirteen days after the end of the session he was given £23 for helping 'in all frendship in preferrying the suete and busynes of the Citie'.[46]

Thus the matters to be pursued by Tothill and Williams were both particular and general. As Tothill's letter also revealed, Exeter's MPs were engaged in promoting measures for the city's merchant adventurers. Indeed, a list of the leading merchants reads like a 'who's who' of the city authorities. In 1597–8 the innocently titled measure 'for confirmation of letters patentes graunted to the Merchantes adventureres of the Cittie of Exeter' perhaps conferred special privileges on them at the expense of those in other towns. Although on the second reading committal it was entrusted to Exeter's recorder, John Hele, it was reported by George Snigge, Bristol's recorder, as being 'not fitt to passe in this howse'. Possibly the Bristol merchants convinced those of York and King's Lynn (who also sat on the committee) that the bill offended their interests as well.[47]

The records of Exeter's merchant adventurers reveal that it was they, rather than any determination by the government, who promoted bills regulating the production and trade of cloth in Devon. In 1581 Geoffrey Tothill, the experienced MP from 1563, was entrusted by the town with the promotion not only of a general bill providing 'that all merchauntes and adventurers beyond the Seas shall dwell in Citties and Townes Corporate' but also a measure for the making of Devonshire kerseys. The first measure had its origin with the merchants of Totnes who proposed the 'joyning with other cities for the exhibiting of a bill at this presente parliament'. They also suggested the bill for the better regulation of the making and selling of Devonshire kerseys 'the principulest commoditie of our countrie'.[48] Two signatories to the letter became Totnes MPs in 1584–5, while both Exeter MPs were leading merchants.[49] Before the session met, the city's merchant adventurers instructed the MPs to initiate a general bill requiring the residence of merchants in corporate towns. The company resolved to pay for all the expenses of the city's MPs within fifteen days of the end of

[46] Devon RO, B 1/3, p. 98; B 1/4, p. 206; 60A, ff. 118–119v.
[47] D'Ewes, pp. 571, 572; *HPT*, II, pp. 187–8, 413.
[48] Devon RO, 58/7/11, ff. 95–6.
[49] HPT, I, pp. 149, 507–8; III, p. 256.

the session and all the company's freemen were to be rated to cover the costs. They were also to promote a bill regulating the length and breadth of Devon kerseys (again the company would cover the charges although now a ceiling of £10 was set).[50]

The size of cloth was a matter of general interest; clothiers of Somerset, Wiltshire, Gloucestershire and Oxfordshire had promoted a general bill to this effect. One experienced MP, Francis Alford, alleged this had been 'laboured for these twenty yeares' and another, William Fleetwood, remembered that in the twenty-seventh year of Henry VIII's reign such clothiers had sought a reduction. Clearly, he claimed, they had confidence in astronomy, hoping 'to have good luck allwayes in the 27th yeare'. Although he had been lobbied in favour of the bill by a draper and alderman of London at the parliament door, Fleetwood felt that those buying a hundred or two hundred yards of cloth for liveries would lose by the bill. After more arithmetic, the house clearly lost patience: 'Do you laugh?', Fleetwood cried, 'Laugh not at me no more than I do at you, you deal uncivilly with me ... it is you allways there in that corner of the house.' Undeterred, he provided a detailed description of a sheep's anatomy, related this to the types of wool produced, and concluded that cloth produced from mixtures of wool would fall apart. If it did not, he temptingly offered, 'then hang me up at the parliament door.' A Somerset clothier sitting for Wells, George Upton, followed. If what he said proved false, Upton told the house, he would not offer himself for a hanging, but was willing to 'gage his credytt' that the bill was a good one. This general measure was successful whereas that for Devon kerseys failed.[51] Devon's clothing interests again tried to get a cloth bill through in 1586–7 with the help of one of the knights of the shire and despite the Commons's preoccupation with the 'Great Cause' of the Scottish Queen. In 1593 Exeter's MPs succeeded in getting a kerseys bill onto the statute book, but another, seeking Devon's exemption from the medieval statutes regulating wool production, failed in the Lords undoubtedly because so many counties sought inclusion that the bill's provisions became effectively meaningless.[52]

Thus Exeter's MPs were entrusted with bills pertaining to the

---

[50] Devon RO, 58/7/11, ff. 121v–122.

[51] SR, IV, pp. 724–5; D'Ewes, p. 368; Trinity College, Dublin MS 1045, ff. 89v, 90v; BL Lansdowne MS 43/72, ff. 174–174v.

[52] D'Ewes, p. 394; SR, IV, pp. 858–60; BL Cotton MS Titus Fii, ff. 53, 71, 76v, 90v; BL Harleian MS 1888, p. 141.

whole county as well as measures for the city itself. The case of the bills promoted against iron mills in Surrey, Sussex and Kent is rather similar. The records of Rye reveal that their MPs in 1581, Henry Gaymer and Robert Carpenter, were ordered to 'prosecute the parliament nowe followinge, for any acte to be made for the preservacon of the woodes lyinge about the townes of Rye, Winchelsey and Hastings' and gave them detailed lists of the woods and mills concerned. They added a list of towns that would be relieved by the bill (including Dover, Sandwich, Folkestone and New Romney) and suggested that their MPs make the burgesses for those towns acquainted with their intentions. The measure that emerged from this was eventually described as 'touchinge yron mylles nere unto the Citie of London and The Ryver of Thames'.[53] Clearly, then, MPs from different towns worked with others over common issues. In 1572 Rye's MPs were asked to

have conference with the residewe of the barons of the portes and also with the burgeseis of Yermouth and Knights of the Shires where are fysher townes, and for the drawinge of a bill to be exhibited this Parliament for the mayntenance of the fishermen of this realme and avoydinge of strangers fyshermen and also for the avoydinge of the fyshe brought into this realme by the Quenis subjects beinge caught on the seies by strangers.[54]

In 1580 the ruling elite in Dover even warned those of Thanet that they had heard of 'matters likely to be prosecuted against them in the parliament' which was to meet shortly and in 1584–5 they paid for letters to be carried to other ports in order to canvas their opinions on the wisdom of having Wednesday declared a fish day.[55]

This survey of the sorts of measures promoted by localities shows that members of parliament such as Exeter's Tothill and Williams or Rye's Gaymer and Carpenter were not narrow-minded localists uninterested in any parliamentary business beyond that directly concerning their town. They were efficient lobbyists able to exploit to the full parliamentary procedure and parliamentary patronage.

[53] East Sussex RO, Rye MS 1/4, ff. 343–344v. This identifies some of the initiatives besides London behind these bills, cf. Elton, *Parliament*, p. 80 n. 101, 244–6.

[54] HMC, *13th Report, Appendix IV*, p. 18, a good transcript of East Sussex RO Rye MS 47/2/35.

[55] Kent Archives Office (Maidstone), Dover Chamberlains' Accounts 1558–80, f. 486; 1581–1603, f. 125v.

It is worth drawing out four particular aspects of this lobbying process which has been illustrated in the discussion above. First, although no real geographical pattern emerges overall, it is true that many more bills pertained to London than to any other town and that northern counties and towns tended not to bother much with parliamentary solutions to their particular needs. Newcastle, Lincoln and York were the only towns to do so regularly. If northern towns and country elites tended to treat the legislative potential of parliamentary sessions rather lightly, there is much evidence that those somewhat closer to the centres of power saw the calling of a parliament as an ideal opportunity to settle a long-standing dispute or achieve specific legislative goals.

However, a second and important point, is that parliament was only one arena of many in which such disputes were treated. Star Chamber, exchequer, the common law courts and, of course, the privy council itself, were more permanent institutions and so dealt very often in the same disputes to which parliamentary bills related. Special commissions of the privy council dealt with such matters, often in the localities themselves. In London, many disputes between the City companies had had a long history in the court of common council and the court of aldermen, besides chancery and exchequer, before they entered parliament.[56] It is also important to remember, as Professor Tittler reminds us, that only a very small percentage of English and Welsh towns ever attempted to obtain acts of parliament.[57]

Thirdly, those localities which did pursue legislation drew not only upon their MPs to promote bills, but very much also on their connections in the upper house. Besides peers possessing local property and bishops exercising local authority and influence, towns could also draw upon their lord high stewards for assistance in pursuing legislation. When Yarmouth sought to obtain legislative restrictions on the importing of herrings in 1581, it turned to its high steward, the Earl of Leicester, for assistance. Leicester was probably responsible for initiating the bill in the upper house and it reached the statute book despite opposition from the powerful Fishmongers' Company of London. The latter promoted a bill of

---

[56] See my 'Public or Private: London, Leather and Legislation in Elizabethan England', *HJ* 31 (1988), 525–48, and Ian Archer, 'The London Lobbies in the Later Sixteenth Century', ibid., 17–44.

[57] R. Tittler, 'Elizabethan Towns and the "Points of Contact": Parliament', *Parliamentary History*, 8, 2 (November 1989), 275–88.

repeal in 1586–7 which was spoken against in the Commons by Yarmouth's MP, William Grice, a client of Leicester's, and although the measure did reach the Lords, it was rejected, undoubtedly with Leicester's encouragement. In 1593 another bill of repeal passed both houses but was vetoed by the Queen; one wonders whether Yarmouth's new high steward, Lord Burghley, persuaded such action as he had done for Conwy in an earlier session.[58]

Thus the House of Lords and its members played a vitally important role in the history of private bills. Of 192 local bills and acts initiated in the last six sessions of Elizabeth's reign, forty-one (21 per cent) were introduced in the Lords. Many of these related to localities who had particular reasons for so doing, their measures affecting the lands or interests of a temporal or ecclesiastical peer. Others recognized that, with the large number of unofficial measures introduced in the Commons, their bills stood a better chance of reaching the statute book by beginning in the Lords. Apart from time – bills initiated in the Lords took far less time to get through the three-reading process than their counterparts in the Commons – it was recognized that measures coming from the Lords were treated by the Commons with a degree of respect, often taking a high priority on the list of bills waiting to be read. Thus whereas only 16 per cent of local bills initiated in the Commons reached the statute book, the success rate in the Lords was 44 per cent.[59]

Lastly, many localities secured the services of London lawyers to assist in their activities. As in their choice of the clients of noblemen, of royal officials or of well-connected local gentlemen as MPs, choosing lawyers often had something to do with a town's desire for specific legislation. Towns also retained London lawyers as counsellors and although only the London records reveal their work in any considerable detail, it is evident that such men worked hard to promote bills for many towns and local interests at

[58] Burghley's successor as high steward, Lord Admiral Nottingham, was consulted by Yarmouth in 1597–8 over its campaign to defeat Lowestoft's assault on its privileges and he made a favourable ruling on Yarmouth's behalf when the matter came before the high court of admiralty in 1601, Norfolk RO, Y C27/1, ff. 8, 43, 54v, 56, 67, 79, 163v, 178, 190, 199v, 211v; Y C19/4, ff. 76v–79; Y C36/7/20. The 1581 act is discussed in G. R. Elton, 'Piscatorial Politics in the Early Parliaments of Elizabeth I' in *Business Life and Public Policy: Essays in Honour of D. C. Coleman*, ed. N. McKendrick and R. B. Outhwaite (Cambridge, 1986), pp. 1–20.

[59] See Dean, 'Bills and Acts', pp. 203, 210.

Westminster. It is likely that York's inability to pursue parliamentary legislation successfully in the early years of the reign might be not only explained by their parsimony, but also by their reluctance to develop powerful legal support which could be called upon. As pressures from the centre increased after the outbreak of war with Spain, the attitude of York's authorities shifted somewhat. The town always seems to have retained lawyers in London to work on their behalf; in 1571 a book of statutes was sent to them by Mr Bell, described as the 'Attorney for City matters in London'. But in April 1590 York decided to obtain the services of Dr Herbert, one of the masters of requests, to assist in their desire for a royal charter to hold a fair in the town and in the following year the corporation resolved to retain a member of the privy council 'to be towardes this Cittye in suche suites and causes as this Corporacon maye hereafter happelye chaunce to have before their Lordships'. Eventually they settled on Sir John Fortescue, whose help was certainly obtained in the dispute over ship money. Whether or not this also had direct consequences for York's parliamentary ambitions is difficult to say, but their MPs in 1601 at least had the job of delivering Fortescue his fee. More certain is York's determination to gain the assistance of one of the county's leading gentlemen, and frequent knight of the shire, Sir John Stanhope. By 1598 his servant Patterson was receiving 40 shillings to act as 'solicitor' for the town.[60]

It seems likely that these more promising links with the centre encouraged York to be more ambitious in its later parliamentary ambitions. The extensive instructions to the MPs attending the last two parliaments of the reign reveal a higher priority being given to parliamentary matters than in the past: the revival of the 1584–5 statute concerning the importation of salted fish, the exemption of York from the 1597–8 tillage act and the abolition of certain patents and monopolies. Indeed, it was in 1601 that the town took the very unusual step of choosing an MP who had few links with the corporation: Dr Bennitt, an official of the archbishop of York. It was he, and Sir John Stanhope, who were among the most outspoken members of the Commons in the attack on monopolies in that parliament. Before the session, the corporation had instructed

[60] *York Civic Records*, vol. 7, p. 33; vol. 9, pp. 95, 98, 112–13; York City Archives, Housebook 30, ff. 220–222v, 234–234v; Housebook 31, ff. 321v, 323, 331v–332; Housebook 32, f. 174. I am very grateful to Mrs Rita Freedman of the York City Archives for lending me microfilms of the housebooks.

its MPs firstly 'to deale with the knightes of the shier and other Burgesses to get the patent for salte overthrowne' and secondly to 'ioyne with some others if so it shall fall forthe for overthrowe if they can of the patent for starche'.[61] Nor is this an isolated example of collaboration between local elites who shared opposition to the demands of central government. In 1601, immediately prior to the outcry in the house of Commons over monopolies, Norwich and King's Lynn were behind a Norfolk petition to the privy council complaining about the patent for white salt.[62]

Thus the local records which have been drawn upon for much of this paper reveal that local interests were the true initiators of general or public bills concerning the West Country cloth industry, regulating overseas trade, the importing of salted fish, providing orders for apprentices. Research into the records of the London companies shows clearly that what appears at first to be public legislation regulating the selling of leather, the making of barrels or the providing of guns is, in fact, attempts by the Cordwainers to keep the Curriers out of a lucrative business, to force the Brewers to use coopers subject to the ordinances of the Coopers' Company and to bring gunfounders under the control of the Armourers' Company. Even the great statute of artificers had its origins with the city of York and probably Exeter and other towns as well.[63]

Thus the distinction between public and private legislation, which parliamentary historians are correct to make in procedural terms and in distinguishing the force which statutes possessed in law, is much less helpful when one turns to the makers and the making of law. Local problems easily and quickly took on national dimensions; national awareness did not preclude particular or localist concerns. Certainly local archives reveal the sort of particular initiatives so often dismissed by historians, following the example of Sir Simonds D'Ewes, as being 'of no great moment'.[64] But they also reveal that localities, through peers and bishops as well as knights of the shire and burgesses, promoted public bills. William Stoughton, Edward Lewknor and John Moore offered petitions on behalf of the inhabitants of Leicester, east Sussex and

---

[61] York City Archives, Housebook 31, ff. 304–5, 323; Housebook 32, ff. 173v–174; HPT, I, p. 428.

[62] Norfolk RO, WLS 17/2, ff. 81–81v, 82, 82v.

[63] Elton, *Parliament*, pp. 263–7.

[64] D'Ewes, p. 505 (referring to a bill for Colchester).

Folkestone by way of supporting general bills for church ministers.[65] Members filled the 1597–8 parliamentary timetable for proposals on poor relief and when it came for the consideration of government initiatives for the promotion of tillage and the curbing of depopulation, local members responded quickly.[66] During the famous monopolies debate in the next session local interest and national interest combined: a York burgess spoke 'in respect of a grievance out of the Citie for which I come' and a Devon man 'for a town that grieves and pines for a Countrie that groneth and languisheth'. When a Sandwich member reported how his town was seriously affected by piracy and moved for a general bill as remedy, he was supported by a burgess from Yarmouth who spoke out of 'the dutie I owe to my Soveraigne and my Countrie'.[67]

The ambiguity of the word 'country' was vital to its ability to draw support from others but it was not considered by its Elizabethan users to reflect a gaping gulf between centre and locality. The study of local legislation in Elizabeth's reign reveals no hard and fast division between court and country or between national and local awareness or, to express it in a parliamentary way, between public and private. Recently some historians have overdrawn such divisions.[68] Country gentlemen and corporate elites were not ignorant provincials suffering from limited horizons. They recognized that national matters had local repercussions and their local experience provoked them to devise and offer solutions for the entire realm. They turned to parliament not only to satisfy their particular needs but also to bring their experience to the making of laws for the commonwealth. In their speeches such MPs referred to themselves as physicians whose job was to cure the ills of the commonwealth.[69] Many towns purchased copies of *all* the acts passed in the parliament and their MPs thought it worth their while reporting back what they had heard of national and even international affairs.[70] And although much of their work was

[65] Trinity College, Dublin MS 1045, f. 79v; D'Ewes, p. 349.

[66] D'Ewes, pp. 552, 560–1; BL Stowe MS 362, ff. 12–12v.

[67] D'Ewes, pp. 645, 645–6, 665.

[68] For a recent discussion of these issues see Antony Fletcher, 'National and Local Awareness in the County Communities' in *Before the English Civil War*, ed. Howard Tomlinson (London, 1983), pp. 151–74.

[69] See, for example, *Salis. MS*, VII, p. 542 and BL Lansdowne MS 73/38, f. 130.

[70] Gloucestershire RO, GBR F4/3, f. 237v; Kent Archives Office (Maidstone), NR/FAC/43, f. 5v; FAC/8, ff. 5, 96; Dover Chamberlains' Accounts 1558–80, f. 252v; 1581–1603, ff. 372, 462; East Sussex RO, Rye MS 47/47/7.

naturally based in the Commons, it is clear that the upper house also had a vital role to play: localities initiated bills there through local peers and high stewards; lay peers and bishops intervened on behalf of the local communities of which they were a part. They could also oppose the interests of those communities.

Yet for some localities parliament had a limited role to play in the Elizabethan polity. Most local legislation pertained to the south – London, Norwich, Plymouth, Exeter, Orford, Dover and Yarmouth lead the list of towns promoting bills; Kent, Sussex, Devon, Berkshire and Gloucestershire the counties. Of the northern towns only York and Lincoln bothered to promote bills with any regularity. In parliamentary legislation, as in religion, the Elizabethan north was only partially integrated in the national outlook. Moreover, all localities saw parliament only as one means to an end and a pretty poor means at that. From a conciliar perspective parliament served many important functions but for local elites it was a time-consuming and, all too frequently, an unproductive place to lobby. It was also very expensive.[71] If they had a choice, most localities preferred to solve their problems locally, or through the more regular and permanent arenas of court and council, or by seeking solutions in the central courts. But if they were determined to, or forced to, seek that most permanent of all solutions, an act of parliament, then many localities demonstrate a sophistication in their lobbying campaigns which meant that local bills became one of the most time-consuming concerns of a parliamentary session.

[71] Wantage's bailiffs' accounts reveal that they had to borrow in order to meet the £88 12s 6d it cost them for an act protecting the town lands and they were paying off those debts for several years to come, Berkshire RO MF 97012 A/2 (microfilm of D/QW/7). Norwich, when they succeeded in obtaiing a bill for the manor of Cringleford of which they were lords, ordered that the purchasers should pay half the costs, Norfolk RO, 16/C/4, f. 124. Some of the London companies levied costs for parliamentary activities on their members, Dean, 'London, Leather and Legislation', pp. 546–7.

7

The Sheriff and County Elections

T. E. HARTLEY

Sir John Neale's picture of the sheriff's role in county elections, though formulated long before the appearance of *The Elizabethan House of Commons* into which it was incorporated, may be seen as part of the general thesis of parliamentary conflict with which his name is usually associated. A thrusting House of Commons, aware of new strength and anxious to flex its muscles in constitutional tussles with Queen Elizabeth, consisted of men eager to serve there, and some of the knights of the shire, in order to further their own local standing and to satisfy a desire to be part of the new political scene, were returned to the house only with the collaboration of partisan and corrupt sheriffs. Neale seems to have echoed a contemporary claim that the sheriff could return 'whom he would ... notwithstanding he were never elected'. The laws governing elections provided inadequate penalties for misconduct at the county court, and in Elizabeth's reign it was the Star Chamber which allowed them to be adjusted to realistic levels, thus making the punishment fit the crime. But despite this distrust of the Elizabethan sheriff, Neale never argued that disputed elections were the order of the day, for many elections were not even contested, let alone disputed.[1]

A trouble-free election could take a number of possible forms. If there were no more candidates than places to be filled, the sheriff would merely have to gain the approval of the freeholders present for their election; and this would be done by acclamation. If a contest for one or more of the seats arose by virtue of a 'surplus' of candidates however, the sheriff would decide the issue by calling on

[1] J. E. Neale, 'Three Elizabethan Elections', *EHR*, 46 (1931), 209–238; J. E. Neale, 'More Elizabethan Elections', *EHR*, 61 (1946), 18–44; Neale, *Commons*, ch. 1 and pp. 69–70, 77–9.

the supporters of each of the candidates to shout their support in turn, deciding by ear, as it were, which candidate carried the majority support. But if this recourse to 'voice' as it was called gave the sheriff no clear indication where the majority lay, he could decide, or be asked, to move on to the 'view', whereby he simply called for the physical division of the supporters into their respective groups so that he could see which side was larger than the other. Finally, if the issue remained doubtful at this stage, the sheriff and the interested parties might then resort to the poll, that is to count the freeholders on each side and possibly examine them, or some of them, to ensure that they were *bona fide* freehold voters.

Mark Kishlansky agrees about the infrequency of contests and disputes, but he has chosen an overall perspective quite different from Neale's: it is only from 1628, or more obviously from 1640, that we can begin to see parliament as a 'political institution in which the rights and liberties of the subject were protected'. This necessarily means that before that time elections, or 'selections' – that is uncontested elections – were part of an 'ecology in which elevations to titles and honours ... marked out the thriving species'. Selection for a seat in parliament was one such mark; the seat was not an issue in itself, for what was at stake was personal worth and magisterial authority. In this world the sheriff was on hand to resolve potential conflict, and it is this role which should be emphasized rather than the 'sheriffs' tricks' of which Neale wrote.[2] Indeed, Neale was too ready to impute guilt to the sheriff; but even where tricks were employed they were a means of adjudication in the very occasional bitter conflicts at elections.[3] Against the background of arguments such as these, it is useful to subject the process of conducting county elections, and the sheriff's role in them, to closer scrutiny, and the following argument re-examines some of Neale's original cases in order to do so; by considering some general evidence relating to elections at the same time we

---

[2] M. Kishlansky, *Parliamentary Selection: Social and Political Choice in Early Modern England* (Cambridge, 1987), pp. 17–18, 22, 23, 57–9.

[3] Kishlansky, *Parliamentary Selection*, especially chs. 3 and 4. The constituency reports in HPT are often informed by the notion of corrupt and fraudulent sheriffs. J. K. Gruenfelder (*Influence in Early Stuart Elections, 1604–1640* (Columbus, Ohio, 1981), p. 15 describes Neale's comment about the rarity of the sheriff's impartiality as an understatement, yet his table of over 900 'stratagems' employed by candidates in 440 elections from 1604 to 1628 notes only forty involving sheriffs, and it is clear that some of these consisted of no more than consultation with the returning officer (p. 21).

may make some tentative suggestions relevant to the current debate.

Neale's account of county elections did not fully describe the sheriff's legal responsibilities. These had been set out by statutes passed more than a century before, though they do not provide a blueprint for close and detailed supervision of the process. Acts of 1406 and 1410 required on pain of a £100 fine that the sheriff conduct elections 'freely and indifferently' and without 'affection' at the next county court after receipt of the writ, and that 'all they that be there present shall attend to the election.' In 1413 it was further enacted that both electors and elected be resident within the county concerned. Further regulation became necessary in 1429 because large numbers of electors, or 'choosers', massing at the court had given rise to fears of 'manslaughters, riots, batteries, and divisions among the gentlemen and people', and the 40/shilling freehold franchise was therefore established, sheriffs being required to make their returns in indentures struck between themselves and the freeholders. The residence qualification for knights was reiterated, and it was further stipulated, as Neale emphasized, that sheriffs who infringed the law were liable to a fine of £100 *and a year's imprisonment*; the earlier stipulation that members of parliament chosen contrary to the statute lose their wages, though not their seats, was upheld. A further act of 1445 tried to remedy the lack of effective sanction by making delinquent sheriffs liable to a second penalty by way of debt to the aggrieved, that is the un-returned though elected, knight of the shire. The residence qualification for knights was again upheld.

Thus the sheriff was bound to return knights elected by the majority of the 40-shilling freeholders present, though the notion of majority is stated almost incidentally rather than as a general principle: it appears only in the 1429 act which instructed the sheriff to return those having the 'greatest number' in the indenture sealed between himself and the 'choosers'. Moreover, if the sheriff was not able to decide the outcome on the basis of the shouted support for the candidates, he was not *required* to proceed to the view, or from the view to the poll, and Neale thought that the Commons may have recognized going to the poll as 'good law' only in 1624, and that there was still no statutory authority for Coke's assertion that the sheriff should, if called upon, do so.[4] The sheriff

---

[4] Neale, *Commons*, p. 88.

was also *empowered* to swear freeholders upon the Evangelists as to their ability to spend 40 shillings a year above expenses, but there was no statutory *requirement* for him to vet his electorate systematically. The sheriff in receipt of a parliamentary writ was bound by his office and his oath to return it, just as he was with all writs he received.[5] Resident knights were to be elected between the hours of eight and eleven in the morning, a duty simply stated, though clearly subject to pitfalls in the execution.[6]

In addition to this legal background we need to consider the nature of the evidence which led to Neale's view of the sheriff's role, for it comes mainly from charges and countercharges lodged in Star Chamber cases, and the outcome of many cases before the court is unknown. A manuscript in the British Library records the decisions in about 600 cases, though only two concerning disputed elections are noted, namely the Wiltshire election case of 1559, and that for the one-member Welsh county town of Haverfordwest in 1571. In both instances judgement went against the sheriff and sentences are given, though they are less straightforward than Neale imagined.[7] The Wiltshire sheriff, Henry Bronker, was found guilty: his sentence – a £200 fine and a year's imprisonment – clearly took account of two offences, though one of them only came to light in the course of the examination of witnesses in the case. It appeared that Bronker was not, strictly speaking, sheriff when he conducted the election, for being 'sick in the head' when the Queen's patent for the office arrived at his house, he had not taken the required oaths, partly because a witness at the time had observed that the sheriff had to have 'so many officers and mynysters under hym as yow must have'.[8] In fact it is said that the sheriff tried to excuse his

[5] 5 Richard II, stat. 2. c. 4 (1382) in *SR*, II, p. 25.

[6] *SR*, II, pp. 156, 162, 170, 243–4, 340–42 for 7 Henry IV, c. 15, 11 Henry IV, c. 1, 1 Henry V, c. 1, 8 Henry VI, c. 7, 23 Henry VI, c. 14. See my note, 'The statute 23 Henry VI, c. 14: the problem of the texts', *EHR*, 82 (1967), 544–48, which deals with the confusion over the statutory hours of election, believed by many Elizabethans (sheriffs and others) to be eight and nine, rather than eight and eleven.

[7] BL Harleian MS 2143, ff. 7v, 30; see J. A. Guy, *The Court of Star Chamber and its Records to the Reign of Elizabeth* (London, 1985), pp. 32, 34 for this manuscript. Estreats of fines for the reign of Elizabeth appear on the Exchequer KR memoranda rolls and offer a more effective way of determining the outcome of suits, according to Guy, though a preliminary search of the rolls for the second half of the reign does not reveal further decisions in cases involving sheriffs and their electoral conduct.

[8] PRO STAC 5/A14/14 (Lawrence Hyde's answers).

conduct at the election by claiming that he was not sworn to his office, which the court 'misliked the more'. The sheriff's penalties were therefore a measure, not of one offence as Neale's account assumes, but two, and we know from Dyer's *Reports* that £100 of the fine was specifically for exercising the office without having been sworn, the other £100 for false return which was the penalty prescribed by the statute of 1429.[9] In this instance then, Star Chamber was not, as Neale suggested, making the punishment fit the crime.[10] The same manuscript records a £20 fine for the sheriff of Haverfordwest, though Neale suggested that this was clearly a clerical slip for £200, in line with what he thought Bronker's fine had been. Sheriff Harries's fine ought perhaps to have been £100 if his offence was comparable with Bronker's, but the more significant aspect of the case is that he was deemed to be guilty of more than merely disregarding voting majorities: he was said to have physically manhandled electors, 'some by the cloakes to passe against Stepneth', his own candidate's opponent, 'for which disorder he was fined £20'.[11] It may well be that '£20' here *is* a clerical error, but we cannot ignore (and neither could Star Chamber) Harries's manhandling of freeholders, a 'disorder' which the sheriff, above all others in the shire, should discourage rather than indulge in. Neale's implication that Star Chamber solved the problem of ineffective fifteenth-century penalties must also be questioned because of evidence he himself cited. The Denbighshire sheriff in 1588 was accused of saying that he would act as he wished because he could well afford to break the law; and in Staffordshire in 1597 the sheriff was said to have been equally disdainful of the legal dangers confronting him in his alleged misconduct. In neither of these two cases does the sheriff seem to have been conscious of, or

---

[9] Dyer, *Reports*, f. 168v in *English Reports*, 73, 369–70.

[10] Neale, 'Three Elizabethan Elections', p. 209; Kishlansky, *Parliamentary Selection*, p. 17 and n. 40, argues that Neale's account of the 'inherent corruption of the electoral system' was based in large part on its supposed absence of remedy, and that the Star Chamber offered ineffectual remedy. This is only partly true, and Neale argued for its offering 'more appropriate satisfaction in terms of punishment, and the opportunity to use the court for proceeding against a number of parties, and not just the sheriff alone'. It only became ineffective as far as he was concerned when the 'emergent' House of Commons offered even more advantages over the remedies on offer from the common law courts (Neale, 'Three Elizabethan Elections' pp. 209–10).

[11] BL Harleian MS 2143, f. 30.

worried by, the prospect of a year's imprisonment, let alone any 'realistic' penalty at the hands of Star Chamber.[12]

It begins to look then as though 'sheriffs' tricks' were being punished – in part at least – on the scale provided by the existing law. It is plain, moreover, that the existence of a number of Star Chamber suits against sheriffs does not prove the reality of the offences alleged. Neale seems to have been prepared to accept almost wholly at face value the charges which were levelled against the sheriffs, but the evidence really tells us little objectively either way about the true guilt or innocence of these men because so much of it was fabricated and 'prepared'. Its real value, however, lies in the revelation that the mechanics of electoral deceit and cunning were well understood, as were the dangers to all concerned at election times, not least to the sheriff as the returning officer.

As one of the county gentry the sheriff was likely to be part of social or political rivalries which had given rise to electoral contests, yet as a sheriff he was legally bound to act impartially. Neale knew this undoubtedly, but it is important to stress it because it accounts for the difficulties on election day and the situation the sheriff had to cope with and indeed *control*; it was *his* county court, and *he* was responsible for executing the writ and *maintaining law and order*. Divisions and disagreements would often be dealt with before the election itself, thus preventing electoral trouble before it arose. The two examples of the elections in Kent in 1597 and 1601 and in Leicestershire in 1601 demonstrate this quite clearly, because in these cases rivalries – the necessary precursor to contests or disputes – had been sufficiently controlled by election day to allow candidates to stand down and avoid contests.[13] Neither did rivalry which reached elections necessitate dispute and shrieval deceit, as the recently studied East Anglian counties of Norfolk and Suffolk show.

Even though Norfolk was rent by divisions, evidence of disputes is hard to come by, even for the 1586 election contest. By this time it seems the deputy lieutenants, Sir Edward Clere and Sir William

[12] Though the sheriff of Hampshire in 1566 asked who would save him from imprisonment if he yielded to pressure to return a nonresident: PRO STAC 5/A39/12, A31/30, L35/27, P30/32.

[13] P. Clark, *English Provincial Society from the Reformation to the Revolution: Religion, Politics and Society in Kent, 1500–1640* (Hassocks, 1977), pp. 262, 264–5; HPT, *sub* Kent, Leicestershire.

Heydon, were prominent among those antagonistic to the more puritanical gentry of the county. Yet even here the contest was only provoked at a late hour by the 'immoderate bragge' of one of the candidates who thereby impelled another to stand though he had previously no intention of so doing. It is true that the sheriff was alleged to have 'proceeded to that election unorderly', indeed, that the freeholders had not been duly summoned, but it does seem that Sheriff Hogan's return in 1586 was an accurate reflection of the freeholders' preferences. And a new writ, quashing the original election, was the result not of shrieval misconduct, but of the lord lieutenant, Lord Hunsdon, persuading the privy council that all was not well in Norfolk in the interests of his deputy lieutenants there. The fact that the privy council reprimanded the sheriff for choosing Farmer, recently dismissed from the bench and therefore an unsuitable candidate, rather than for deceiving the 'choosers' adds weight to this suggestion.[14] The second election was apparently conducted under the supervision of the deputy lieutenants backed by the privy council; under those circumstances the sheriff returned Heydon and Gresham, the lieutenancy candidates. But in the event the *original* returns stood, and the Commons and the lord chancellor, both of whom had adjudicated on the matter of the source of writs in such cases, thus vindicated Sheriff Hogan.

Even when rivalry deepened later in the reign with the advent of Sir Arthur Heveningham[15] no *disputes* seem to have disturbed the elections. Attorney General Coke did travel back to the county in 1597 and took a major role in restraining the 'common people' at the election, though it is not clear what was behind this apparent concern about the massing populace, or that there was any suggestion of electoral malpractice.[16] And in Suffolk, apparently less divided than Norfolk, we have no evidence of disputed elections at all. Nearly half of Elizabethan county elections may have been *contested* (1584, 1586, 1597 and 1601), but there is no word of disputes or sheriffs' tricks. Generally speaking, the 'cosy consensus' apparently prevalent among the Marian gentry of Suffolk seems to

---

[14] A. Hassell Smith, *County and Court: Government and Politics in Norfolk, 1558–1603* (Oxford, 1974), pp. 319–20; HPT, *sub* Norfolk. The issue of a new writ was itself the cause of debate in the Commons, of course: Neale, *Parliaments*, II, pp. 184–7.

[15] A. Hassell Smith, *County and Court*, pp. 323–9.

[16] HPT, *sub* Norfolk.

have continued and elections could well have been settled by discussions among the oligarchy.[17]

The approach of an election and the business of conducting it could present problems, even without the ill intent of those involved. Once a new parliament had been decided on, writs went out which required the election to be held at the next county court after their receipt. The final rallying of supporters for candidates was thus signalled, though rumours clearly circulated beforehand, and the freeholders could be put on stand-by far in advance. In 1601 anticipation lasted for months before writs confirmed speculation, simply because the Essex rebellion caused a postponement of a parliament which had been expected earlier in the year. All the same, the writ itself was necessary before firm arrangements could be made for the marshalling of one's supporters at the right time and in the right place.[18] Sometimes little time was left for sheriffs to give adequate notice of the impending election, and this could create real difficulties. It was said, for instance, that the sheriff of Hampshire received the writ for the by-election in 1566 too late for him to proclaim it adequately, and that he accordingly stayed away from the county court on the day despite the presence of at least several hundred people; Sheriff Molineux of Lancashire sent the writ back in 1597 because he claimed he had no time to execute it before the start of the intended parliamentary session.[19] These may have been ploys designed to allow one side to gather its strength to the disadvantage of the other, or to avoid the obvious strength of the other side in a contest.[20] Conversely, interception of the writ before it reached the sheriff was a possible means of catching the other side unawares.[21] Two points are clear though: the writ was a tool which could be used by parties opposed to the sheriff and his alleged partisan stances; and attempts to keep the writ secret could not in any case prevent would-be voters turning out at the county

---

[17] D. MacCulloch, *Suffolk and the Tudors: Politics and Religion in an English County, 1500 to 1600* (Oxford, 1986), pp. 81, 89–90, 335–6.

[18] A. Hassell Smith, *County and Court*, p. 326.

[19] HPT, *sub* Hampshire, Lancashire.

[20] See Radnorshire too in Neale, *Commons*, pp. 80–1, where, incidentally, despite accusations of writ delay, the sheriff still allegedly had to resort to other 'tricks' to avoid electing Roger Vaughan, who claimed a majority at the two county court days involved.

[21] HPT, *sub* Hampshire suggests this as a possibility: and interrogatories to be put on behalf of Sheriff Pexall seem to be based on the assumption: PRO STAC 5/P30/32.

court when there was a whiff of election in the air. As long as the process of election was tied to the county court – whose time of meeting was well known to all – rather than to a special day following a fixed interval after the decision to assemble parliament, the arrival of writs was problematic from time to time: coming immediately before their next courts it might be deemed that sheriffs had acted too quickly so as to favour one side; while delaying the business for a further month also exposed them to charges of acting partially.

However, it does seem to have been acknowledged that the timing of the writ could be genuinely problematic, even for instance in Warwickshire in 1601 where the privy council clearly suspected the sheriff of 'some turne of faction and parcialyty', but nevertheless agreed that another writ be issued.[22] In Shropshire in 1593 the writ came to the sheriff the day after his county court, and parliament was due to begin before he could hold the next: in this case the privy council assured him that he could nevertheless proceed with the election at the next meeting of his court.[23] As we have seen in the case of Norfolk in 1586, the Commons committee investigating the matter encountered the complaint that the sheriff had not given due notice of the election to the freeholders, though it was clear to them that the sheriff had received the writ only the day before the county court, and that he was bound to execute it at that time, there being about 3000 people present even though due warning had not been given. In this instance the election went ahead; and the committee concluded that the writ and returns were 'in matter and form perfect and duly executed'.[24]

The sheriff's own preferences, as we have seen, ought not to influence his conduct of elections, and the privy council expected him to avoid 'passion' and to act impartially as he was a 'publique mynister', in short, to be 'upright and indifferent'.[25] But he also invariably had influence over other freeholders, both tenants and friends: his own voice might well remain unheard in a properly conducted election, but those of his own circle could not be disqualified by virtue of his holding office. Aggrieved parties could clearly seize on this, however, and suspect or suggest sinister

[22] *APC, 1601–04*, pp. 247–8; Neale, *Commons*, pp. 52–3.

[23] *APC 1592–93*, p. 48.

[24] D'Ewes, p. 396; A. Hassell Smith, *County and Court*, pp. 319–20.

[25] *APC 1601–04*, pp. 247–8, 251, 271 (Warwickshire, Worcestershire, Hampshire).

machinations whether they existed or not. Thus before the Denbighshire election in 1588, the sheriff was asked for his support for John
Edwards, who was in the event returned, and to secure that of his
friends. Sheriff Brereton is alleged to have said that he would give
his support as far as it was consonant with his oath of office;
moreover it was stressed that the other candidate had not asked for
Brereton's help. Again, we can never know certainly if the sheriff
acted as honestly as is claimed, but this matters less than the fact of
the admission of his preference.[26]

Freehold status – and resident status too – were at a premium at
election times, and 'fraudulent elections' could be made as a result
of freeholds fraudulently given or claimed by partisans of one or
both sides, though these were not directly the work of the sheriff:
and unless the sheriff had the time and the knowledge to determine
the eligibility of all who turned up he might unwittingly allow
invalid voices. Charge and countercharge in election cases frequently focused on the issue of who was entitled to have a voice, but
the general truth is clear enough: the device of introducing non-
freeholders of one sort or another into the county court was
obvious and readily understood, and, as in the case of Montgomeryshire, could be resorted to in some measure by both sides.[27]
So the sheriff could be vulnerable to the charge of too readily
accepting unqualified voters, or refusing – because he was partisan
– to enquire too closely into the status of those giving their voices at
his court.[28] But even if he could safely assume that those assembled
before him were all true freeholders, he still confronted the difficult
task of determining which side commanded the greater voice, for
voice was clearly the first resort in the process. The numbers
involved in county elections appear to have varied considerably
across the country. From something like the 500 to 600 implied by
the figures given in the disputed Hampshire by-election estimates
of attendances at the county court run into thousands.[29] The

[26] PRO STAC 5/A39/12 (John Edwards's answers).

[27] Neale, 'Three Elizabethan Elections', pp. 214, 230, 232.

[28] Freehold status could be difficult to determine too: Neale's view that
'marginal freeholders' existed – men who were willing to be considered eligible for
the privileges of the status, but not its duties – tells us little in itself of the *true*
position of such men; and the very concept of a forty-shilling freeholder was not
always readily grasped at the time. (Neale, 'Three Elizabethan Elections', p. 237;
'More Elizabethan Elections', pp. 41–2).

[29] Neale, *Commons*, pp. 83, 108–10, 115; HPT *sub* Hampshire, Monmouthshire,
Norfolk, Staffordshire, Yorkshire.

sheriff's task in the first instance was to decide which side had the greater voice, and even in a crowd of a mere 600 it is easy to imagine the genuine difficulty in deciding which side had the greater vocal support, and, more importantly, in making a judgement which the losers would accept. Where numbers were larger, so were the problems, even for those on the same side: in Montgomeryshire in 1588, estimates of an alleged majority varied from 300 to 600 where the total electorate on the day was said to be about 1600.[30] And this is before one considers ways in which this first noisy stage could be perverted. The Staffordshire sheriff at the 1597 election was said to have been persuaded by the 'inordinate clamors, lowde voyces and great outcryes' of non-freeholders brought in to win the day for John Dudley, and thereafter to have refused appeals by justices of the peace present to proceed to the poll. It was subsequently alleged that the sheriff had allowed recusants currently in his custody, and their wives, into the election to make a 'confused noyse'. It was also said that in Yorkshire in 1597 Sir John Saville tried to name his own candidates and to distract the voices of the freeholders from the others named, so that the voices at the initial election were confused for two hours or more.[31] Confused sound might be followed by confused sight of course, and separating the sides for the 'view' was not always so easy, for in this case those on one side easily became mingled with women and children from York, making matters even worse.

The requirement that knights be residents of the counties they served – reiterated, as we have seen, in the evolving electoral legislation of the fifteenth century – emerged in a number of cases: in the Wiltshire election in 1559 (as we shall see later), in Hampshire in 1566 and at the end of the reign in Rutland.[32] The bill filed in the Star Chamber against the sheriff of Staffordshire over the 1597 election made much of the fact that the parliamentary writ required him to return two knights, fit men *of the county*, and Edward Littleton, the unsuccessful candidate and complainant in the case, therefore alleged that Dudley's election was irregular because of his position as a mere 'sojourner' at Lord Dudley's house. Several of the questions to be asked of Sheriff Whorwood – his answers do not survive – focused on whether Dudley had any

[30] Neale, 'Three Elizabethan Elections', p. 236.
[31] PRO STAC 5/L11/24, L35/27; BL Microfilm 485, reel 33: Hatfield MS 139, f. 74.
[32] HPT *sub* Hampshire; Neale, 'More Elizabethan Elections', p. 37.

houses or freehold lands in the county, and where he was *most resident*, and whether he dwelt in any house *of his own* there. In Yorkshire Stanhope and Hoby, the two unsuccessful candidates, were not regarded by many as true locals, and Sir John Saville, their opponent, required the under-sheriff on the day of the election to read the statutes stipulating that only residents of the shire be elected.[33]

Such complaints could be dismissed as technical quibbles[34] which were designed to cloak malicious and fraudulent intent, but residence does generally seem to have been regarded as a requirement, despite the refusal of members of the Commons to do anything about the wholesale disregard of the law as far as the boroughs were concerned.[35] We may turn to Burghley himself for a view on the matter. In Nottinghamshire the privy council was confronted with the spectacle of deep division between the Earl of Shrewsbury and Sir Thomas Stanhope, the rivalry which was reflected again in Yorkshire in 1597. Burghley himself wrote to Shrewsbury on 27 January 1592/3 ahead of the election to be held the following Monday, expressing a clear concern about rumours that Shrewsbury intended to go to the election with some 'great extraordinarie companies' to lend support to Sir Charles Cavendish, his brother-in-law. Burghley believed, apparently wrongly, that Shrewsbury was also supporting a 'gentleman not well-reported for religion', a Mr Pierpoint. His opinion was that others were more suitable for the county if the freeholders 'might have theire free libertie', though he said he understood it would be difficult for Shrewsbury to change his mind at such short notice; if 'contention' were to arise however, Shrewsbury should avoid a breach of the peace. Burghley's fear of disorder seems to have outweighed his concern for the free election of well-qualified men, but his preference for men of sound religious outlook who were resident within the county was clear, for he had noted that Cavendish was 'noe possessioner within the countie'.[36]

[33] PRO STAC 5/L11/24, L34/34; BL Microfilm 485, reel 33: Hatfield MS 139, f. 74.

[34] As Neale was inclined to do in the case of Wiltshire: Neale, *Commons*, pp. 97–8.

[35] Cf. Kishlansky, *Parliamentary Selection*, p. 25; Elton, *Parliament*, pp. 227–8.

[36] Welbeck seems to have been given him by Shrewsbury after the election: HPT, *sub* Cavendish, Sir Charles; HMC *Bath 5: Talbot, Dudley and Devereux Papers, 1533–1659*, pp. 116–17; and see Neale, *Commons*, pp. 63–8, where Neale, again without direct evidence, believes the sheriff to have acted as a Shrewsbury

Closer examination of a number of election cases allows us to observe the difficulties we have been considering in general. Neale provides a good example for Wiltshire for 1559, and thus gets the reign off to a bad start for the reputation of sheriffs as fair and scrupulous returning officers. This election proved the occasion for bitter rivalry between Sir John Thynne and the first Earl of Pembroke, who supported George Penruddock against Thynne: a recent quarrel between Thynne and Penruddock over an advowson presumably added spice to the contest. For Neale, the situation in Wiltshire in 1559 is clear enough: the 'wretched sheriff' deliberately overturned Penruddock's election in favour of Thynne.[37] Lawrence Hyde, one of Thynne's leading supporters, did indeed admit that many at the election considered Penruddock had the better part of the voices on the day. But doubt arose as to whether they were all resident, and all freeholders; and when asked whether he had advised the sheriff to reverse his own first declaration of Penruddock as the victor and to return Thynne instead, he responded that he had urged Sheriff Bronker to do so because he considered 'the lawes and statutes of this realme, the case being as it was, wold warrant the same.' He also claimed that while he had helped the sheriff to note the names of Thynne's supporters – while the sheriff's deputy sat elsewhere and recorded those for Penruddock – as many were actually sworn for their freehold (and therefore eligibility) 'as John Hoper and John Michell who stode ther for Mr Penruddock did require to have sworne'. Other witnesses for the sheriff expressed some doubts about the eligibility of some of Penruddock supporters, but one of the main objections was that Penruddock himself was thought not to be resident within the shire, but in Hampshire. Another leading witness, Francis Chocke, who had bound himself to the sheriff to pay any legal expenses or fines which might ensue from his returning Thynne – to 'save him harmless' as the saying went – also testified to a majority of thirty-seven for Penruddock, though it was reported, he said, that not all were freeholders, and he said his promise to the sheriff was made for 'frendshipp that of old tyme hath ben bitwen Sir John

---

partisan, and to have moved the place of the election to the castle outside the town 'presumably' keeping Stanhope in ignorance: 'it was a gross fraud.' Neale does not doubt, however, that Stanhope's side was armed, but he fails to consider the situation thus confronting the sheriff.

[37] Neale, *Commons*, pp. 97–8; HPT *sub* Wiltshire.

Thynne and hym', and because he thought the law clearly indicated that Thynne be returned.[38]

Penruddock's witnesses on the other hand could be expected to assert that he was qualified for election by virtue of his residence in Wiltshire, which they duly did. It is interesting, however, that all of them thought him resident by virtue of his position as the Earl of Pembroke's man, and *in the earl's house at Wilton*, the problem being, apparently, that he had virtually shut up his own house at Ivechurch since his wife's death a year or so before the election, even though his duty as a justice of the peace brought him to the county; and even John Hoper, one of Penruddock's close advisors stated that since the death of his wife he 'hathe lyen personallye more at Wilton in my lorde of Pembroke's house than he hathe at Ivechurche.'[39]

There are a number of interesting points in all this. In the first place, the change in Penruddock's personal circumstances since last serving as knight seems to have been significant. His domestic arrangements had clearly altered, and his living had changed its focus from Ivechurch, his own home, to Wilton, someone else's. The complaints of nonresidence made by Thynne's men may seem pettifogging, but they appear to have been offered as serious objections to Penruddock's election in Star Chamber. Indeed, in the case started in the exchequer by the attorney general against Bronker we know that the sheriff's stand was quite simply that the law required him to return a resident in the shire and that Penruddock failed the test.[40] Neale's view that this was a quibble may be correct if it was in fact an excuse by a partisan sheriff to exclude a candidate, but equally to return Penruddock under such circumstances invited legal retaliation from his opponents. Faced therefore with a fair probability of legal action whatever he did, it is understandable that the sheriff adhered *strictly* to the law, especially if it favoured his friends. Secondly, the complexity of ascertaining who gained the greater voice, and difficulties in determining which voices were legitimately given, are features of this election dispute which are ground common to both sides: they should be stressed when we encounter a reluctance to proceed to the poll, for such reluctance is often treated in itself as evidence of corrupt intent. Thirdly, it is clear from this case, whatever the decision in Star

[38] PRO STAC 5/A14/14.
[39] PRO STAC 5/A14/15.
[40] PRO E 159/340, Hilary, membrane 9.

Chamber, that the sheriff's position at the election was an uncomfortable one. The outcome of the election was far from clear, and given that the sheriff was bound by the writ to make a return, it is understandable that both sides in this case were prepared to 'immunize' him from the harmful results of a return which the other side might challenge at law.

At least two aspects of the office of sheriff help us to seize the point here. First, it was much preoccupied with the execution of hosts of writs of all kinds, and the work required a steady legal brain to ensure that procedure was followed correctly, otherwise the sheriff could find himself sued for undue process. Secondly, the sheriff himself, generally no legal expert, transferred much of the business to his under-sheriff, and the two men then made an agreement, the deputy undertaking to protect the high sheriff – to 'save him harmless' – against all actions at law which could follow allegations of incorrect procedure on writs. Serving as sheriff of one's county may have been seen as prestigious, but the work involved was both tedious and a potential legal minefield.[41] Finally, as far as the Wiltshire election was concerned, Thynne did serve in the event, elected irregularly or not: despite what is called the 'palpable misconduct' of the sheriff, Penruddock only resumed his parliamentary career in 1572.[42]

The 1588 Denbighshire election case further illustrates the difficulties confronting sheriffs. Neale believed that sheriff Owen Brereton changed the customary election venue at the county hall in order to return John Edwards, despite a majority among the freeholders for William Almer, and of further refusing Almer's request to poll, or indeed to hold the election again. Neale knew that the Edwards clan, of whom the sheriff was one, saw Almer as unpopular and litigious and balked at the prospect of his return. So they resorted (Neale believed) to trickery: they moved the site of the election from under Almer's nose so that his supporters could not be counted, supporters who (Neale also believed) constituted a majority, despite Edwards's claim that Almer had dragooned all and sundry – whether they were eligible or no – to voice their support for him.[43]

What is played down here is Almer's own action on election day,

[41] T. E. Hartley, 'The sheriffs of the county of Kent, c. 1580–c.1625' (PhD dissertation, London, 1970), pp. 133–6, and ch. 7.

[42] HPT sub Wiltshire.

[43] Neale, 'Three Elizabethan Elections', pp. 211–18.

namely filling the county hall with his own men before the start of proceedings. Brereton claimed – as he might – that Almer's supporters threatened order, that 'riot' was imminent, so that the election had to be moved to maintain peace: thus it was decided to hold the county court at William Edwards's house, and John Salusbury, one of Almer's leading supporters, was not told of the change though he met the sheriff on his way (as he thought) to the election. In fact, Sheriff Brereton freely admitted that Salusbury was not informed for fear that the news would reach Almer's supporters at the county court and produce the very disorder he was trying to avoid, and he was careful to claim that there was no *intent* to hinder those wanting to vote. For his part, Almer based his action, says Neale, on the belief that Edwards might pack the hall beforehand. But in the attempt to justify his conduct, which was *prima facie* the mobbing of the election venue, no substantial evidence of such moves among Edwards's men appears.[44] All Edward Theolall, one of Almer's witnesses, could say at this point was that Almer was so confident of winning the day that only 'sinister practice' could deny him victory, and that it was suspected that 'the sherif and others ... shuld practice to putt into the said shirehall beforehand all the nomber of the freeholders that came with theme to th'elleccion.' It is hard to reconcile a belief in an Edwards plan to pack the county hall with a presumed intention by the same side to move the election to the Edwards's house. The evidence as Neale cites it is in fact equally open to the interpretation that *Almer* sought to pack the county court and intimidate the sheriff.[45]

Neale also dismissed the sheriff's claims that difficulties arose because a meeting of the quarter sessions was planned for the afternoon of election day. The sheriff said he feared that the quarter sessions would be hindered by the election which, under that

[44] PRO STAC 5/A31/30,/A39/12 (John Edwards's answers to interrogatories and Almer's bill against Brereton). Almer's bill does not make explicit claims about the place of the election. It glosses over the question of intentions concerning the location, claiming only that freeholders had been created for the purpose of defeating Almer of his undoubted majority.

[45] PRO STAC 5/A23/22. John Puleston's evidence that John Edwards intended to have the county court at his uncle's house is not reflected in the evidence of other witnesses for Almer who were driven instead by the fear, they said, that Brereton and Edwards would pack the usual venue in the shire hall: Neale, 'Three Elizabethan Elections', p. 217, n. 2; PRO STAC 5/A23/22, evidence of John Puleston, Edward Theloall, Pyers Salusbury, Robert Salusbury.

morning's circumstances, could become a lengthy process. He did not deny that the election was traditionally held at the shire hall, but he said if he had held it there, he should 'not have bin able to have chosen the said knight that daye, nor the next daye followinge as he thinketh, and therefore it must needes have bin a hyndrance to the said quarter sessions.'[46]

John Edwards, the successful candidate, believed, moreover, that his own support from between 600 and 700 freeholders gave him a majority. Neale's figure of 1000 or more for Almer does not seriously deal with his opponents' claim that he had dragooned massive support from non-freeholders, and the under-sheriff, John Kenrick, instructed by Brereton to go to Edwards's house to hold the election there, said that support for Almer and Edwards was such that he 'cannot iustly thinke which syde should have had the greatest nomber.' David Powell, a justice of the peace and cleric, another of Edwards's supporters, agreed that Almer would have had the majority if the election had been held in the shire hall simply because 'he had taken up all the roome in the said shire hall and laye there all nighte.' But he added that this was not to say that the majority of the freeholders in the town that day were for Almer.[47] Under-sheriff Kenrick was scrupulous in his reply to the crucial question about holding the election in Edwards's house: was it, said the interrogatory, a means to 'defraud' Almer of his place? The answer was clinical and precise. Forasmuch as some were gathered at Edwards's house in support of John Edwards, rather than Almer, 'the said county courte was kepte at the said Edwards' howse to th'entent the said John Edwardes should be chosen knight of the said county.' Neale regarded this as a confession, but the words were carefully chosen and can be seen as saying nothing beyond the fact – surely unexceptional as it stood – that Edwards's supporters wanted him returned.[48]

No one denied that Almer had adversaries in this election, but the hijacking of the county court by his supporters presented the sheriff with the golden opportunity, should he need it, to claim that the election could not under such circumstances be a 'free' election. It surely even presented him with the prospect that had he proceeded with the election there, then he might have found himself at the wrong end of another lawsuit by Edwards's side for

[46] PRO STAC 5/A31/30.
[47] PRO STAC 5/A43/29.
[48] PRO STAC 5/A43/29.

being unduly influenced by the massed might of Almer's men. The added complication of the impending quarter sessions that afternoon only strengthened the sheriff's apparent hand, and placed the onus even more firmly on Almer's side – given that they suspected partisan dealing by the sheriff and trouble from their opponents – to behave in a way which left them with 'clean hands'. Suspecting some conspiracy by Edwards and his friends, Almer's side took action which allowed the sheriff and Edwards to steal a march on them elsewhere. As things turned out, he seems to have met the possibility of a sheriff's trick with one of his own. Neale reinforced his notion of the sheriff's treachery here by recalling what happened when Almer later took action against Roger Puleston for his part in the election and was consequently charged with prejudicing the Commons's privileges, because Puleston was then a member of the house himself. Almer is said to have received 'lenient treatment' from the house.[49] Almer did indeed behave well before the Commons and said his offence was committed without intent, but he was still adjudged to have committed a contempt, and some members thought that Puleston's own ill-advised action in responding to Almer's suit at law *without the privity of the house* had cut the ground from under the Commons's feet; Almer's treatment may have been a reflection, then, not so much of his own position and case, as of Puleston's behaviour.[50]

Shrieval tribulations are well illustrated in Denbighshire: contending candidates marshalling their forces (sometimes literally) against each other, and one of them probably enjoying the sheriff's allegiance, if not his partiality; an electorate not readily ascertainable under these circumstances; and a statutory duty to make a return. In circumstances which looked likely to lead to a difficult and controversial outcome, it is not surprising that the sheriff here, as in other cases, received assurances of financial support should he become subsequently embroiled in legal battles: Almer's litigious reputation perhaps made the need more pressing here. But one of the most frightening aspects of the unusual situation of the contest – especially to an officer charged with conserving the peace – was the threat of imminent violence, riot or disorder. The sheriff spoke of it here, but it seems to have been a greater danger in the Montgomeryshire election of the same year, where other aspects of

[49] Neale, 'Three Elizabethan Elections', p. 218, n. 4.
[50] D'Ewes, pp. 431–2, 434–5.

the Denbighshire contest were also reflected. Here too there were accusations of intent to capture the county hall so as to justify the presence of armed supporters, though no substantial evidence was produced. Neale believed the claim that Sheriff Lloyd intended to halt the process of polling to disadvantage his enemy, yet this is no more intrinsically probable than the counterclaim that noisy, armed men from Arthur Price's side harassed their opponents as they came to be polled, and that they set up a rival court at the other end of the hall. The sheriff's qualms about law and order should not be dismissed in this situation: some of his witnesses named individuals who had already given and received violence in the melee.[51]

We have three accounts of the Yorkshire contested election of 1597, yet the story is still unclear, not only because of the usual confusion which arises from conflicting and incomplete partisan reports, but also because we cannot say why Sir John Saville reversed an earlier decision not to stand. What is clear, however, is that by election day he was intent on opposing Stanhope and Hoby, the two candidates with the apparent support of the council of the north. He appealed to local clothing interests with the notion that, paired with Fairfax, he would be preferable to Stanhope and Hoby who were not really residents and were not considered supporters of local issues. Underlying the whole episode was the rivalry between Stanhope and Saville's patron, the Earl of Shrewsbury, a spill-over from the Nottinghamshire trouble already mentioned.[52]

It is remarkable – and so far inexplicable – that the sheriff himself was nowhere in sight at this time; and the under-sheriff who was left with the conduct of the business failed in the task presumably given him by the president of the council, Archbishop Hutton, namely, to see to Stanhope's return at least.[53] We must remember, however, that criticism of the officer was nonexistent, or at least muted. No one complained about his dividing the sides for the view so that Saville's was swelled by inhabitants of York, passers-by as it were, including women and children; or indeed claimed that the officer acted other than under duress from

[51] Neale, 'Three Elizabethan Elections', pp. 227–38; PRO STAC 5/P57/30, membranes 4, 6, 8, for Harry Vaughan, Hugh Pugh, John David ap Gwillim, Rees ap Richard and David Lloyd ap Pugh.

[52] Neale, *Commons*, pp. 86–93; HPT, *sub* Yorkshire: consitituency report based on a draft by Neale; Kishlasnky, *Parliamentary Selection*, pp. 49–55.

[53] Kishlansky, ibid., pp. 50–1, 53.

Saville.[54] Neale's suggestion that he failed to complete the poll in connivance with Saville is not reflected in the complaints lodged by the Stanhope partisans to the privy council, though the impression may arise that the under-sheriff was weak in resisting Saville's harassment. Even so, the burden of their complaint was that Saville's conduct was threatening to life and limb, and that the under-sheriff had been virtually kidnapped from his own court and taken off by Saville, only to return and declare him and Fairfax elected. Despite all this, Saville and Fairfax had the majority according to the election return, and indeed took their seats in parliament. In their version of events, the Stanhope and Hoby partisans naturally argued otherwise, believing they would have had a majority if the poll had proceeded as proposed and agreed by the under-sheriff. But nothing was offered to support this claim other than that Stanhope's side 'did thinke in there consciences that ... the nomber on the parte and side of Sir John Stanhope and Sir Thomas Hobbey wolde in lawfull freeholders exceede the others 300 at the least or more.'[55] Saville's side, however, had suggested another means of breaking the deadlock of the doubtful view of the electors, namely, a second view to be taken by men nominated by Stanhope and Hoby, along with an examination of any elector whose qualifications seemed in doubt to them: polling every man would have taken too long. The suggestion was turned down, and the under-sheriff therefore duly made his return as the initial view had indicated, in favour of Saville and Fairfax.[56]

What can we safely say about this election? First, although Hutton and the council suggested the under-sheriff had acted in Saville's favour, this was not reflected, as we have seen, in what was said of events by Stanhope's supporters. They claimed in fact that he made preparations for the poll, and they recalled his telling Saville that he wanted to proceed with it as agreed. There is nothing to justify Neale's opinion that Saville had colluded with the officer, who became his 'willing tool'.[57] Secondly, the Saville and Fairfax side stressed that the examination of voters in the case of dubious eligibility had been refused by their opponents, even though they claimed to have offered them the right to nominate the triers themselves. No apology was made for the denial of polling in

[54] Ibid., pp. 51, 53 and n. 14.
[55] BL Microfilm 485, reel 33: Hatfield MS 139, f. 74v.
[56] BL Microfilm 485, reel 35: Hatfield MS 141, f. 190.
[57] HPT, *sub* Yorkshire; BL Microfilm 485, reel 33: Hatfield MS 139, f. 74v.

view of the huge numbers which overwhelmed the under-sheriff; and he was within his statutory rights in refusing it in so far as he was not compelled to undertake it.[58] Plainly, the difficulties surrounding the process of polling and dividing the sides, whatever Kishlansky says about the ability of Elizabethan society to compute accurately, are demonstrated here.[59] The privy council – which for Neale was the one institution of sixteenth-century life capable of unseating fraudulently elected members – allowed Saville to take his seat, releasing him, indeed, from a token imprisonment for his misconduct so that he could do so.[60] Marginal comments on a document listing reasons why Saville's election was 'unlawfull and unorderly' suggest that 'disorder' was as much – if not more – the issue here as whether the sheriff had made a false return.[61] Saville had broken up the proceedings with force and intemperate language, had removed the under-sheriff from the meeting leaving the assembled freeholders for some two hours, possibly a cause for concern in its own right.

The Yorkshire election of 1597 involved not so much a tricky sheriff as an overbearing candidate standing against others who seem to have been ineptly chosen: and it may be that in the face of local resentment the privy council considered that despite Saville's overreaction and near-riotous behaviour discretion was the better part of valour. We have no information, moreover, on the action, if any, which the council said it would take against the under-sheriff here.[62] We might add that, generally speaking, the privy council's intervention in election troubles appears to have been for various reasons, and not just because of alleged or proven shrieval misconduct. Fears of disorder, as we have seen in Yorkshire and Nottinghamshire, must be counted a major concern: from time to time it surfaced in Essex, especially in 1588 when the council wrote to a number of the participants – not just the sheriff, be it noted

---

[58] BL Microfilm 485, reel 35: Hatfield MS 141, f. 190; 8 Henry VI, c. 7 (*SR* II, p. 243).

[59] Kishlansky, *Parliamentary Selection*, p. 62.

[60] HPT, *sub* Yorkshire.

[61] The first reason – that non-freeholders and nonresidents were among Saville's supporters – is followed by six others which focus almost wholly on disorderly conduct, such as Saville's preventing the sheriff from conducting the poll, his threatening to break down the castle gates and his abusive language, likely, it was said, to cause 'quarrell and bloodshedd'. (BL Microfilm 485, reel 33: Hatfield MS 139, f. 76).

[62] HPT, *sub* Yorkshire.

– urging caution. In Denbighshire in 1601 violence was threatened to the point where the election was abandoned, thus prompting council investigation of the leading parties, and even earning Neale's sympathy for the sheriff. On the other hand, when the council demanded impartiality from the sheriffs in Warwickshire and Worcestershire in 1601 it may be that its action was prompted by the wish to promote favoured candidates, and that alleged shrieval trickery was stressed as a justification for intervention.[63]

Indeed, Neale commented on the fact that the privy council appears to have had little time or inclination to deal with recalcitrant sheriffs; Star Chamber did not apparently make the punishment fit the crime, nor can it be said to have remedied the deficiencies of the existing legal position as defined in the fifteenth century.[64] Why was the law not changed so as to deal with the matter? The legislation of Elizabeth's reign which had a bearing on the English shrievality was concerned principally with the mundane business of controlling sheriff's officers and the fees attaching to the office. Further acts passed in the earlier part of the reign reduced the number of counties paired under one sheriff – though this was increased again in 1571 when Surrey and Sussex were exempted from the act continuing the initial statute of 1566. We know little about the reasons for these acts, or their initiators, and it would be particularly interesting to know why the two shrievalties were recombined in 1571. The motive may have been administrative efficiency, and they may have arisen from gentry pressure in the counties concerned: there is no apparent reason to believe that the object was to attack shrieval corruption at elections. It has also been suggested recently that sheriffs may have been responsible for some of the Elizabethan borough enfranchisements, sending their election precepts to boroughs not previously electing burgesses. In 1571 no fewer than eight boroughs sent members for the first time, but there is no suggestion that if sheriffs were involved they were castigated, at this or any other time, for irregular conduct, or for furthering the borough interests of great men on whose instructions they may have acted. And the boroughs continued to send members up.[65] Even in the case of Ludlow, where in 1597 it seems the

[63] HPT, *sub* Essex; *APC 1588*, pp. 318–19; *APC 1601–04*, pp. 342, 374, 379, 380; Neale, *Commons*, pp. 127–8; *APC, 1601–04*, pp. 247–8, 251.

[64] Neale, *Commons*, p. 79.

[65] G. R. Elton, *Parliament*, pp. 194–5; J. Loach, 'Parliament: A "New Air"?', in *Revolution Reassessed*, ed. C. Coleman and D. Starkey (Oxford, 1986), pp. 123–5, 128.

sheriff of Shropshire may have misdirected his precept – thus allowing the Earl of Pembroke to return his own man to the disadvantage of the city and its candidate – it seems there was no general feeling that he had behaved corruptly. There was merely a suggestion from some quarters in the house that he may have acted in haste and from want of experience.[66] All in all then, there was no apparent general hostility to sheriffs' conduct at elections, nor a desire to tighten control. There were perhaps many in parliament who were content to leave matters as they were. Many members of the Commons in particular served as sheriff at some point in their lives: about two-fifths of Kent's, two-thirds of Northumberland's and three-quarters of Leicestershire's knights for the reign took on the office for example, though by no means all would have had experience of supervising elections themselves. Borough representation in these counties showed far less shrieval experience, though Newcastle-upon-Tyne provides a striking exception to this because it seems to have been the rule for the town (a county in its own right) to elect former sheriffs to serve in parliament, there being only one exception.[67] The Commons at least were not likely to support legislation against their own kind, and the foregoing argument has stressed that elections were by no means solely in the sheriff's control, that there were occasions when the dynamics of society in county, and borough, could manifest themselves in a sometimes dramatic way. The study of borough disputed elections shows that, *mutatis mutandis*, the same difficulties appeared there as in the shires: disputes over residence qualifications among candidates, over the voting rights of individuals and over determining majorities in the hubbub of voices.[68] The evidence again confirms that sheriffs' tricks were not essential to electoral dispute, and we must stress the privy council's concern at elections which was often with the participants and their supporters rather than the sheriff himself. All that we now know of the involvement of the gentry – with or without contest or dispute – and the difficulties and obscurities facing the sheriff in his legally vulnerable position must, when taken together, suggest a sufficient answer to the question as to why the law was not tightened up by an enraged parliament, whatever the Commons may have done to increase its own involvement over such cases in the seventeenth century.

[66] Neale, *Commons*, pp. 163–4; HPT, *sub* Ludlow.

[67] HPT, *passim*.

[68] Cf. Elton, *Parliament*, pp. 193–4; Neale, *Commons, passim*; HPT, *passim*.

Our discussion also prompts one or two reflections on the nature of elections and their significance.[69] Although the instances are few, views about the nature of parliamentary representation sometimes appear in the disputes; and they must be placed alongside Kishlansky's view that there was no relationship between the 'putative franchise and the actual process of selection'.[70] The statutory qualifications for knights of the shire seem from time to time to have been live issues, and reflect an idea of a candidate's suitability for the task of serving the county, for example Penruddock's insufficient status (he was not a knight) and his alleged nonresidence in Wiltshire: both these elements are known to have reappeared in Somerset in 1614.[71] The Staffordshire and Rutland disputes of 1597 and 1601 respectively also reflect objections to nonresidence; but the Denbighshire and Montgomeryshire cases of 1588 seem to indicate more positive requirements than knowledge of the community through residence. Here the claim was that Almer was unsuitable for election in Denbighshire, being quarrelsome and likely to cause dissension in the county – he was 'lewde and unsemely for his calling' – though his own complaint to the Star Chamber was that his defeat amounted to a conspiracy against the freeholders. And in Montgomeryshire some of Herbert's witnesses considered him a better 'commonwealth' man than Price.[72] The fifteenth-century law, imprecise as it was, was clearly concerned with majorities, and it was in that sense that it was upheld, in the courts at least.[73] Moreover, a man's 'fitness' – by virtue of his knowledge of his county, as well as his character – for the task of parliamentary service again implies a notion, albeit imprecise

[69] See especially D. Hirst, *The Representative of the People? Voters and Voting in England under the Early Stuarts* (Cambridge, 1975); J. K. Gruenfelder, *Influence in Early Stuart Elections*; Kishlansky, *Parliamentary Selection*.

[70] Kishlansky, *Parliamentary Selection*, p. 15; individuals, we are told, represented communities because of their personal qualities and standing, rather than reflecting special interests or the ideals of a particular group of constituents.

[71] Neale, *Commons*, pp. 97–8; Kishlansky, *Parliamentary Selection*, p. 99.

[72] See above, p. 176; Neale, 'More Elizabethan Elections', pp. 34, 37; PRO STAC 5/A39/12; P57/30; Neale also shows that there was concern in the Cinque Ports that 'outsiders', ignorant of the privileges of the ports, had been unable to prevent their being undermined in parliament (*Commons*, p. 218 and *passim* for other concern over 'outsiders').

[73] See Plowden in *English Reports*, 75, pp. 182–201 for the case of Buckley v. Thomas (Anglesey 1553), and the judges' reference (pp. 198–9) to a case from Henry VII's reign.

perhaps, of a verdict exercised by the 'choosers'.[74] It is only in these circumstances, of course, that problems about personalities, and what they came to stand for, could begin to emerge later. By the latter half of the reign moreover, it is possible to detect 'issues' on the electoral scene, albeit on a limited scale. So in Denbighshire (1588), and Rutland (1601), as well as the Staffordshire case in 1597 already mentioned, antipathy to alleged Catholic candidates or their supporters is apparent. None of this should surprise us in view of the exclusion from the Commons since 1563 of all avowed Catholics and the privy council's preference, stated in 1584 and effectively reiterated in 1586, for members who were 'well-affected' in religion.[75] But the Yorkshire election of 1597 is perhaps the most interesting, for there seem to be no fewer than three points of contention: the nonresidency of Stanhope and Hoby; a feeling that they were backed by the council of the north and the privy council; and Saville's support of the clothmakers of the West Riding.[76]

Neale's case studies of elections were based largely on the assumption that what happened at the county court was decided by the sheriff because it was his court. If the foregoing review of some of those cases is correct, however, then we need to shift the emphasis and modify our concept of elections. The term 'election' is conventionally used to signify the events which occurred at the county court, and yet, as we have seen, the court's proceedings were merely the last stage in a process which had been going on for some time, and which need not involve the sheriff at all. The process of choosing knights of the shire was a long one, and only the final stages occurred in the sheriff's domain, the county court. In contested elections the sheriff's duties had to be performed in circumstances which, if the parties were keen to exploit the fertile ground for charge and countercharge, could lead him into troubled waters.[77] The arrival of the writ itself could cause initial difficulties, and should there be a contest with an uncertain outcome, going to

---

[74] Cf. D. Hirst in *Albion*, 19 (1987), 429–30.

[75] HPT, p. 29; Neale, *Commons*, pp. 290–1; PRO STAC 5/A31/39, A39/12; Neale, 'More Elizabethan Elections', pp. 39–40; above, p. 173. There seem to have been other religious dimensions in Norfolk of course, and see D. MacCulloch, 'Catholic and Puritan in Elizabethan Suffolk', *Archiv für Reformationsgeschichte*, 72 (1981).

[76] Neale, *Commons*, pp. 90–1; HPT *sub* Yorkshire.

[77] Fear of disorder was alleged, as we have seen, in Denbighshire and Montgomeryshire in 1588, in Yorkshire in 1597, and in Denbighshire again in 1601.

the poll could be problematic, both legally and logistically.[78] Even so, on occasion there were energetic calls for the poll from interested parties.[79] A massed gathering of men, women and children could naturally cause the sheriff concern in its own right; and the prospect of dividing large numbers of freeholders (true or not) into two 'camps', which in turn could be swelled by nonvoting bystanders, where men on one or both sides were armed, where violent activity had preceded the election itself and where the hubbub, badinage and sheer verbal, if not physical, abuse were being hurled about, was presumably even less attractive. The absence of a regularized system of registering voters – an electoral register – made any process of checking which was called for (though not mandatory as we have seen) very cumbersome, even where small numbers of voters were concerned, as the Hampshire by-election of 1566 shows. So when the numbers present or eligible to vote ran into thousands, we can well believe that sheriffs were too weary to continue.

There is no reason to believe that disputed elections were very common occurrences, but there are difficulties in being able to recognize the existence of uncontroversial contests.[80] We should not believe that absence of tension and conflict necessarily indicates overwhelming harmony, where the gentlemen of the shires were hesitant to join issue with each other in the quest for a parliamentary seat. As we have seen, there is sometimes no evidence of contested elections in Kent and Lancashire, yet there is good reason to suppose that there was pre-election competition for nomination which had been resolved by election day. In Kent too, as Neale showed, there was energetic canvassing of voices in the process: so absence of a contest

[78] All this is apparent in Kishlansky's account of the Somerset election of 1614, *Pariamentary Selection*, pp. 85–101.

[79] Kishlansky, *Parliamentary Selection*, pp. 61–2; we do not have to stress their alleged and unacceptable egalitarianism to appreciate why they were not so welcome to others.

[80] Kishlansky (*Parliamentary Selection*, p. 12, n. 31) correctly states that positive evidence of uncontested elections is unusual, and that 'it is impossible to prove a negative.' His argument is subsequently dependent on the assumption that uncontested elections were 'normal': 'normal conduct is generally unremarkable and unremarked upon.' But we could equally argue that we do not hear very much of uncontroversial contests, smoothly administered – rather than disputes – because *they* were normal. His comparison with marriage and divorce (pp. 76–7) is appropriate: because all marriages do not end in divorce we cannot simply believe that those which do not are all successful and harmonious. It is not clear, moreover, if Kishlansky uses 'normative' (pp. 12, 22, 74) to mean 'normal' (i.e. the practice) or to describe a set of rules preferred by society (i.e. the goal, or ideal).

cannot always be evidence of unwillingness to initiate at least a competition.[81] Writing around for support may clearly be seen as an attempt to solve the issue by gathering enough backing to leave the field clear on the day. The point is that respect for the integrity of the community – the wish to avoid disruption of the peace – was not inconsistent with a struggle for honour and place.[82]

The fact of the matter was that the sheriff's actions were dictated by fifteenth-century laws which were based on fears of public disorder, but which had not been adjusted to assist him in his task which was by now made more difficult by the processes of population growth, inflation and a growing interest in parliamentary service itself, by, in short, an enhanced electorate which could be dragooned by key constituents. Perhaps the most surprising aspect is that, despite all the allegations of pre-election violence and conspiracy, of false returns against manifest majorities, of armed men and crowds whipped up to a frenzy of partisan solidarity, there is no evidence of mayhem following a declaration of such an election, the time at which one might have expected an eruption of frustration and indignant anger. It does look as though Elizabethan England was generally well under control at election time, despite Star Chamber stories of conspiracy and riot.

[81] Kishlansky, *Parliamentary Selection*, pp. 24–5, 62–3, 65, 74, and especially p. 29 where we hear of clearing the way of potential competitors; Neale, *Commons*, p. 74.

[82] L. Peck, 'Goodwin v. Fortescue: The Local Context of Parliamentary Controversy', *Parliamentary History*, 3 (1983), 44; Kishlansky repeatedly acknowledges the quest for peace (e.g. *Parliamentary Selection* pp. 63, 68, 92, 97, 99 n. 105), but he places too much emphasis on the formal declarations of 'friendship' by contemporaries. In the Somerset election of 1614 Berkeley and Poulett expressed their amity towards Phelips, but they could find no sympathy with his attempts to win support for himself (Kishlansky, p. 91).

8

English Parliaments 1593–1606: One Epoch or Two?

CONRAD RUSSELL

Twenty years ago every schoolchild knew that at the opening of James VI and I's first English parliament, a number of members of the Commons were shut out from hearing the King's opening speech.[1] We used to hear innumerable essays which invoked this incident as a symbol of what went wrong at the beginning of James's reign. We never heard of the occasion, instantly recalled by Martin, when exactly the same thing happened at the beginning of Elizabeth's last parliament, in 1601.[2] The difference in the treatment of two similar incidents strongly suggested a double standard of judgement. Similarly, when I wrote, in 1971, that the 1604 session 'produced the portent of a contested election for the Speakership', I both somewhat dignified the confused 'muttering' of different names in 1604 by calling it a 'contested election',[3] and had not remarked the parallel, if better resolved, confusion in 1584, when Fleetwood ended a confused silence by telling the members: 'cry Puckering.' This incident was taken by Neale (probably rightly) as evidence of an inexperienced house, not of the inadequacy of Elizabethan parliamentary management.[4] It is hard to believe that if the same incident had happened under James, historians would have managed to be so restrained.

However, to cry 'double standard', good sport though it may be, is no answer to the question what conclusion we should reach if we apply a single standard. Since the beginning of the new approaches

---

[1] S. R. Gardiner, *History of England* (1893), I, p. 165.

[2] *CJ*, 921; D'Ewes, p. 599.

[3] Conrad Russell, *The Crisis of Parliaments* (Oxford, 1971) (hereafter Russell, *Crisis*), p. 266: *CJ* 141.

[4] Neale, *Parliaments*, II, p. 25.

loosely and collectively known as 'revisionism', we have had no sustained discussion of the differences between the last parliaments of Elizabeth and the opening parliamentary sessions of James. This essay cannot maintain a claim to be a definitive answer to that question. It rests only on a consideration of the obvious sources, and involves no attempt to make the sort of detailed study of non-parliamentary sources which would be necessary before we could see the events concerned in the round. It should thus be taken as advancing hypotheses, to be tested by future research in greater depth.

An immediate and casual impression from reading D'Ewes's *Journal* for 1601 followed by the Commons's *Journal* for 1604 tends to suggest that there is not very much difference between the sessions they describe. Very much the same members took the leading part in both sessions, and behaved in a way very much like themselves. Sir Francis Hastings was equally concerned to protect the poor or to reform religion in the two sessions. Sir George More was equally concerned to produce a careful enunciation of the conventional wisdom, and Lawrence Hyde equally concerned to oppose financial burdens on the country. The Lawrence Hyde who initiated the monopolies debate in 1601 is not visibly different from the Lawrence Hyde who sponsored the purveyance bill in 1606. Sir Henry and Sir Edward Montagu were equally concerned for re-sponsibility and balance on the two sides of the chronological divide, Sir Robert Wingfield equally concerned to square his loyalty to the Cecils with his duty to the country, Richard Martin equally ready to pop up unexpectedly and Francis Bacon equally sententious. Of the really prominent figures in the session of 1601, perhaps only Ralegh suffered for being 'left over from the previous reign'.

Nor does a comparison of the business (with a few headline exceptions) suggest a very dramatic change. Drink and alehouses, like the poor, are always with us, and swearing bills seem to have been a permanent background feature from the later part of Elizabeth's reign right through to the statute of 1624. The 1601 bill against adultery, like Ignatius Jordan's bill in 1628, did not com-mend itself to the house. The bill provided for a man committing adultery to lose his tenancy by courtesy, and a woman to lose her dower. Serjeant Harris said it allowed ecclesiastical courts to determine inheritances, which was *ultra vires*, and that a poor man would not be punished because he had nothing to lose, whereas a poor woman would be. This was enough to move all the house to cry 'away with it.'[5] The resistance to fining husbands for their wives' recusancy continued unabated, and the only striking features of the issue in Jacobean times which were not present under Elizabeth were the eloquence of Lewknor's image in 1604, that it was like making a husband do penance in a white sheet for his wife's adultery, and the fact that the resistance continued after the Gunpowder Plot.[6]

It is a good cross-check on such superficial impressions to study the essays in this collection and ask how far they could, *mutatis mutandis*, be put on a reading list for early Stuart parliaments without misleading the reader. In the process of identifying our '*mutanda*', we may understand a bit more what changed in the passage from one reign to the other. Professor Graves's essay, in particular, seems to describe a picture Stuart historians should find familiar. His insistence that many bills failed 'due to sheer lack of time' and his picture of a 'frequent logjam' of bills are true for any time before parliamentary sessions became continual.[7] I have not compiled a table of the proportion of bills which failed in the early Jacobean sessions, but a casual impression suggests that the picture he gives, of a slightly rising graph of failure, remains true up to the first clogging of the legislative pipeline, in 1614. This does not seem to be because there were more opposed bills, though the resistance to bills for the reformation of morals should not be underrated. It seems to be rather due to an increase in the number of bills put forward, though without quantitative information such a suggestion should be advanced tentatively. The number of bills succeeding suggests a legislative machine whose productivity was more influenced by the length of the session than by any variation in the political temperature. In 1597 twenty-six public and fifteen private Acts became law, in 1601 nineteen public and ten private, in 1604 thirty-three public and thirty-nine private, and in 1606 twelve public and seventeen private. The flood of naturalization bills after 1604 is the only obvious political circumstance accounting for

[5] D'Ewes, p. 641.

[6] Heywood Townshend, *Historical Collections* (1680), pp. 228–9; *CJ*, 239, 992–3; *The Parliamentary Diary of Robert Bowyer, 1606–1607*, ed. D. H. Willson, (New York, 1971) (hereafter *Bowyer*) p. 23 and *CJ*, 263.

[7] Above, pp. 38, 41. On the problem of logjams of bills in later parliaments, see Conrad Russell, *Parliaments and English Politics 1621–1629* (Oxford, 1979), pp. 41–8.

much change in these figures. Two possible differences strike a Stuart historian. One is that Elizabeth's use of the veto on seventy-two bills and thirteen sessions seems a good deal higher than Stuart use of the veto, though this is a tentative impression.[8] The other is that Professor Graves's picture of the Lords as 'the more efficient chamber' depended on the fact that they were the smaller house. By the 1620s this was no longer as true as it had been, but the change is not significant during the period covered by this essay.

Dr Dean's picture of legislation, which logically belongs with Professor Graves's picture of business management, again seems to portray a broadly similar picture. It emerges both from Dr Dean's contribution and from Dr Hartley's that the sense of accountability to a wider country, described by Professor Hirst,[9] is not a Stuart linear development, but something well established before the Queen died. Sir Hugh Beeston, in 1601, was in the unusual position of having his county unrepresented, because its election dispute had not yet been resolved, but his ringing declaration that 'if I should not speak something on behalf of my country, I dare not go thither again,' seems to be only an unusually dramatic statement of a member's working assumption.[10] Sensitivity to country feeling was not a revolutionary Stuart development, but a normal part of the working parliamentary atmosphere, as a study of the subsidy debate in 1593 or 1606 will quickly illustrate.

Professor Jones's stress on the capacity of religion to become involved in all issues is equally true all through the period. Sir George More's speech in 1601 on the bill for the better settling of the watch, that 'those that be night-walkers offend God, do the commonwealth no good, and sin in both' is a typical example of the point.[11] Beyond this, the five sessions compared here seem to show very little change in the religious atmosphere. The same bills for religious reformation remained on the agenda throughout. The House of Commons, much more than the Lords, though not exclusively, remained concerned about pluralities, the Sabbath subscription and the provision of a learned ministry.[12] Yet, though there was a steady head of steam for these bills, they were not

[8] On the veto in the 1620s, see Russell, *Parliaments and English Politics*, p. 44.

[9] Derek Hirst, *The Representative of the People?* (Cambridge, 1975), *passim*.

[10] Townshend, *Historical Collections*, p. 210.

[11] Ibid., p. 193.

[12] For the texts of some of these bills, see HMC *House of Lords*, XI pp. 89, 91, 96, 98–100, 101–3 and other refs.

coming from the whole house: there was an equally steady under-current of resistance to them, which helps to establish that the commons was not an exclusively puritan house. In 1606, when Nicholas Fuller reported a bill to restrain arrests on the Sabbath, Hakewill dismissed it as 'the absurdest bill that ever passed from a committee', and asked what should be done with two people fighting on the Sabbath. In spite of Fuller's efforts, the house followed Hakewill, and thew the bill out.[13] The only occasion when we can see a measurable trial of strength between godly and ungodly factions in the house is on the motion to sit on Ascension Day in 1604, which must have mustered the full godly voting strength. It was carried by the narrow margin of 137 to 128.[14] This division may be a reasonably accurate measure of the strength of the advocates of 'further reformation' in the house.

The impression of limited change in the religious atmosphere is one in which the parliamentary sources are likely to be deceptive. The sameness of the bills misses the excitement generated by Hampton Court, and even more by the canons of 1604 and the enforcement programme which followed them. In many ways, 1604 produced a degree of tension in religious matters which had not been seen since the last similar campaign for subscription, in 1584. It did not produce a wave of tension on the level of 1584, partly because it was a second round, and the participants knew the moves, but the effects of the deprivations were serious enough. What is interesting then, is how little of this appears in the parlia-mentary sources: it is possible that the withdrawal of the Eliza-bethan ban on religious discussion was only slowly assimilated. It is also possible that Robert Cecil, James Montagu and others kept much of the discussion within court circles, by being willing to listen before a parliament asked them to. For our purposes, it is as interesting that the parliamentary sources give an impression of no change as that the evidence from outside the walls shows that impression to be false.

This essay attempts no comparison of Dr Hartley's material on elections with the early Stuart period. This is because the 1604 election, which is the only Stuart election within the period of this essay, is an ill-recorded election, and, the election of 1614 is too far into the new reign to make a very useful comparison in a study

[13] CJ 307.
[14] CJ 972.

designed to isolate the effect of the change of dynasty. That said, Dr Hartley's essay does not give a picture which looks particularly unusual. Professor Elton's essay is also not discussed at length here, because it raises issues which were exhaustively ventilated in the Long Parliament debate on the canons of 1640, and are therefore discussed at length in my forthcoming *Fall of the British Monarchies*.[15] The issues raised by Dr Alsop and Professor MacCaffrey, which concern war, peace and money, are too far-reaching to be discussed in the form of an extended gloss: they need to be discussed in full. Dr Alsop is correct in stressing that the requests for multiple subsidies from 1589 onwards showed 'a generally indulgent and responsive Commons'.[16] He is clearly right that there was never much doubt that the subsidies would be voted. However, it is possible to see, on closer scrutiny, an undercurrent of discontent at the exceptionally heavy weight resting on the poorer taxpayers, and it is possible that some of the discontent which surfaced in the purveyance and subsidy debates of 1606 had grown logically out of Elizabethan dissatisfaction, and needed only the less restrained atmosphere of peace to reach the surface. It is at least possible to ask whether the financial reflexes of early Jacobean parliaments are in part a re-action after the weight of Elizabethan wartime taxation, and there-fore whether they might have been very much the same if Elizabeth, and not James, had still been on the throne.

It is not an altogether fanciful hypothesis to see the falling yield of the multiple subsidies in the 1590s as a silent expression of foot-dragging at the growing burden they implied. Members, when they discussed the burden of the subsidies, tended to take the line that the burden on the rich was not severe, but that the burden on the poor was causing considerable difficulty.[17] Lord Keeper Puckering, opening the parliament of 1593, touched on both points together:

The aid that formerly hath been granted unto her Majesty in these like cases, is with such slackness performed, and that the third of that which

---

[15] Conrad Russell, *The Fall of the British Monarchies 1637–1642* (Oxford, forthcoming), chs 2, 5, 6 and *passim*.

[16] Above, p. 109.

[17] I am grateful to Dr Ian Archer, whose work on the burden of taxation is in pro-gress, for a very valuable discussion of the subject. On the declining yield of the sub-sidy, which was of course only part of the total burden of taxation, see Roger Schofield, 'Taxation and the Political Limits of the Tudor State', in *Law and Government Under the Tudors: Essays Presented to Sir Geoffrey Elton On His Retirement*, ed. Claire Cross, David Loades and J. J. Scarisbrick (Cambridge, 1988), pp. 227–55.

hath been granted cometh not to Her Majesty ... Her Majesty thinketh this to be, for that the wealthier sort of men turn the charge upon the weaker, and upon those of worst ability, so that the one dischargeth himself, and the other is not able to satisfie what he is charged withal.[18]

Later in the same session, Fulke Greville also drew attention to the burden on the poor and expressed a fear, characteristic of the period, of association between high taxation and political disorder: 'the poore are greeved be being overcharged this must be helped by increasing of our owne burthen for otherwise the weake feet will complain of too heavie boddie. It is to be feared if the feet knew their streght [sic] as we doe their highnes they would not beare as they doe.'[19] For the moment, Greville said, it would have to suffice that the time required it, yet the harder members bit on the bullet that the times required it in 1593, the more convinced they were likely to be that the time did not require it in 1606.

It was no help that these escalating war costs were falling on a country with what has been described as a 'low-tax philosophy',[20] and it was no help to James that Elizabeth's personal frugality was constantly stressed as a reason why the sums should be granted. When Sir John Fortescue opened the subsidy debate in 1597, it is often hard for a modern reader to be sure which Sir John Fortescue is speaking:

wee knowe wee live in a government more happie because free from extreme and miserable taxes, the time being not to be compared to the daies of Queene Marie, when everie man was sworne to the uttermost of his landes and goodes, neither to King Edward the 3rd his time, in wch everie fowerth parte was given to the king towards his conquest of Fraunce, neither will I speake of the dangerous impositions of Fraunce, where 6d was given for everie chymney, and soe for every burying, christning and churching, all those are fitter for a regall than a politique government, for an austere and strange borne conqueror, then a mild and natureall Queene.[21]

This association of high taxation with arbitrary, and above all with unsuccessful, government showed in a less polite way in 1606, when

---

[18] D'Ewes, p. 458.

[19] BL Cotton MS Titus F ii, f. 47r.

[20] The phrase is that of Dr Ian Archer, and is closely similar to phrases used by the late Professor Joel Hurstfield. I am grateful to both of them for discussions of this topic.

[21] A. F. Pollard and Marjorie Blatcher, 'Hayward Townshend's Journals', *BIHR*, 12 (1934–5), pp. 12–13.

William Noy complained that subsidies went from the poor to the rich, and compared the situation with the parliament of 1450, when 'the subjects answered, what by takings excessive etc, they were near destroyed.' Dyott followed him, asserting that exactions upon subjects in Henry VI's time were the cause of what followed. It was a historical myth, but a highly potent one, and the Elizabethan successes in gaining subsidies had been won at the expense of giving it a new lease of life. With this philosophy went an insistence, warranted by many medieval precedents, that retrenchment, rather than taxation, was the right way to deal with a financial crisis.[22] This tradition too was not a Stuart rediscovery: it was fully visible in Sir Henry Knyvett's speech in the subsidy debate of 1593. He proposed, among much else, that the Queen's debts be called in, and that she be given power to sell debtors' lands, that stewards should answer for fines they received and that the Queen should sell coppice wood to increase revenue. He also proposed the main Tudor and Stuart addition to the ideology of retrenchment finance, that the Queen could have great financial benefit by a new statute of recusants. Financially, these were no doubt all sound proposals in a minor key, but they did not match well with Knyvett's own proposal that the Queen should send out, not weak forces, but a royal army. In this speech, he is at times the spiritual ancestor of Sir John Eliot.[23]

The subsidy, of course, was very far from the whole weight of Tudor and Stuart taxation, and some of the undercurrent of discontent surfaced about payment for other things. In 1597 Sir Thomas Coningsby expressed himself freely against the bill to erect a bridge over the Wye at Ross. He opposed it because of the poverty of the country, 'the multidue [*sic*] of taxes and imposicons', because they would need to repair it after floods so often that it would 'utterlie impoverish them' and because 'everie quarter sessions there be taxes sett and imposed by the Justices for the repairing of them.'[24] Is this the other side of the coin to the willingness to vote subsidies recorded by Dr Alsop?

---

[22] I am grateful to Dr David Starkey for drawing my attention to the extent to which high taxation and deficit finance were identified with failure, rather than with success. The point, once made, is confirmed even by the most cursory study of members' use of precedents. For these examples, *CJ* 284 and *Bowyer*, pp. 79–80.

[23] BL Cotton MS Titus F ii, f. 35v. Knyvett's speech contains a constructive vein usually absent from Eliot's, but the devotion to retrenchment ideology is common to both.

[24] 'Townshend's Journals', p. 15.

The most famous example of resentment fastening on other payments which were not regarded as necessary to national defence is of
course the monopolies debate of 1601. In a house which had just voted
four subsidies with startling docility, the monopolies debate was an
excellent opportunity for displacement aggression. Sir Edward Hoby
dwelt on the effect of monopolies on prices, and Martin said he spoke
'for a town that grieves and pines, for a countrey that grooneth and
languisheth'. These members, at least, could go home and say they
had done something to relieve their constituents' burdens.[25] The
pattern of the monopolies debate, and the golden speech which
followed it, is perhaps not quite that which later mythology has made
it. It is not quite, as it appears, a case of a loving Queen overruling her
heartless ministers, nor does it seem that at the time members were
much deluded that it was any such thing. Like any major government
concession, it was clothed in rhetoric, and demanded a reciprocal
rhetoric, but neither obscures the traces of stage management, nor
absolves us of the need to look for the stage manager.

The resentment generated by the issue did not spare the Queen.
At the beginning of the session, when she left after her opening
speech, 'very few said God save your Majesty, as they were wont in
all great assemblies.'[26] At the height of the debate, Sir Robert
Johnson, not one of the most provocative members, wished the
Queen had heard one-fifth of what was said that day.[27] Robert
Cecil, facing this debate, had already been involving in moves to
persuade the Queen to suppress monopolies before the parliament.[28]
He was, then, in the unfortunate position of a minister forced to
defend a policy he had already unsuccessfully opposed. He did so,
in the usual style of ministers in such a position, out of both sides of
his mouth. He told the Speaker that he should perform the Queen's
command not to receive bills of this nature, while at the same time
saying men who desired patents which took from subjects their
birthrights were wicked offenders. Under these circumstances, one
may wonder whether his famous protest that the behaviour of the
house was 'more fit for a grammar school than a court of Parliament' was meant to still the storm, or to ensure that he could report
to the Queen that it was uncontrollable, although he had tried.[29]

[25] D'Ewes, pp. 644–8.
[26] D'Ewes, p. 602; Townshend, *Historical Collections*, pp. 178–9.
[27] D'Ewes, p. 647.
[28] *Salis. MSS*, vol. XI, pp. 324–5.
[29] D'Ewes, pp. 649, 651.

The next day, immediately after the Queen's concession had been announced, it was Cecil who was on his feet to spell out, as only its architect could have done, exactly what it did and did not mean.[30] As with any major government concession won in hard battle, there was some suspicion concealed under the overt thanks. Mr Donhault, the lord keeper's secretary, said the speech was worthy to be written in letters of gold, lest it might be 'not so happily effected'. It would be nice to know whether Sir John Neale was right to call him the lord keeper's 'undisciplined' secretary. Lawrence Hyde, the mover of the bill, seconded him on the ground that records would be a lively memory in ages to come – or, in other words, because it would make it harder for the Queen to go back on her concession.[31] It was Cecil, not the Queen, to whom Sir Francis Hastings expressed his thanks in private.[32]

In fact, the sceptics were quite right in their suspicions about the value of the Queen's concession. The majority of the monopolies of which they complained, though they were suppressed, had sprung up again before the death of Elizabeth, and had to be suppressed once again by Robert Cecil. This time, he persuaded James to act by proclamation before his first parliament met, and thereby saved him from another nasty dispute.[33] The achievement was cited in the preamble of the subsidy act of 1606 as a justification for the grant of subsidies.[34] James, of course, did not succeed in suppressing monopolies either, and the real question (not suitable for discussion here) is about the institutional pressures which kept them going. What is clear is that the monopolies debate of 1601 cannot be cited to support the view that Elizabeth was better able to handle parliaments than James. The dramatic character of her concession is a measure of how deeply she had got into trouble.

One monopoly on which there was no redress was saltpetre, a symptom of the growing administrative burden of early modern war. On this, Robert Cecil could only say: 'for this I beseech you be

---

[30] D'Ewes, pp. 652–3.

[31] D'Ewes, pp. 652–7; Neale, *Parliaments*, II, p. 387.

[32] *Letters of Sir Francis Hastings*, ed. M. Claire Cross, Somerset Record Society, vol. 69 (Frome, 1969), p. 78. Hastings said Cecil's 'vearie honourable carriage' had 'affected the whole House much', and would increase his reputation 'throughout all parts of the land' ... ' when it shall be brought down to them'. He wrote on 29 November, four days after the event.

[33] N. R. N. Tyacke, 'Wroth, Cecil and the Parliamentary Session of 1604', *BIHR*, 50 (1977), pp. 121–2.

[34] 3 Jac. I c. 26.

contented.'[35] His argument that the kingdom was not so well furnished with powder as it should be was one that no one who remembered the Armada could well deny, and the grievance of saltpetre was still going in 1606 when Hoskins, ever the mischief-maker, proposed to put it into the purveyance bill.[36] The whole area of militia law was one where the Commons made little serious attempt to bring the law up to date. The Marian militia statute specified an obligation to provide a number of weapons which had become obsolete, and in 1597 one of the Moores 'made a motion to the house for the repealing of the statute of unnecessary armour and weapons.'[37] It was thoroughly in the spirit of the House of Commons that he was not recorded to have made any motion for an up-to-date obligation to provide necessary armour and weapons. Serjeant Hele's motion, the same year, to make it felony to refuse the press was more constructive, but no one showed any wish to act on it.[38] The 1604 house, in leaving the King without any secure legal basis for the militia, was acting entirely in the spirit of its Elizabethan predecessors.[39] Serjeant Harris's motion, in 1593, to base military obligation on tenures, was an interesting antiquarian proposal, and possibly part of the reason why James was reluctant to accompany any abolition of wardship with the abolition of feudal tenures.[40]

At the beginning of James's reign, with the conclusion of peace, it became safe to express a great deal of feeling which national security had kept bottled up in time of war. Robert Cecil warned James:

Your Majesty may therefore please to remember first that you found a people worn with great and heavy burdens, which they endured the better in hope of the change of your blessed government, which in matters of

[35] D'Ewes, p. 653.

[36] *CJ* 261.

[37] 'Townshend's Journals', p. 11 and n. It is not clear whether this was Francis Moore or Sir George More. On the general issues involved, see A. Hassell Smith, 'Militia Rates and Militia Statutes', in *The English Commonwealth 1547–1640: Essays in Politics and Society Presented to Joel Hurstfield*, ed. Peter Clark, Alan G. T. Smith and Nicholas Tyacke, (Leicester, 1979), pp. 93–110.

[38] 'Townshend's Journals', p. 21. The difficulties arising from the failure to pass any such bill were tackled, in unpromising circumstances, by the Impressment Act and the Militia Ordinance of 1642. S. R. Gardiner, *Constitutional Documents of the Puritan Revolution* (Oxford, repr. 1979), pp. 242–7.

[39] The crown appears to have contemplated a bill in 1604, but there is no record of its appearance. Hassell Smith, 'Militia Rates and Militia Statutes', pp. 100–1: SP 14/6/99.

[40] BL Cotton MS Titus F ii, f. 49v.

payment continues yet not a little burdenous to those that expected ease in contributions, feeling the weight of so many in the days of peace.[41]

Cecil's wording is close to that of the Apology of the Commons, that there was a general hope that 'some moderate ease should bee given us of those burdens and sore oppressions under which the whole land did groane.'[42] It is perhaps not surprising that this reaction in favour of lighter burdens in time of peace should be particularly explicit in the matter of the militia. Sir Henry Poole, in his complaint against the Wiltshire muster-master in 1606, said he was charging subjects against their wills 'in this tyme of peace'. The 1606 petition of grievances said the saltpetremen proceeded 'in more violent and unlawful sort now, then in tyme of warr', and the same petition attacked the levy for muster-masters under the heading of 'taxes sett in tyme of warr, and still continued'.[43]

If James appears to have faced rather more resentment at financial exactions than Elizabeth did, this appearance may be in part deceptive, and the result of Elizabethan resentments now more freely expressed. Yet James's own notorious liberality was not a helpful addition to the mixture. Thanks to Dr Croft, we now know beyond any doubt that Cecil, in private, expressed himself very freely to James on the need to control his liberality.[44] James offered the ideal excuse to draw out and encourage the retrenchment philosophy which had become widely enunciated during the war and added to its credibility as it became obsolete. Someone, whether Cecil or not, seems to have reproved James for his liberality even before his first parliament met. In his opening speech, he said he could not exhaust the fountain of his liberality, and 'I rather crave your pardon, that I have been so bountiful.' The bounty, he said disarmingly, proceeded from 'mine own infirmity'.[45] He expressed the hope that time would teach his subjects not to be so importunate in craving, but time required royal assistance, which was not forthcoming.

In 1606, as in the 1340s, resentment at financial burdens

---

[41] Pauline Croft, 'A Collection of Speeches of the Late Lord Treasurer Cecil', *Camden Miscellany* vol. XXIX (1987), p. 289.

[42] *Salis. MSS*, vol. XXIII, p. 142.

[43] *Bowyer*, pp. 130, 131, 154. I am grateful to Dr Richard Stewart for these references. Also Hassell Smith, 'Militia Rates and Militia Statutes', p. 100.

[44] Croft, 'Collection of Speeches of the Late Lord Treasurer Cecil', pp. 284–7 and *passim*.

[45] *CJ* 146.

surfaced in the attack on purveyance, led, like the monopolies agitation, by Lawrence Hyde. When Hyde and his allies attacked purveyance outright, what they appear to have been arguing was that purveyance *below the market price* was illegal. Since the purveyors proudly insisted that their prices had been unchanged for 300 years,[46] the establishment of this principle would have cost the crown a large sum of money. A draft bill, possibly drafted by Lawrence Hyde, would have bound the purveyors to pay the market price or as they could agree with the party.[47] Hare may have been making the same point when he argued, in 1604, that purveyance had been against law since the reign of Henry VIII, since in Henry's reign, purveyors had still been paying the market price.[48] Yelverton, in 1606, was making the same point when he insisted that the King 'hath no prerogative in price', and was answered by the attorney general with the counterclaim that 'the King hath more than pre-emption'.[49] Dr Lindquist appears to be right that the Cecilian efforts at composition foundered because some of the leading figures in the Commons thought the King was trying to sell a right they did not believe he had. He may well also be right that the outright attack on purveyance was not something in which the Commons hoped to succeed, but rather a 'face-saver', to preserve their credit in their countries.[50] Equally, the attempt of the crown and the judges to argue that the parliament could not take away purveyance may well have been equally meant as a face-saver. The lord chief justice, who has usually been quoted to this effect, argued that 'Acts of Parliament may expound, and limitt the prerogative, but not take it away absolutely *without recompense.*' John Chamberlain, proving that even Homer can nod, for once missed the two crucial words of qualification, and generations of historians have been misled with him.[51] What needs explaining is why Salisbury's persistent efforts at composition met with so little

[46] *CJ* 216.

[47] Yale University, Beinecke Library, Osborn Files, Parliament. I am grateful to Dr Eric Lindquist for help in placing this document, which he has printed in 'The Bills Against Purveyors', *Parliamentary History*, 4 (1985), 38–40.

[48] *CJ* 202; Russell, *Crisis*, p. 37.

[49] *CJ* 276–7.

[50] Eric N. Lindquist, 'The King, The People and the House of Commons: The Problems of Early Jacobean Purveyance', *HJ*, 31, 3 (1988), 549–70. For a fuller account of these debates, see Pauline Croft, 'Parliament, Purveyance and the City of London', *Parliamentary History*, 4 (1985), 1–34.

[51] *Bowyer*, pp. 134–5 and n.

success, and here the desire for ease after the war, the low-tax philosophy and the retrenchment ideology are all important.

So also is the fact that taxation was still seen as an occasional, rather than a regular, phenomenon. This is the only meaning we can give to Ridgway's insistence, in 1604, that 'we have no precedent for taxes by Act of Parliament.'[52] Sandys was making the same point in 1606, when he said: 'it maie be dangerous in that it will make all the lande tributary.'[53] Hoskins similarly insisted that: 'our ancestors passed bills – never an imposition of inheritance demanded.'[54] The point, of course, was not strictly true: the creation of tonnage and poundage refuted it. However, that was a precedent which fell mainly on merchants. Out of date though this attitude was, neither the postwar mood nor the King's famous liberality helped to create a climate in which it was easy to tell the public that it was necessary to change it.

In the 1606 subsidy debate, the same concern with the amount of taxation dominated the discussion. There was no attempt in 1606 to trade supply for redress of grievances, and the concern with the amount shows clearly in the difference between the first two subsidies, which were carried without dispute, and the third, which was forced through by a majority of one. It must be stressed that, in terms of the conventions governing the grant of subsidies, the justifications of 1606 were as weak as those of 1601 were strong.

Only the Gunpowder Plot, by its reminder that the popish threat had not stopped with the coming of peace, and by giving occasion to celebrate the King's merciful deliverance, gave occasion for a subsidy-giving mood. Ridgway, who moved the subsidy, invoked 'the mass of treasure exhausted by Ireland', which was a good reason, but not an easy one to put over to the house. The invocation of the blessings of peace may have sounded hollow to an assembly conditioned to demands based on the exigencies of war, while entertainment of ambassadors, the great charge of the household and rewards to both nations all invited a response based on the retrenchment ideology. The Queen's funeral was a marginal case. It was, in terms of conventional justification, perhaps the easiest to refuse of all the subsidy requests of the seventeenth century. It is,

[52] *CJ* 214, 274.
[53] *Bowyer*, p. 71.
[54] *CJ* 274.

then, a mark of considerable underlying good will that members did not do so.[55]

Instead, they set out, like sensible politicians, to get the best bargain they could in return for granting it. They were aware that they had done something exceptional, and they wanted credit for it. Yelverton said there was 'never any example of two subsidies in time of peace till now',[56] and he was correct. After the third was voted, Salisbury noted that 'they have ... carried themselves very lovingly and dutifully to his Majesty, haveing given him three subsidyes and six fifteens, which is no other precedent in time of peace.' A very similar phrase was inserted in the preamble of the act.[57] It was this sense that they had done the King an exceptional favour which led to the petition of grievances.[58] In sheer form, the petition of grievances is something to which there is no Elizabethan parallel, but it does not represent, in any crude sense, an attempt at redress-supply bargaining. The motion for a collection of grievances was made, immediately *after* the first two subsidies had been granted, by Sir Robert Wingfield.[59] It was perhaps relevant that Wingfield was the son of Burghley's sister and a Cecil client. Robert Cecil was known to believe in an exchange between contribution and retribution, a notion of *quid pro quo* a good deal more amicable than redress-supply bargaining, and there is no reason to believe that Wingfield's motion was displeasing to his patron. There are occasional hints of bargaining, such as Martin's proposal, 'no mention of subsidy until there be some remedy for the purveyors, and other grievances'. This seems to have been too strong for the house, and was answered by Ridgway saying that 'that king could not be safe, that was poor.'[60] When the grievances

[55] *CJ* 266, *Bowyer*, p. 31 and nn. There is truth in the comments of Gardiner, *History*, I, p. 299. On the conventions and the 1606 grant, see G. L. Harriss, 'Mediaeval Doctrines in the Debates on Supply, 1610–1629', in Kevin Sharpe (ed.), *Faction and Parliament* (Oxford, 1978), pp. 76–8, 81–2.

[56] *CJ* 289.

[57] *Bowyer*, p. 84n; 3 Jac. I c. 26.

[58] See the remarks of Harriss, 'Mediaeval Doctrines in the Debates on Supply', p. 78: 'the less urgent and evident the danger the greater was the scope for excuses by subjects, for pleas of goodwill and promises of redress of grievances by the king, and for hard bargaining over the abuses of royal government'. This remark is made generally, but it also encapsulates the differences between the last years of Elizabeth and the first years of James. See also Schofield, 'Taxation and the Political Limits of the Tudor State', pp. 228–30.

[59] *Bowyer*, p. 33; *CJ* 267.

[60] *CJ* 272.

came, they were mostly not very far-reaching, involving a few surviving monopolies. Sir William Brouncker's patent for the issues of jurors, which bore a charmed life, was named and survived. These things were hardly the stuff of major drama, and the only worrying note was that almost all of them, if remedied, would to some extent diminish the King's revenue, and thus the net value of the grant for which their redress might be a reward.[61] All in all, the 1606 subsidy debate shows a serious reluctance to reform an outdated financial system, but no very great rise in the political temperature. In this, it is the direct and lineal successor of the subsidy debate of 1593, which shows exactly the same thing. If the situation was a little worse under James than it had been under Elizabeth, this is not the result of a radical transformation, but simply that it had been going on that little bit longer. There is no recognition that defence, especially in Ireland, had become a regular peacetime cost, and there is no recognition that the burden of debt left by the war was more than the crown could shoulder unaided. Hedley argued that 'the king's debts no cause subsidies – a dangerous precedent – it may be always alleged.'[62] In terms of traditional and conventional wisdom, Hedley was probably correct. Yet in the face of the overwhelming increase in costs the crown had faced during the war with Spain, leaving behind a diminished income and an increased debt, such an attitude was seriously out of date. The members who sat through the later Elizabethan parliaments had, it is true, always granted subsidies when it was demanded of them: the conventions of the old system demanded that in wartime they should do no less. Yet, just *because* Elizabethan demands had been so carefully couched in terms of the old system, the experience had not provided any significant financial education for the members who had passed through it. When peace returned under James, this uneducated state must have made them more welcome to their countries, as it made them more infuriating to the lord treasurer. The lord treasurer perceived himself, correctly, as wrestling with the legacy of an Elizabethan problem: 'it is not a thing that all men know, that the late time had much ado to save itself from the effect of want, even whilst the late Queen of happy memory lived.'[63] Had she been still alive in 1606, much of the parliamentary atmosphere would probably have been very much as it was.

[61] *Bowyer*, pp. 109ff.
[62] *CJ* 282.
[63] Croft, 'Collection of Speeches of the Late Lord Treasurer Cecil', p. 285.

Yet it would be seriously misleading to present the opening years of James VI and I as entirely in line with the last years of Elizabeth. Such a view would be highly Anglocentric, since it would leave out the biggest single issue of James's first parliament, that of the Union. The Union, because it carried, as no other issue did, the prospect of major constitional change, created anxieties about how the country would be governed which did a great deal to shape the atmosphere of James's first English parliament, and probably did so in many more ways than are now apparent. How far James at first intended to push in the matter of Union is not entirely clear: his aims were probably far more limited than they have been taken to be. Yet he did mention, during 1604, both the prospect of union of laws and the prospect of union of parliaments.[64] Either of these was enough to cause considerable alarm to most English members of parliament. The legal implications of creating a new state could be far-reaching: 'the change of style will be, as it were, the erecting of a new kingdom, and so it shall be, as it were, a kingdom conquered, and then may the king add laws and alter laws at his pleasure.'[65] Sir Edwin Sandys, who seems to have been more fully aware of the potential implications than most, urged the house to 'proceed with a leaden foot',[66] and there may be a serious comment on the session of 1604 concealed in the remark ascribed to the Earl of Northampton, that 'King James's hope was like to be cast away not on Goodwin Sands, but on Edwin Sandys.'[67] Sandys raised the problem of legislative sovereignty in a united Britain: 'we can give no laws to Brittaine because we are but parcel: Scotland cannot, because it is another part. Together we cannot: severall corporations. By this our Parliament dissolved.'[68] At a stroke, the Union could downgrade the English parliament from the status of a national parliament to that of a provincial estate. It would also, by merging two kingdoms with different laws, put the survival of any individual law or legal principle at the mercy of a process of

[64] *CJ* 171; SP 14/9/35.
[65] Brian Levack, *The Formation of the British State* (Oxford, 1987), p. 38.
[66] *CJ* 950.
[67] Bedford Estate Office, Bedford MSS Fourth Earl vol. 25 (unfoliated). Bedford does not date the remark, and records only that he heard it from the Earl of Bath. The surrounding material appears to date from 1640, so this appears to be oral history, recorded well after the event. It is tempting, though necessarily tentative, to link it with the conference on the Union in 1604 when Northampton 'posted after Sir Ed. Sandys from place to place'. SP 14/7/74.
[68] *CJ* 186 and 958.

negotiation which the King would inevitably dominate. Hedley was quite right that 'the King cannot preserve the fundamental laws by uniting, no more than a goldsmith, two crowns.'[69] Sandys asked who could make laws for the new Britain, or who would interpret an act of union: 'there will be none to do that, but ye k. of Britany.'[70] He thought interpretation by usage would be, as always, to the King's advantage. It makes a serious point that Cowell's *Interpreter* was a unionist tract. Speaker Phelips, opening the 1604 session, was giving voice to a general anxiety when he insisted that James was not a conqueror, and 'the ark of government ... hath ever been steered by the laws.' New laws, he said, could only be made by parliament, and only by parliament could old laws be abrogated[71] – a rejection of the principle of 'desuetude', by which Scottish laws might be deemed to have become obsolete.

The issue of the Union perhaps contributed more than we have realized to two of the headline events of the session of 1604: the Apology of the Commons and the case of Goodwin v. Fortescue. Thanks to Professor Elton, it is now common knowledge that the Apology was never approved by the full house, and cannot be taken as representing the views of all its members. After a debate, it was referred back to committee on the motion of Sir William Strode, and never re-emerged.[72] Yet, even when we have dethroned the Apology from the status of a great constitutional document, it remains a political event, and one which, in the new terms of political history, remains to be explained. Who was responsible for it, and why was it written? In the usual way of historical explanation, 'why' must wait upon 'when'. The committee which drew it up was set up on 1 June, as a result of a motion from Sir Thomas Ridgway 'to take a survey of the proceeding of the House and to sett down something in wryting for his Mats. satisfaction', and of another, immediately following, from the Speaker, for a petition 'with reasons of satisfaction for the proceeding in matters of wardships, etc'.[73] In terms of chronology, it appears likely that these motions may have been a response to James's speech of 30

---

[69] *CJ* 187 and 958.

[70] SP 14/7/63.

[71] Levack, *Formation of the British State*, p. 82; *CJ* 146.

[72] G. R. Elton, 'A High Road to Civil War?' in *Essays in Honour of Garrett Mattingley*, ed. Charles H. Carter (London, 1966) pp. 325ff. On the reference back, see *CJ* 248 and *Salis. MSS*, vol. XXIII, p. 152.

[73] *CJ* 230: *Salis. MSS*, vol. XXIII, p. 139.

May, and since that speech seems to be wholly lost, any explanation of the Apology must be in part conjectural. Some hint of its
contents may perhaps be gained from the abrupt change of front of
the Lords at the conference on wardship reported on the morning of
1 June, when they offered 'expostulation or friendly reprehension'
of the Commons for pursuing the project of compounding for
wardship which they themselves had encouraged the Commons to
take up. Any attempt to deduce the content of James's speech from
presumed answers to it in the Apology runs a dangerous risk of
circular reasoning, but for what it is worth, such reasoning suggests
that James may, as he often did under stress, have delivered his
standard anti-Melvillian speech, attacking the notion of any jurisdiction in the realm independent of his own.[74]

What had just happened, on 30 May, which might have aroused
such fears in James? On 26 May Sandys had offered the heads for a
petition on wardship, in which he said that 'our desire is, the taking
away of the tenures *in capite*.'[75] To Sandys, such a proposal was a
mere synonym for the abolition of wardship, for which the Commons had been encouraged to negotiate by Sir Robert Wroth,
probably on the initiative of Cecil.[76] On that reading, the Commons were entitled to some indignation if they were reproved for
meddling because they had followed the lead of one of the King's
most prominent councillors. To James, on the other hand, tenures
were something very much apart from wardship, which was merely
one of their incidents. Tenures, as Serjeant Harris had suggested in
1593,[77] might be a ground of military obligation, which, after the
failure to renew the militia statute, might become very necessary.
They were also, as a careful reading of Calvin's case suggests, a
possible ground of allegiance, and therefore something whose

[74] I am grateful to Dr Jenny Wormald for helping me to understand how
James's Scottish experience may sometimes have left him and his English subjects
divided by a common language. On what follows, she is entitled to observe that
'you know my methods, Watson,' though I hope I have followed them to rather
better effect. See also HMC *Buccleuch* iii 89. The proceedings of 4 June raise the
question whether the English clergy had been inflaming James's suspicions, as
Bancroft was well qualified to do.

[75] *CJ* 227.

[76] N. R. N. Tyacke, 'Wroth, Cecil and the Parliamentary Session of 1604',
BIHR, 50 (1977), pp. 120–5. Wroth's unexpected remark that 'impossible that
any good could come of this course in the matter of wardship, etc.: he foresaw it: he
knew it' follows immediately after the speech by Sandys quoted above. *CJ* 228.

[77] Above, pp. 192–3.

removal might be a very sensitive subject to James. In the same speech, Sandys had also said that 'it is but a restitution unto the original right of all men by the law of God and nature; which is, that children should be brought up by their parents and next of kin, and by them directed in their marriages.'[78] Here Sandys spoke as the pupil of Hooker, invoking a Thomist doctrine of natural law. To James, who had a very Burkean insistence that rights had to be granted by someone, the invocation of 'original right' may well have raised visions of Buchanan and popular sovereignty, and so inflamed the fears which surfaced in the speech of 30 May. There is thus the possibility of an Anglo-Scottish culture clash in the misunderstanding over wardship which gave rise to the Apology. The invocation of natural right, moreover, carried an implied threat to wardship the other side of the border.[79]

There was also a more direct link with the Union in another issue which surfaced on the morning of 26 May. Tey raised the question of the book published by the bishop of Bristol on the Union, which was a long attack on the Commons's unpublished objections to the change of name. He was eagerly supported by Sir Edward Hoby, who claimed the book was the worst scandal since Arthur Hall. James was always sensitive to attacks on the Union, but the question of the bishop of Bristol's book was more serious than this, since the bishop claimed, in his dedication, that James had read and approved the whole book.[80] The book thus became a royal attack by proxy on the Commons, and that on an issue which had already convinced Sandys and Fuller that 'the prerogatives of princes may easily and doe daily growe. The priviledges of subjects are for the most part at an everlasting stand.' It may not be a coincidence that this passage in the Apology is placed immediately after the attack on the bishop of Bristol's book as a contempt of the house.[81] Yet this was not all: if the book was for the house a direct attack on the Commons, the attack on the book was for James a direct attack on himself, and James did not take such attacks lightly.

He was also sensitive to anti-Scottish feeling, and only eight days earlier, had warned the Commons not to bewray their dislike of

[78] *CJ* 227, 981.

[79] This may be why the Lords reminded the Commons of the existence of wardship in Scotland. *CJ* 230.

[80] John Thornborough, *A Discourse* (1604), dedication. *CJ* 981, 226–7.

[81] *Salis. MSS*, vol. XXIII, pp. 144–5.

Scots. In his letter of 1 May, described by Edward Montagu as 'somewhat ... sharp',[82] James had told the houses that 'you do both me and yourselves an infinite wrong' by their opposition to the Union, which he said must proceed from distrust either of him or of his mother. When he told them not to spit and blaspheme in his face by preferring war to peace, hatred to love, more experienced James-watchers than they could yet have become would have seen a storm coming.[83] Over the bishop of Bristol's book, the personal hurt of James and the constitutional fears of Fuller and Sandys clashed head on, and the contribution of that clash to the Apology may have been very large indeed. The note of constitutional alarm which first endeared the Apology to Whig historians is constant in the debates on the Union in 1604, and is not perceptible in the debates on any other subject. That alone would have been a good reason for linking the Apology with the Union, and with the appearance of the bishop of Bristol's book, the link seems to have been clearly forged.

The other headline issue to which the Union may have contributed is the case of Goodwin v. Fortescue. In 1971, I wrote that 'the important question ... is why both sides considered the issue worth a serious dispute.'[84] In Anglocentric innocence, I was then quite unable to answer my own question. The adjective apart, the question still stands. What may be the key item of evidence was discovered by Dr Bruce Galloway, who found that Francis Bacon was advising James to use his prerogative to create parliamentary constituencies to summon the Scots to the next session of the Westminster parliament.[85] Any such intention could have made the English parliament's insistence on judging its own election returns into an issue, not merely of privilege, but of sheer survival. James had already exercised his power to create new constituencies freely, and Speaker Phelips's first act on his election was to issue a warrant for new seats, 'by reason of more charters granted by his Majesty'.[86] The house remained sensitive for some time to the notion of Scots at Westminster, and in 1606 it was proposed to add a general clause to naturalization bills that those naturalized should have no voice in parliament. This was 'generally liked and

[82] CJ 975; HMC Buccleuch iii 93.
[83] SP 14/8/2.
[84] Russell, Crisis, p. 267.
[85] Bruce Galloway, The Union of England and Scotland (Edinburgh, 1986), p. 41.
[86] CJ 141.

assented unto', but appears not to have been done, on the ground that no parliament could bind its successors.[87] A fear that the judgement of election returns was being used as a smoke screen to bring about the union of the parliaments might explain the otherwise incomprehensible fear that 'this may be called a *Quo Warranto* to seize all our liberties.'[88] When James had not yet abandoned the hope of union of the parliaments, such a fear was not entirely absurd. Liberties were English, and there were as yet no British liberties. The Union, then, is the biggest difference between Elizabethan and Jacobean parliaments, and accounts for a very large proportion of the constitutional evidence which once convinced Whig historians that the Jacobeans were living in a new age. That evidence was perfectly genuine, but historians of England were unable to explain it: it is one of the birth-pangs of Britain. How deep the constitutional questions raised by the Union went, and how long the resultant fears lasted, are questions which require further investigation.

The other way in which the first Jacobean parliament was very different from the last Elizabethan parliament is that it was living under a different law of succession. In any society, the society's ideas on what confers title to supreme power must inevitably influence that society's ideas on legitimacy and authority in general. So long as the succession had been governed by Henry VIII's will, supreme power had, in the last resort, been enjoyed by parliamentary title, since Henry had insisted that his right to bequeath the throne be enacted by the parliament, 'and by authority of the same'. The 1571 act, which made it treason to deny the authority of an act of parliament to determine the succession, merely underlined the point.[89] Burghley, a good Elizabethan, was simply following this line of thought in his draft interregnum bill of 1584, which frankly described any period between the Queen's death and the choice of a successor as an 'interregnum', and proposed to enact that the last parliament which had met should declare the right candidate 'in forme of an Act of Parliament'.[90] Without the royal assent, such a proposal came very near an ascending theory of power.

In 1604, with the accession of James, all this was instantly

[87] *Bowyer*, p. 167.
[88] *CJ* 159.
[89] *35 Henry VIII c. 1; 13 Elizabeth I c. 1.*
[90] SP 12/176/22.

changed. James could not afford any truck with parliamentary titles: if they were valid, Henry VIII's will still stood, and the Stuart line was excluded. James's claim rested, not on an act of parliament, but on the claim to be the next heir in blood, and on the further claim that the title of the next heir in blood was automatic and indefeasible. The Jacobean act of recognition spelt out this principle with ruthless clarity: the parliament recognized, 'being bounden thereunto by the lawes of God and man' (not 'by authority of the same'), that 'immediately upon the dissolution and decease of Elizabeth, late Queen of England, the imeriall crowne of the realme of England ... did by inherent birthright and un-doubted succession, descend and come to your most excellent Majesty.'[91] Parliamentary authority was entirely excluded. Sir Edwin Sandys could recognize a major change in political ideas when he saw one. It may have been he who said, perhaps significantly when speaking on the Union: 'this House hath trans-lated the Crown from one line to another, which it could not do.'[92] The judges in Calvin's case now insisted that there could be no interregnum by the laws of England, and when the notion of an interregnum went out, a large measure of parliamentary authority went out with it.[93] A careful study of the reports of Calvin's case on the naturalization of Scots born after the Union goes a long way to validate Sandys's fears about the consequences of the Union for parliamentary authority. The key point of the judgement in Calvin's case was that allegiance was owed to the person of the King, and not to the laws. Loyalty was to an individual person, not to a body politic, and, as Sandys had feared, the effect of the Union on the law was to strengthen the crown as the one British institution. It is very hard for anyone reading the reports of Calvin's case to see the early seventeenth century as a period of growing parliamentary power.

[91] *1 Jac. I c. 1.*

[92] *CJ* 178, 951. We are given no name for the speaker, but the argument that 'we cannot make any laws to bind Britannia,' which this follows, was one of Sandys's regular points.

[93] Sir Edward Coke, *Seventh Report*, p. 11.

Notes on Contributors

J. D. Alsop is Associate Professor of History at McMaster University. He is a graduate of the universities of Winnepeg, Western Ontario, and Cambridge, and the author of articles on Tudor finance and financial administration. He is presently researching a book on Elizabethan taxation.

David Dean is Lecturer in History at Goldsmiths' College, University of London. He is a graduate of the universities of Auckland and Cambridge and has held research fellowships at Clare Hall, Cambridge, and the Institute of Historical Research, London. He is reviews editor for *Parliamentary History*. The author of several articles on Elizabethan parliamentary history, he edited *Interest Groups and Legislation in the Elizabethan Parliaments* with Norman Jones and is currently writing a book on the legislation of the later Elizabethan parliaments.

Sir Geoffrey Elton is Regius Professor Emeritus of Modern History at the University of Cambridge and Fellow of Clare College. He has been a Fellow of the British Academy since 1967, was President of the Royal Historical Society (1972–6) and of the Seldon Society (1983–5). He is the author of nearly twenty books, including *Studies in Tudor and Stuart Government and Politics* (3 vols, 1974, 1983) and *The Parliament of England, 1559–1581* (1986).

Michael A. R. Graves is Associate Professor of History in the University of Auckland. He is the author of *The House of Lords in the Parliaments of Edward VI and Mary I* (1981), *The Tudor Parliaments* (1985) and *Elizabethan Parliaments, 1559–1601* (1987), as well as two general political histories of early modern Britain. His study of *The Early Tudor Parliaments* is in the press and he is presently working on a biography of the Elizabethan MP Thomas Norton.

T. E. Hartley is Senior Lecturer in History at the University of Leicester, and his doctoral research was concerned with the sheriffs of Kent in the reigns of Elizabeth and James. The first volume of his edition of Elizabethan parliamentary documents – *Proceedings in the Parliaments of Elizabeth* – was published in 1981, and he is currently working on the second volume, covering the parliaments from 1584 to 1601.

Norman L. Jones was educated at the College of Southern Idaho, Idaho State University, the University of Colorado and Cambridge. His first book, *Faith by Statute. Parliament and the Settlement of Religion, 1559* (1982) won both the Whitfield Prize and the Archbishop Cranmer Prize. His second, *God and the Moneylenders, Usury and Law in Early Modern England*, appeared in 1989. He and David Dean edited *Interest Groups and Legislation in Elizabethan Parliaments*, a special issue of *Parliamentary History*. In 1982–3 he was a Mellon Faculty Fellow at Harvard University. He is currently Professor of History at Utah State University.

Wallace MacCaffrey has been Professor of History at Harvard since 1968. His publications include *Exeter, 1540–1640, The Shaping of the Elizabethan Regime* (1968) and *Queen Elizabeth and the Making of Policy, 1572–88* (1981). He is currently working on *War and Politics, 1588–1603*.

Conrad Russell is Professor of History, King's College, London, and was formerly Astor Professor of British History, University College, London, Professor of History, Yale University and Lecturer/Reader in History, Bedford College, University of London. Author of *The Crisis of Parliaments: English History 1509–1660* (1971) and of *Parliaments and English Politics 1621–1629* (1979), he delivered the Ford Lectures, University of Oxford (1987–8), on 'The Causes of the English Civil War', to be published by Oxford University Press, and has written a book, which is about to go to press, on *The Fall of the British Monarchies, 1637–1642*.

Index

Index by Ann Barrett